WAKE-UP CALL

WAKE-UP CALL

The POLITICAL EDUCATION of a 9/11 WIDOW

Kristen Breitweiser

WARNER BOOKS

NEW YORK   BOSTON

Warner Books
Hachette Book Group USA
1271 Avenue of the Americas
New York, NY 10020

Visit our Web site at www.HachetteBookGroupUSA.com.

Printed in the United States of America

First Edition: September 2006
10 9 8 7 6 5 4 3 2 1

Warner Books and the "W" logo are trademarks of Time Warner, Inc., or an affiliated company. Used under license by Hachette Book Group USA, which is not affiliated with Time Warner, Inc.

Library of Congress Cataloging-in-Publication Data

Breitweiser, Kristen.
    Wake-up call : the political education of a 9/11 widow / Kristen Breitweiser. — 1st ed.
       p. cm.
    ISBN-13: 978-0-446-57932-2
    ISBN-10: 0-446-57932-7
    1. Breitweiser, Kristen.   2. September 11 Terrorist Attacks, 2001—Personal narratives.
3. National Commission on Terrorist Attacks upon the United States.   4. Widows—
New Jersey—Biography.   5. Terrorism victims' families—New Jersey.   I. Title.
    HV6432.7.B743A3   2006
    973.931092—dc22
    [B]
                                                                            2006010593

To Caroline, because your smiles, your giggles, and your bug-hugs inspire me to never give up.

And to the moon and stars who follow me always and give me a reason to look up and smile.

Acknowledgments

Mindy, Patty, Lorie, and Monica—the girls—I would not be alive today without our friendship. You have taught me how to survive and how to fight. How to laugh. How to be strong. And how to cry. Together, we have achieved so much. I am so very deeply proud to have you as my closest and truest friends.

Sara—my best non-widow friend—you keep me grounded with your sparkling wit and enthusiasm. If there was ever a name that meant both little sister and very best friend, that name would be you, Sara.

Dad and Gail—for the many, many times that you came through for me with your simple advice, your babysitting and dogsitting, or just providing for Caroline and me a place to call our home.

Judy Lynn—my sister—I can never repay you for having the strength in times when I had none. You carried me through.

Mom-Mom—my grandmother—for teaching me about the most important things in life . . . because of you, I will always have a lilac bush under my bedroom window.

Gail—your advice, support, and guidance are the very best. But your friendship means the world to both Caroline and me.

The Siller family—you are like a family to Caroline and me. Thank you for everything that you do for us and for truly giving Caroline her second home.

Jamie Raab—my editor—you are the best publisher/editor/ friend a person could have. Thank you for keeping me motivated and inspired by your never-ending support for this book.

Laura Palmer—thank you for helping me get out of the starting gates and keeping me on track. Without you I might never have started writing this book.

Monika—thank you for taking such good care of my two most prized possessions on this earth, Caroline and Cooper.

And for Mom and Ron—thank you for being Caroline's angels and my conscience.

Contents

Sweets,

Where to begin. Well, I am going to work under the assumption that you know that you are dead and that you might not know why. Explaining why you were murdered, how it happened, and what has happened to our world since that horrific day is a long story.

But first I want to tell you that Caroline, Sam, and I are okay. Caroline talks about you often. Yes, she talks. I know that must seem unbelievable to you, because when you were killed she was two and a half and suffering from speech delays. Well, she talks now—she talks a lot. We still have speech issues, but for the most part she is a happy and healthy five-year-old girl.

What is most important for you to know about your little girl, our little doodlebug, is that she still smiles and giggles all the time. Ron, she is so happy. She continues to be our little sunshine. I tell her stories about you all the time. I tell her that when she was a tiny infant you would walk around the house with her when she couldn't sleep and sing her the "birthday song" because you didn't know any lullabies. I tell her that when she would awake during the night you rubbed her back until she fell off to sleep. I tell her how we used to walk on the beach with Sam and take him swimming—even in winter. And of course I tell her how we so loved our walks together in the woods.

Caroline is no longer shy. Remember how she would never let people hold her and our friends and family worried that she was too attached to us? Well, that has changed. She has become a very confident, outgoing, and adaptable little girl. Her hair is long and blond. Her face is exactly like yours. When I look at her, I see all of you in her. And, although it makes me sad that you are not here to see her, on some level I have to believe that you are keeping an eye on her and getting such a kick out of how she dances through life. There were moments early on when she would look up to the ceiling or look out the window and giggle. It was as if she was seeing something, someone. I hoped it was you. Was it, Sweets?

She loves to play dress-up; her favorite is a fairy princess. She's athletic, too, and adores riding horses. You'd be so proud to see her sit up straight on the horse and concentrate on riding. Her soccer team has only boys—she scored three goals last week. And she is learning how to read; her favorite book for now is Green Eggs and Ham.

She tells people without even really knowing them, "My daddy's dead." Very matter-of-fact. I guess that is what happens to you when your father dies and you have to share it with the whole world. It becomes a cold reality. She is too young to realize the startling impact this has on people when so bluntly delivered by such a little girl who for all intents looks "normal." I guess, for her, she doesn't quite know what it is to have a daddy, so she cannot understand the devastating meaning behind having a "dead daddy." All she knows is that her "dad" is an image trapped inside a photo.

For a while, all of the photos around the house of the

two of you confused her. She kept looking at the pictures and realized that she was a baby in all of them. In her little mind, she thought that if she were a baby again, you would exist again. Consequently, she spent some weeks behaving like a baby. I finally asked her why she was behaving that way and she said, "If I am a baby, Daddy will come back." She ran and got a picture of you with her and said, "See, I am a baby. That's Daddy. If I am a baby, I will see Daddy again. Daddy will come back."

Yes, Ron, we have many, many conversations like this. Conversations that rip out my heart, leaving me bewildered, speechless, and searching for answers. And I know that at some point I might not have those answers or "fixes" to make our little girl feel better. And that is what my life is like. I worry about the future. I worry about not having answers that will make Caroline feel safe and secure.

For now, though, I am still getting away with dodging Caroline's increasing curiosity about what happened to you. I give her vague answers that sound reassuring. I do my best. Often I will have tears in my eyes as I talk to her about you. Noticing my sadness and tears, Caroline instinctively cradles my face in her hands and says, "No, it's okay, Daddy is in heaven and I can see him in the moon."

Yes, Sweets, she thinks that you are in heaven and that you live on the moon and amongst the stars. She often asks if she can go visit you. I try to explain to her that she cannot go to heaven because once she goes, she cannot come back. And then this goes into a very convoluted conversation that leaves me searching for even more answers. It's hard to explain to her that there are no visitors in heaven, and that if she goes there, she has to stay. Caroline promises and promises me that she'd come back after her visit but that she just wants to see you, her daddy.

Every night she looks to find the moon in the sky. She confidently finds it and says, "That's where my daddy is." Depending on her mood that day, she either shouts or whispers, "Mommy, Mommy! There's the moon. I see Daddy. I love you, Daddy. I love you!" as she blows kisses up to the night sky.

The last three years have transformed me in many ways. I have learned how to live as a single mother and as an activist. I don't know which transformation has been more difficult to undertake. I didn't really have a choice in either one. And neither transformation has been easy. For example, what is harder: staring down the director of the FBI and catching him in a flat-out lie or looking Caroline in the eyes and trying to tell her that not all planes are meant to crash into buildings?

I am still learning how to raise our little girl without you in her life, just as I am still learning how to be a fully engaged and better American citizen. I have learned how to fight Washington and win small battles, just as I have learned how to answer some of Caroline's less probing questions about what happened to you and why you died. In truth, I am scared of the many things I have learned in the past three years while marching through the halls of Washington. I am scared of the many questions that don't seem to have answers.

Sweets, my "wake-up" call came in the form of your being senselessly murdered by hijackers flying planes into

*your office building. I doubt that I will ever feel totally
safe again in any environment. How can I, when steel
turns to dust and all that is left of you are your two arms
and your small gold wedding band?*

*But your wedding ring, that small shiny gold band
scratched yet still perfectly round and intact, was found
in that horrific pile of death and destruction by rescue
workers—just normal men and women working their
hearts and guts out for the pride of our country. And,
sweetheart, I look at your wedding band as a symbol.
Much like it was found buried beneath the smoldering
rubble and ruins, I believe our country is buried
somewhere beneath the current chaos, waiting to be
discovered, so it, too, can shine again.*

—December 2004

The only thing necessary for the triumph of evil is for good men [and women] to do nothing.

—attributed to Edmund Burke

CHAPTER ONE

A Love Affair That Almost Never Happened

A S RON TOLD IT, he first saw me in 1994 while I was playing beach volleyball at the Jersey Shore. He said he'd had his eye on me from that very instant. I, on the other hand, was completely oblivious to his presence. In those early days, I wouldn't have paid much attention to him because he simply was not my type. Blond, strong, and blue-eyed, Ron was the straitlaced, wholesome all-American guy—a Fourth of July parade, complete with bursting fireworks.

That same summer, I was hanging out with a close-knit group of friends and we had a regular routine. Our summer life revolved around sunbathing, playing beach volleyball, surfing, and partying. We would religiously arrive at the beach by 10:00 A.M., eat breakfast, which usually included ham, egg, and cheese sandwiches and cheese fries, apply our sunblock, line up the volleyball schedule, and gossip about the parties that had taken place the night before. Sometime around five o'clock, the mass exodus from the shoreline would begin. Everyone would filter slowly off the beach, drop their beach chairs on the front lawn of the small beach bar called the Yankee Clipper, and walk inside barefoot to grab a plate of nachos and a few Long Island iced teas. Everybody knew everybody else. It was a small, exclusive club of friends. Everyone was tanned, gorgeous, and looking to have fun.

The Yankee Clipper was an institution. You could feel the gritty floor underfoot—a combination of dropped peanut shells, spilled alcohol, and vagrant sand. The bar smelled like cocoa butter and suntan lotion. The music was always the same—cheesy, upbeat, and happy. When songs like "Rockin' Robin," "Sweet Caroline," or "Margaritaville" were played, everybody drunkenly chimed in. Arms were wrapped around waists of the people standing next to you. Haphazard conga lines would form. And every evening would end with the same last song: "The Summer Wind" by Frank Sinatra.

Around 11:00 P.M. what we called "the crawl" would begin. The crawl was the long walk either home, to the next bar, or to a private party at someone's beachfront home. Buzzed, sunburned, and feeling the cool ocean breeze on our faces, we would stumble along still barefoot, covered in sand, and wearing our bathing suits. There were no fancy outfits, no designer handbags, and nobody spent time primping and fussing with their hair. Baseball caps, cut-off shorts, and wrinkled linen shirts were all we needed for our three-month "come as you are party."

It was the summer after my first year in law school, right before I was leaving for Europe, when I first met Ron. I was drinking with a group of friends at the Yankee Clipper, and each time one of my friends or I finished a drink, the waitress appeared with another. And another. And another. As the evening wore on, so did the mystery as to who was sending over all of our drinks. The waitress soon began bringing over trays of shots and handing them to everyone. She continued to bring tray after tray after tray. It was verging on the ridiculous. Finally I asked who was sending over the drinks. She told me she was sworn to secrecy, but that our mysterious benefactor was in the bar and an admirer of mine. I was spooked, uncomfortable, and, frankly, wanted to leave immediately. My friends were intrigued and insisted that we stay—in truth, they were just enjoying all the free drinks.

Sometime after midnight, a very inebriated guy showed up with a tray of drinks. He knocked into me, nearly spilling the entire tray. He was pretty drunk. I looked at him, annoyed, and asked him if I could help him out with anything. He righted himself, looked me straight in the eye, and stammered: "I just want you to know I love you." Ron Breitweiser had spoken his first words to me. He was drunk, his eyes were bloodshot, and he was barely standing. All I wanted to do was to get away from him.

Nervously I looked over to the waitress, who pointed to him knowingly. I looked back at Ron as he stumbled some more and asked, "Will you go out on a date with me?" Quite put off by his forwardness and his drunkenness, I brushed him off by saying that I was leaving for Europe the next day, not to return until the end of the summer. I then turned to my friend Paul and asked him to walk me to my car. My only hope was that the crazy drunk guy (I still didn't know his name) would think I was dating Paul and leave me alone. Paul smiled at me, whispered into my ear, draped his arm around my waist, and ushered me out of the bar. The next afternoon I got on the plane and flew to the south of France to study law.

Deciding to take a summer abroad and study in Aix-en-Provence was one of my better law school decisions. It lightened my load for the following semester back at Seton

Hall, and it provided me with an excellent opportunity to travel throughout Europe. Ironically, among the classes I took that summer was "Terrorism and International Law." It wasn't anything I was drawn to; it just happened to fit into my schedule. Since we had classes only three days a week, there was plenty of time to take off and travel. I spent the rest of my summer biking around Provence, rock-climbing and glacier skiing in Switzerland, hiking in the French Alps, swimming along the coasts of the Italian and French Mediterranean, and partying all night long before the running of the bulls in Pamplona.

Returning home, I started my second year of law school. It was rigorous, but I always liked the challenge of being a student with a goal to achieve. I wasn't sure I wanted to be a lawyer—as an undergraduate I'd been drawn to the sciences and dreamed about being an astrophysicist or even a neurosurgeon. But the many years of training and medical residencies that a medical degree required made me feel restless and impatient. Law school felt like a smarter and much more practical choice. Besides that, I liked the idea of having three more years of educational structure—I knew it would give me more time to grow up before having to settle down and get a real job.

It was the fall of my second year in law school when Ron's and my paths crossed again. I'd been partying with my law school friends in Hoboken, New Jersey, and we decided to spend the rest of the night clubbing in Manhattan. Ron was a few years older than I, and he was already working on Wall Street. According to Ron, who told me the story of our encounter afterwards, it was on this night that he saw me stumbling through the PATH station with my law school pals. When he told me the story, I didn't believe him until he described what I was wearing and the people I was with. Once reminded of the occasion, I did recall the random night of partying (but not Ron), because it turned out to be an outrageously fun night and one of the rare occasions when my law school friends and I ventured into Manhattan. When Ron recounted to me how he had seen me that evening it struck me as strange, but more so, it struck me as fate. Now it gives me chills because I think about how serendipitous it was to run into Ron in the subway station of the World Trade Center on a night when I was out partying happily with my friends. If only he had known or I had known or anyone had known that so many years later thousands of people would perish in that very spot.

Six months later, Ron and I crossed paths again, but not by coincidence. He had finagled my phone number from a colleague at the law firm where I was clerking that summer. Ron called up cold—totally out of the blue. He first introduced himself as the guy from the Yankee Clipper who'd told me that he loved me. This immediately spooked me. Annoyed that one of my work colleagues would be so stupid as to give Ron my phone number, I was curt with him on the phone. Ron then began to tell me that he had seen me in the WTC/PATH train station that fall. I began to wonder if this guy was stalking me. Ron then asked about law school and whether I had a boyfriend. Wanting desperately to brush him off at this point, I told him that I had several—which wasn't exactly a lie. Completely undeterred, Ron asked me for a date. I declined. Hanging up the phone, I hoped that would put a stop to the pesky stalker named Ron Breitweiser.

But Ron was persistent. He would periodically call or send flowers. He seemed to pop up constantly wherever I was. I guess his persistence was a survival skill for him. Growing up in a rigidly Catholic family without any advantages, Ron knew that if he was going to make a life different from his parents, he'd have to blaze his own trail. He went to the University of Delaware and majored in business. He didn't get an MBA after college, he got a job. Hard work and perseverance were his ways of competing with those who had the privileges of wealth, class, and Ivy League educations. He got his first job by writing a letter to a man on Wall Street who'd written a book Ron admired. The man invited Ron to lunch, and by the time it was over, Ron had his first job. All he needed was a chance to prove himself.

I had several great guy friends in law school who were like older brothers to me. When Ron's persistence about dating me became an annoyance during the winter of my third year of school, I asked the boys what I should do. "Go out with him. Chain-smoke, suck down straight vodka, and act obnoxious." The boys assured me that the only way I was going to get rid of the "stalker" was to scare him away. Armed with my new strategy, I accepted the next time Ron asked me out.

We went to dinner at a crusty Irish pub named Harrigan's. When the waitress came to take our order, I told Ron I didn't eat and hoped he wouldn't mind if I continued to smoke. Ron was a militant antismoker. He was disgusted with my constant inhaling, and he didn't hide his utter disdain. I felt like my plan was working. I ordered another vodka on the rocks with two limes and then another. I lit another cigarette from the one I was about to extinguish. Ron tried to make conversation, but I refused to engage with him at any level. When he asked if I ever wanted to get married, I made it crystal clear to him that I had no interest in ever getting married or having children. Ron ate. I smoked and swilled vodka, playing the part of the ultimate bitch to perfection.

Unbelievably, the next day Ron sent me flowers and called to thank me for accompanying him to dinner. He was more than cordial. I was stunned. I'd expected never to hear from him again. Finally I ended the conversation by thanking him for the flowers and telling him that I was so immersed in my final year of law school that it would be impossible for me to even consider seeing him again. Ron left me alone for a while. I thought my plan had worked.

I graduated from Seton Hall Law School in May of 1996 and immediately began studying for the bar exam. One night at the Parker House, another favorite beach-bar hangout of mine, I was taking a much-needed study break with some of my law school friends. On my way to the ladies' room, I quite literally ran into Ron. I apologized for crashing into him.

As I looked up, I saw his blue eyes looking back at me and his amazingly huge, bright smile. He gushed, "Wow! How are you? Remember me?" I stumbled, took a step backwards, threw a quick smile, and said, "Sure. How are you? Would love to talk, but I'm just leaving." I used the bar exam and the studying I had to do as my excuse for rushing away.

The New Jersey bar exam was four or five weeks away. In the interim, Ron did his detective work and found out the date of the exam. He was hatching another plan. When I returned home after the two-day exam, I found a huge double bouquet of long-stemmed red roses on my doorstep with a note that said: *Hope you did well on the bar exam. Ron.* For the first time, Ronald Breitweiser had caught me off guard—in a nice way, something that rarely happened to me.

My aunt and my best friend, Paul, came over and saw the enormous bouquet. I asked them what they thought I should do. My aunt said, "Give him a shot." Paul agreed. They looked at me, laughed, and said simultaneously: "He is persistent." I called to see if the florist had Ron's number.

She said Ron was hoping I would call and had told her it

was okay to give me his number. I immediately called to thank him for the flowers and he immediately asked me out to dinner. I hesitated. He said, "Come on, you have to. Today is my birthday." It was August 4, 1996.

This time I actually put some effort into getting ready and wore something other than my usual uniform of jeans and a little white T-shirt. When Ron arrived, I was in a short, simple black dress and flat black sandals. He was wearing ripped jeans and a wrinkled blue shirt that looked like it was plucked straight out of the laundry bag. I was incredulous. "This is how you dress to take me out on a date? On your birthday? Are you joking? Couldn't you have at least ironed your shirt?"

Immediately, I decided to change into something more casual. As I was threw on my own pair of ripped Levi's and wrinkled shirt, I was thinking that he was clueless, totally clueless. Ron stayed in the kitchen chatting with my grandmother about working in New York City. She and my aunt told him that he was crazy to work in such a filthy, dangerous place. They asked him why he wanted to work in the city. There was so much crime and it was so stressful. Did he really want to commute every day? The World Trade Center had been bombed three years before, on February 26, 1993. My grandmother asked Ron what he would do if something like that happened in his building. "I'll tell you what I would do. I'd run like hell and get outta there."

We said good-bye to my family and drove to his parents' house, which was about an hour away, to have birthday cake. I should have realized the significance of meeting Ron's family on our first date. But I was oblivious. Ron had told his family, particularly his older sister, a lot about me. So when I walked into their home I felt very much under the microscope and uncomfortable.

We finally left his parents and drove to a quiet Italian restaurant. During dinner, the conversation was playful and easy. Ron confessed to me that he thought I'd been a real bitch the first time we went out. I said that I had been trying to make him leave me alone. He smiled broadly and beamed, asking, "Aren't you glad I didn't?" I answered him honestly: "Yeah. Actually, I am glad you didn't let me scare you away."

Early the next morning, I stopped at a farm stand and picked out a huge sunflower and placed it in an Evian water bottle. The night before, I'd learned that Ron was training to be in the Golden Gloves, an amateur boxing competition. After the farm stand I stopped at a card store and found a vintage postcard with a photo of a small blond-haired boy with boxing gloves on his hands. On the back of the card I wrote, *Thanks for being persistent.* I drove over to the beach house Ron had rented for the summer and left the sunflower and the card on his back doorstep. From that moment on, we were inseparable.

Ron was working in the city, and I was living on the Jersey Shore. By the end of our second month of dating, in September 1996, Ron had moved in with me at my aunt's guest cottage and was commuting to New York City every morning by bus. It was a romantic whirlwind. Every week Ron sent me two huge bouquets of flowers. One went to the courthouse where I was a judicial clerk, and another was sent home. He left me little notes and cards in my brief bag, in the car, on the mirror in the bathroom, and even on the container of half-and-half I used for my morning coffee.

Ron had discovered a very romantic side of himself. When we couldn't see each other, we talked for hours on the phone. After we watched a movie, Ron would brainstorm to figure out a romantic follow-up related to the movie. After seeing *Braveheart* with Mel Gibson, Ron bought an antique white lace handkerchief and a flower similar to the one Mel Gibson receives from his love in the movie. Ron wrapped the flower in the handkerchief and left it on my pillow one evening. After we saw *Message in a Bottle*, I opened the refrigerator three mornings later and found an antique blue bottle with a note from him inside.

But probably the most romantic thing he did was on our first Valentine's Day. We had gone out for a romantic dinner and he gave me a beautiful bracelet from Tiffany that was classic—just what I liked. I hardly expected anything more. When we arrived home, a trail of at least a thousand rose petals made a path lit by small votive candles from the front door to the bedroom. I was overwhelmed. We had left the house in darkness and returned to find it aglow. (Later I learned that my grandmother and aunt did the decorating while we were at dinner.)

When I walked into the bedroom, I found even more rose petals strewn on the bed in the shape of a heart. And sticking out of the covers, propped up on a pile of pillows, was a huge surfboard (my dream surfboard) with a big smiley face that Ron had drawn in bright red lipstick. I gushed. I turned and realized how completely in love I was with this man. The thousands of rose petals, the flickering candles, and the bracelet from Tiffany were all wonderful and certainly touched aspects of me. But the surfboard with the big, bright, silly smile drawn on it was pure me. It was cute, romantic, and fun. Ron had dazzled me with the perfect gift for Valentine's Day.

After we started dating, one of Ron's friends told me about a conversation she had had with Ron several years before Ron and I had officially met. They were at a beach bar hanging out with a group of people and the conversation turned to marriage. Ron announced that he was never going to do it. He was tired of women looking for successful husbands to marry. In fact, when women approached him and asked him what he did for a living, Ron told them that he worked in a cannery. It was his litmus test. If the woman walked away immediately, he knew she wasn't the woman for him. When pushed and prodded by the girls in his crowd who kept telling him that he had to get married someday, he'd finally pointed to me across the crowded beach bar and said, "Okay, I'd get married if a girl like that would marry me."

I'd never met anyone as upbeat and energetic as Ron. I was touched by his kindness and entranced by his brilliant smile. He would constantly chide me for being so negative in thought. He urged me to be more optimistic and to think more positively. It used to exasperate me that he could be so utterly upbeat all the time. One of his favorite phrases was "Sweets, bad shit just doesn't happen to me." If Ron had a pound of manure dumped at his feet, he'd start thinking of using it to fertilize bulbs that would bloom into beautiful flowers.

When I think of Ron on my doorstep in those ripped jeans and rumpled blue shirt, something still moves in my heart. Ron had spent a lifetime waiting to be cherished. He was sweet and vulnerable but also confident and assured. He never called me Kristen. He only called me Sweets. "Oh, you will marry me," he said from day one, square one. I wasn't so sure. He said he'd convince me. And he did.

Pink lemonade in a Thermos, peanut butter sandwiches, and sandy nectarines with sweet juice dribbling on my chin are part of the happiest memories of my childhood summers at the beach. My sister, Judy, and I used to ride our bikes to the beach

behind our mother, whose rickety black English bicycle somehow made it from one summer to the next.

We lived only a few blocks from the beach. The summer
ritual was as predictable as the tides. As soon as school ended,
mothers and their children flocked to the beach like sand-
pipers. The women sat in circles and the children played. The
younger the kids, the closer the mothers were to the water. The
babies and toddlers played in the tide pools, and then as
the kids got older, they graduated from making drip castles to
burying each other up to their necks in the sand to riding boo-
gie boards and finally surfboards. Babies napped under tents
made from beach towels and chairs. We ate sandwiches while
the moms drank sun-sweetened iced tea. No one read books,
magazines, or newspapers. Everyone just talked.

It was the same perfect summer from one year to the next.
We'd go home and have dinner with our fathers and then go
back to the beach for a post-dinner stroll on the boardwalk. My
parents would get coffee and my sister and I would have ice
cream. We watched as the boats floated in and out of the inlet.
We waved to the boat captains, who sometimes would honk
their horns, to my sister's and my great delight. We could see
the stars and the moon drip over the ocean and it was pure
magic to me.

My father was the mayor of our town, Manasquan, New
Jersey, during my entire childhood and teenage years. It was
mortifying for me. I hated the attention it brought our family.
As someone who is inherently shy, I found it embarrassing. It
was my dad's part-time job; he also worked as an advertising
executive in New York City. I didn't know much about that aspect of his life. What I did know was that I detested that he was
Manasquan's mayor.

Manasquan is a small town. When I was growing up, the

population was never more than 5,000 year-round. My dad was elected to five terms as mayor. His public persona stripped me of my privacy and cut into our time together. Whenever we walked downtown, people stopped to talk with him about their complaints: streetlights that needed to be fixed, irregular garbage collection, tree limbs that had to be hauled away. At night the phone rang regularly, interrupting our dinners. I resented the intrusions and sharing my father with everyone else. I grew to hate politics.

My sister, Judy, was two years older than me. Her nickname in the family was "the perfect child." Her room was always neat; she did her chores without ever being asked a second time. Diligent and conscientious, she was never late with her homework and her grades were always good. Judy had had the same group of friends since she was in kindergarten. My friends were always boys; hers were always girls

We were both straight-A students, but I was the one determined to buck the system, while Judy wanted to know the rules so she could follow them. My mother was an immaculate housekeeper and it annoyed her that I would dare leave a pile of neatly folded clothes on the foot of my bed. She called it "the tree," and it became a sore point between the two of us. But there were many of those.

From the time I was five, my mother said she knew I'd be a lawyer. The skills I eventually developed as an attorney were honed by our contentious relationship. My mother and I were always arguing. "Could you please unload the dishwasher?" "No." "Could you please take the laundry upstairs and put it away?" "No." My sister looked for ways to comply; I wanted to spar. I'd talk my mom into circles, flipping issues around until in exasperation she would say, "I hate it when you do this to me." My dad would get home and ask about the day and my mom would say, "She's driving me crazy." For me it was a game. Arguing was a sport and I was very competitive. It was nothing personal. It was entertainment. And I enjoyed it.

There wasn't a sport I didn't play. The school year for me revolved around soccer, basketball, softball, field hockey, and/or tennis. I would come home every night at six o'clock; we'd eat dinner and talk about what Judy and I did in school. As much as I loved sports, by the time I was a junior in high school I was thoroughly burned out. I was tired of listening to coaches as I'd done since about the third grade.

Despite having been diagnosed with ulcerative colitis as a teenager, I still kept up a rigorous athletic schedule. When I started cutting back, I realized there were other after-school options. I could read, hang out with my friends, and watch TV. I still got straight As, but the tension with my parents escalated, especially with my mom. When I was nineteen, I had a huge falling-out with my parents and basically left the house to live with my aunt in her guest cottage.

Some of the security of my childhood disappeared when my mother was diagnosed with breast cancer during my sophomore year of high school. Judy was a senior and on the verge of leaving for college. My mother had been the ballast in our family, cooking lovely, perfectly balanced meals every night that drew us together as we talked and shared what had happened to us that day. We'd occasionally have pizza, but we were not a takeout family and never went to McDonald's. My mother would spend an afternoon slowly cooking a pot roast and serve it with gingersnap gravy, red cabbage, mashed potatoes, two vegetables, and something for dessert that she'd made while the pot roast was simmering. My mom delighted in being a homemaker. She was smart and accomplished, a teacher by training, but she knew that the center of her life would always be her family, and so it was.

Her cancer complicated our already combustible relationship. I was still rebellious, my sister was leaving home, and my mom's body was betraying her. She was a woman who liked to be in control, and now she was losing it in the areas of her life that mattered most to her. The older I get, the more I appreciate how devastating this time must have been for her. She was stoic and held a lot of her emotions inside.

In her twenties, my mom had a partial hysterectomy because of a precancerous condition. When she was diagnosed with breast cancer in her late thirties, she elected to deal with it by having a double radical mastectomy with reconstructive surgery. I remember her in the hospital swaddled with bandages and the tubes that drained her wounds. It was excruciating to see my mother—a five-foot-nine-inch-tall Swede—so vulnerable. If she was afraid, she didn't show it.

It would be easier if I could say my mother's breast cancer diminished the volatility between us, but it didn't. She went on to have her reconstructive surgery, which was unheard of in our town. My mom was determined to get her body back. She loved her life and us beyond measure and was not going to surrender any aspect of her life to cancer. She smiled and carried on. I don't know how her anger and despair were expressed or if they ever were. She was not the type of woman who would go to therapy or seek outside help of any kind—to her that would have been a sign of weakness.

Fortunately my mother's surgery was successful, and although the recovery was arduous, she rebounded, at least outwardly, in about a year.

While it was frightening to think that my mother had cancer and could die, once she recovered I slipped back into believing that everything was fine. For a time it was, and I continued on in my rebellious ways.

But four years after my mother's mastectomy, when she was forty-two, she was diagnosed with cancer of the mouth. It was a second cancer, completely unrelated to the first. She never smoked or drank. We weren't an introspective family. I don't remember long conversations about Mom's second cancer. I don't even remember her in bed. The mouth surgery to remove the cancer had left her with a tongue that was mangled and a somewhat slurred speech that embarrassed her. She had also lost some of her taste for certain foods. This frustrated her because she was someone who centered her life around nourishment. She was always tasting and testing the foods she cooked, adjusting them for taste. Now she found it difficult to discern which ingredient was in need of tweaking.

During this time, my relationship with my mother remained strained. I was still trying to push away and carve out my own identity, but at the same time, my mom's illness and ongoing battle with cancer were always in my mind. Both my mother and I felt more than we said. My mother's biggest worry about me was that I would never settle down. She was crazed with the thought of me living a life alone. Of course, my behavior during this period gave her plenty of reasons to think she was right. She abhorred my lifestyle. She didn't trust me or the gentlemen I kept company with. Nor did anyone else in my family. In fact, when my sister was married, I was specifically invited without a date. The reason? My family feared I'd bring a mobster to my sister's wedding.

I was in law school when my mom got sick again. I remember the many long drives to Philadelphia for her radiation treatments. The specialists in this type of cancer tend to be at big inner-city hospitals, and it's a cancer commonly found in heavy smokers and drinkers. My mother never was either. But sitting in the waiting area and looking at the people afflicted with this type of cancer left quite an impression on me. Their faces were grossly deformed. No noses. Cheeks missing. Tracheotomies. It was scary and devastating. My mom, of course, remained strong and uncomplaining.

When we walked into the waiting room, my mom would be in a polo shirt and khaki pants with a sweater tied over her shoulder, a striking Swede whose blond hair had turned gray prematurely. We would sit among (mostly) men with their noses gone, their faces carved out by this awful disease. Sometimes the cancer would grow on their necks—ugly signposts of imminent death. It was unbearable to sit there and think that my mother's face would soon be ravaged in similar ways. Within a few months, it was—her face became swollen and malformed, her throat unable to swallow food. She needed a tracheotomy and a feeding tube for the last nine months of her life.

But her dignity was non-negotiable. While she was being kept alive by whatever viscous formula was injected into her feeding tube, she continued, for those last nine months of her life, to cook dinner for us every night. The smells, the texture, the taste of food was something she would never again experience. But my mom still presided over her kitchen and our table, cooking meal after meal while she sat there and watched the rest of us devour her delicious creations. (She also stocked the freezer with frozen meals with detailed labels so my father would have something to eat after she died.)

My sister was already married with a young son and seven months pregnant with her second child when my mother took a turn for the worse. Judy was living in Virginia, and since I lived only half an hour from my parents, I was able to help with more of Mom's day-to-day care. I learned how to clean her trach by putting a tube down her throat and suctioning up the phlegm. I learned how to inject her with her food supplements. And I spent time with her making amends for the many, many years of battle I had put her through.

My mom adored Ron. He seemed like the stable and reliable man she was sure I would never date, let alone marry. Because Ron's family could be so cold and unreliable, he was drawn to the warmth and laughter of my parents' home. He enjoyed talking politics and business with my dad, and he loved my mother's cooking. It gave me enormous happiness and a sense of closure to know that my mother would die assured that I was married to a man I loved and that I would not live out the rest of my life alone.

It took Ron and me three years to start dating. But it took him only four months to propose marriage. I accepted immediately. We started dating in August just after I'd taken the bar exam. He proposed on December 1, 1996, after we'd watched a movie at home. He had a stunning diamond ring hidden in our bedroom, which was cut by a Belgian man who came out of retirement just to do it.

We decided to elope and marry in the Caribbean. We told our family and friends that we were taking a January vacation. We'd researched what we needed to do to marry there. We flew to the Grenadines to get a marriage license and walked into a city hall with chickens running about.

We stayed in a beautiful resort on Petit St. Vincent that was romantic and private. The hotel provided a priest of some persuasion that we paid to have flown to the island. He was in a suit and tie and barefoot. I wrapped a sarong around my bikini and tied a white shirt around my waist. Ron looked as happy

as I'd ever seen him. He was wearing khaki shorts with an
open blue shirt and a handmade sea-glass necklace.

A small boat took us to a spit of land that appears only at
low tide. One of the hotel managers came along as a witness.
We were married at sunset, the gilded light making the water
shimmer. I felt radiant and connected to a deeper peace than I
had ever known or imagined possible.

Ron's smile was incandescent. We said the traditional vows,
promising to love, honor, and cherish each other till death us
did part.

When we returned from our romantic idyll, we had the delight
of telling those we loved that we were, well, married. We went
over to my parents' home deliberately not wearing our wedding bands. My mother was eager to see our pictures and she
was flipping through, admiring our cottage, the beautiful
beach, and the sea, which can be described only as blue beyond belief. Even when reduced to four-by-six glossy prints,
the place was paradise.

Suddenly my mom came to a photograph of the two of us
beneath this little makeshift white arch the resort provided for
our wedding ceremony. Mom looked at the photo of the two
of us standing in the sand before a barefoot priest and said,
"You did it, didn't you? I knew it!" She was absolutely delighted
and not entirely surprised. She knew how intensely private I
am and how just the thought of parading myself down the center aisle of a church in billowy, frilly white gown with people
staring at me was just not my cup of tea. My mom was elated
and we immediately started talking about having a big party
later that fall for all of our family and friends.

My marriage was an enormous relief for her and gave her

a sense of security and peace at a time in her life when hopes for the future were rapidly diminishing.

Her cancer began a final and monstrous assault on her body. It was gruesome to behold. But she refused to relinquish any of her dignity. A few weeks after we got back from the Caribbean, my mom needed to get a feeding tube. And for those last nine months of her life, she did not sip a drink of water or taste a morsel of food. She continued to cook, guided by her instinct and her sense of smell but, most of all, by love.

Her quiet valor was heartbreaking. Ron and I decided to move in with my parents, mostly to spend more time with my mother but also because we were still in the process of finding a home for ourselves. When springtime arrived, we decided to get a golden retriever puppy. We worried about not having a home to bring our new puppy to, but my mom assured us that we could bring the puppy to her home. Besides, she knew that both Ron and I worked full-time and someone needed to take care of the little bundle of warmth who became known as Sam. My mom went with us when we picked him up. She held him in her lap for the entire drive home, just smiling and giggling at his absolute puppy-ness. Even if we factored out the natural exuberance of puppies, Sam was still over the top. He leaped, he licked, and he made us laugh so much with his antics. He was pure joy, and my mother reveled in him. Sam was a comfort to her that words could never be. As life was ebbing from her, Sam came rushing in.

It was excruciating for my mom. She was being tortured by a disease that could not be stopped. Her two daughters were thriving in the midst of new lives and my mom knew she wouldn't get to share those lives with us. She was angry about what was happening to her. In retrospect, I can now see how it would have helped if she'd gone to therapy or had some kind of outside support. But that was not the way she coped. While she wasn't part of the 1950s generation, she was of that mindset that shunned therapy and opening up to outsiders. You combed your hair, put on some lipstick, and got on with it.

That summer of 1997, my mom and I planted bulbs together that she knew she'd never live to see bloom. There was great comfort for her in nature, and she did find solace sitting on our back deck and staring at the thousands of oak trees that towered over Ron's and my new home. Ron and I had purchased a home filled with light and surrounded by forest. There were paths that began just beyond our doorstep, and we took daily hikes together.

Ron had never connected with nature before. It seemed almost incomprehensible to me until I understood how shortchanged his childhood had been. He had never noticed nature or slowed down enough to appreciate the beauty that was before him. I made him look at leaves and appreciate the texture and complexity of something so seemingly simple as bark. He learned to smell the air, the moist, sweet fragrance of the earth after a rain. He had never noticed how crisp and invigorating a breeze could be as it stirred through the leaves. The more Ron saw, the more he wanted to see. He wanted to immerse himself in nature. We rode mountain bikes a lot together through the woods and reveled in the sunsets with Sam bounding along beside us.

We never stopped talking. Our marriage was a nonstop conversation. Ron would follow me into the bathroom while I took a shower just to keep talking to me. We did errands together on Saturday not because we both needed to, but because we wanted to be together all the time. Part of what would become consoling to me in the years ahead was that when I looked back, I knew there wasn't a moment wasted.

Ron was an unabashed romantic and I so was I. We both left Post-it notes to each other around the house with silly messages. I would open my wallet to pay for groceries and find a yellow note with red writing that said, *The bearer of this note is entitled to five puppy kisses.* Or I would go to gather my gardening gloves and find another note that enclosed a Shakespearean sonnet about roses. And then there were the more racy notes that were written along the lines of *Naked! You, me, and a bottle of whipped cream!*

For someone who'd insisted for years that she never wanted to be married, I morphed into a domestic diva almost overnight. I was so thoroughly happy that I wanted to give as much to my life as I was getting from it. I don't do anything halfway, and once it was clear that I was going to stop work and care for my mother and make a home for Ron, that's what I joyfully did.

Welcome to my bubble. I tuned out the outside world. I stopped reading the *New York Times*. Ron despised it—he called it the "liberal rag." He read only the *Wall Street Journal* and the right-wing *New York Post*. He was a conservative Republican, idolizing and reading books about Ronald Reagan. During the Clinton years, we both thought Bill and Hillary were shameless liberals who were taking the country in the wrong direction. For someone who had always been independent and able to think for herself, I adopted my husband's politics and views as easily as inhaling my next breath. Ron and I were in sync in so many ways that it seemed natural to me that we would share this aspect of life, too.

I saw absolutely no reason to care about politics. It just didn't matter to me. I have vague, almost nonexistent memories of the Clinton-Dole race in 1996. In 2000, I knew that Al

Gore was running against George Bush but could not have told you three things about Gore. I found him dull and not very intelligent. I voted because Ron voted. I remember Sunday mornings when Ron would watch the political talk shows on the television. He loved Dick Cheney. When I would raise concerns about George Bush not receiving good grades in college and not seeming to be so bright, Ron would allay my fears by saying that Cheney was a man who knew what he was doing and who would make sure George Bush didn't screw anything up. How ironic.

Living in the bubble was easy. We had a beautiful home with floor-to-ceiling windows, skylights that brought the clouds, the blue sky, and the thousands of oak trees surrounding us into our home. Every appliance was gleaming and state-of-the-art. Our furniture was an eclectic mélange of antiques that all seemed to come together in a warm, inviting way. The colors were deep, dark, and earthen. One of our rooms was designed around Ron's hobby of fly-fishing. The deep green walls were covered with antique fly rods and creels. Fly-fishing books were piled up to make impromptu end tables, and paintings of old Irishmen fishing in the Irish countryside with their Labrador retrievers covered the walls.

Another room was decorated along the theme of hunt country. I found old riding jodhpurs, boots, hats, and saddles that I piled up in corners and on top of armoires. Oil paintings of horses hung on the walls. Our home was shared with family and friends who often came over to enjoy an elaborate meal, a simple cup of tea, or a fun cookies-and-cocoa sledding party.

Decorating our home both inside and outside became my passion. The young girl who dreamed of being a neurosurgeon was now changing her decorative pillows with the seasons. I agonized over ways to grow my prized English roses in the shady garden. I would spend hours researching the varieties of roses that would thrive in deep shade.

The garden became my canvas, and I decorated it with every possible seasonal theme. Mums and scarecrows would lead up to goblins and pumpkins for Halloween. When Thanksgiving approached, turkeys would be sticking out of the planters still blooming with mums. Wreaths, garlands, and hundreds of lights would be out for Christmas. I put handmade wooden signs on the trees around our house. With the first big snowfalls I would decorate with snowmen and sleds. Hearts and red ribbons graced the trees for Valentine's Day, and by Easter there were bunnies and eggs.

I was obsessed with making our home picture-perfect. I remember buying garlands of fresh boxwood and other greens to decorate every mantel and every room of our house for our first Christmas. Ron would walk in the door and be overwhelmed by the smell of the fresh greens, the Swedish glog simmering on the stove, and the roaring, romantic fire in the fireplace.

When we entertained, I would always incorporate some elements of the outdoors into the dining table. Pinecones would become place-card holders; gigantic oak leaves would be laid under clear salad plates so that when the first course was complete, you would find the surprise of a beautiful leaf peeking out at you. Gnarly twigs became a fascination, and I'd bring huge bundles into the house to make enormous, elaborate arrangements. And of course, edible flowers such as nasturtiums and pansies sparkling in fine sugar always adorned dessert plates.

I played classical music in the house all day—opera, orchestral, and piano were my favorites. These were the sounds from my grandparents' home. Fresh flowers were found in antique silver cups in every room. I would arrange and change them every few days. My grandmother's house always had large, beautiful bowls filled with flowers throughout each season, and I was discovering her traditions within myself. One of the best pieces of advice my grandmother ever gave to me was "Always plant a lilac bush beneath your bedroom window." Shortly after Ron and I moved into our house, we did.

My grandmother and my mother had always made the holidays feast days. We had enormous celebrations for Thanksgiving, Christmas, and Easter. Waterford punch bowls came out with the fine crystal, elegant china, sterling silver, and of course porcelain figurines to match the season.

At Easter you would always find oodles of daffodils and hyacinths overflowing the table and small European figurines of bunnies and Easter eggs strewn about. At Christmas, there was always the enormous crystal punch bowl filled with gigantic bright red antique ornamental Christmas balls. My grandmother would insert green sprigs of holly and pine that would peek out from the glimmering centerpiece. Set in little scenes on the large dining table would be small wooden figurines of children caroling, sledding, or carrying bundles of gifts. The tablescape was always magical.

As my mother was dying, my homemaking became a way to keep me tethered to her. She didn't have to tell me how happy she was to see me settling into a life with echoes of her own. And my total immersion into domestic life was also a way to absorb some of the agony of my mother's final months. We were both angry at the cruelty of this disease that seemed determined to steal her dignity before it destroyed her life.

Sometimes we would talk about what was happening to her, but mostly we did not. There were moments when she would break down and say how unfair everything felt, but those were short-lived. For the most part, we just found it more comfortable to surround ourselves with nature—whether that meant taking short walks on the beach or small hikes in the woods.

My mother lost the ability to speak toward the end of her life. Even if she held a finger over her trach, sounds did not emerge. She scribbled on pads, and the angrier she got, the faster she wrote. Her eyes spoke for her. My mother was a tower of strength that was imploding. My father seemed to manage my mom's illness by going on as he always did. His routine of working and moonlighting as mayor seemed to hold him together. My sister and I felt helpless. But helpless is too easy a word: We felt wild and complicated emotions that we will be untangling for the rest of our lives.

My mom died the day before Thanksgiving 1997. I remember I was running late that morning on my way down to the house. My mother and I had planted some bulbs the week before, and I wanted to sit with her and sketch out a picture of how the flowerbeds would look in the spring. I remember rounding the corner toward my parents' home and seeing the flashing lights of police cars.

My heart sank.

I walked up to the front door, and a police officer stopped me and suggested that I not go inside. I pushed my way through and saw my sister covered in blood. Judy was eight months pregnant and had come up to spend the week with my mom. I remember climbing the stairs of the house and seeing my very pregnant sister sitting on the couch in her maternity sweatshirt covered in blood. It was on her cheek, on her hands, and in her hair. I grabbed Kip, my parents' dog, and said that I needed to take him for a walk. Before leaving, my father walked down the hallway. He looked stunned. He asked me if I wanted to see my mother before they took her away.

I looked at my sister. She said, "Don't. Don't do it. Kris, it is really bad." I saw in her eyes how bad the scene must have been. For one of the few times in my life, I took her advice and walked out the front door with the dog.

I headed straight for the beach. I guess I was gone for about an hour. It seemed like a long enough time. When I turned the corner heading back to my parents' house, I saw the coroner walking beside the gurney that carried my mother's dead body. My memory is of the black body bag rolling down the front walk. Tears streamed down my cheeks. And a pit formed in my stomach. It seemed impossible that my mother could be inside that black, scary bag being slowly wheeled away.

When I returned to the house, I met my father's best friend walking down the stairs. He had an armful of towels, the bathroom rugs, and the shower curtain. They were all covered in blood. He asked me to help him load them into the washing machine. I looked at him and said, "Just throw them out. Please. Just throw them out."

My mother had suffered a pulmonary embolism. My sister had been helping her into the shower and said that she seemed fine. Judy had left her alone and walked out to the kitchen when she heard a thump. She went into the bathroom to find my mother hurriedly wiping up blood from the floor. My sister slipped on the blood and tried to help my mom. Judy realized that blood was coming out of Mother's trach. She awkwardly tried to stop the flow, but our mother collapsed into her arms and died.

I don't quite know how my sister didn't go into spontaneous labor right at that moment, but she didn't. She is one of the strongest women I have ever known, to endure our mother's dying like that in her arms. When she told the story of what happened, she assured me that our mother was not scared or panicked in her final moments. Judy said Mom was just wiping up all the blood as it continued to spill out of her neck. The image of our mother calmly and neatly accepting her death, even cleaning it up, leaves me shaken and bewildered. Our mom stayed true to herself to the very end, quietly tidying up, doing what needed to be done.

Knowing Mom's death was coming did not minimize the impact. Her suffering had been unbearable, and so was knowing that I was twenty-seven years old and would never spend an afternoon with my mother again. I would never walk into the kitchen and talk to her for hours as she cooked. And the beach—the beach where we spent the happiest days of my childhood—would always feel incomplete without her.

I remember going for long walks with Ron after my mother's death as I struggled to grapple with its unfairness. When I was thirteen, my family had decided to get a new dog. We'd named him Kip. When Ron and I were walking one day, I remember trying to explain the feeling I had about my mother's incomprehensible death. I kept saying to Ron, "People aren't supposed to die before their dogs. How is Kip alive and my mom dead? It would be like you dying and Sam still being here. It's not the order of things. It's not the way things go." Ron, in his upbeat and reassuring voice, said, "Don't worry, Sweets, I'm not going anywhere, don't worry." He then looked at Sam, who was trotting along beside us, and said, "Sorry, little boy, you're going before I do. That's just the way it is."

And I believed him.

In time, my mother's death began to feel like the bolt of

lightning that decimates one beautiful tree in the forest but leaves every other tree exquisitely untouched. Her death was a cruel and awful blow, but my forest was still standing. Ron and I would hike through the woods almost every day after he came home from work. He'd change into what we called his "comfy clothes" and we'd hike through the sunset. I opened his eyes to nature and its extravagant beauty: fall leaves that looked like stained glass, the graceful loops of hawks, and the shimmer of an early moon. I taught him about deer tracks in the snow and showed him how to find Orion. On days we didn't go hiking, we'd take Sam to the beach. Ron would throw a stick or ball into the waves that Sam always gleefully returned to us.

With a sandy, messy, and panting dog, Ron and I would head home, open a bottle of wine, and have supper. After dinner, we'd read. Ron would study a corporate report on Nextel or PepsiCo from a decade ago. He had to know the biography—the ins and outs—of companies to develop the investment strategies he needed as a money manager. I curled up beside him, reading *Town & Country* or *House & Garden*. The bubble was a pretty fine place to be.

A year after my mother's death, I became pregnant. While Ron had *always* known he wanted children, I wasn't so convinced. It seems incomprehensible to me now, but I can remember exactly how I felt. Ron was thrilled and I was scared to death since we hadn't planned on my getting pregnant just yet.

My identity was shifting and I wasn't ready. For years I'd said I didn't want children. At some level my mother's death might have intensified that feeling in a way I couldn't articulate. I understood the equation between love and loss and knew the terrible vulnerability that one demands of the other.

But when my obstetrician said, "We do have other options," the axis in my world shifted profoundly. "This pregnancy" became "my baby" and "our child." I realized that I was becoming a mother—in fact, I already was a mother to my unborn child, and it was very important that I be the best mother I could be. As I settled into the idea, I became thrilled. I loved being pregnant.

Mine was an ideal pregnancy. No morning sickness or aversions to food. Ron and I continued hiking and walking on the beach. Hiking and talking. Walking and talking. Ron and I never ran out of things to say. It was the hallmark of our relationship; in the 1,644 days of our marriage, we spent only a handful of days separated from each other and talked away the hours in the rest of them.

I had a high-risk pregnancy because of my ulcerative colitis and lupus, an autoimmune disease I was diagnosed with during my pregnancy. There were no real problems, only potential ones. Nevertheless, I was happy to have a scheduled C-section. The date we chose was the earliest date possible—I couldn't wait to meet our new daughter.

And on March 18, 1999, Caroline Whitney Breitweiser took her first breaths in this world.

⊷⊷⊷

How can six pounds and thirteen ounces of anything release such enormous and boundless joy? Once I emerged from my cesarean fog, I stared at the warm little bundle of love beside me, my daughter, Caroline. Her blond hair arranged itself into a quirky Mohawk. She was all head and no neck, which made her a commanding presence, right from the start. Everyone agreed that she looked exactly like Ron. I had never seen him happier.

He had made it past the boundaries of his unhappy childhood and now thoroughly belonged to a family of his own.

The nurses taught Ron how to change Caroline's diapers at the hospital, and for the first few days at home he was in charge while I recovered from the C-section. Ron and I had been happy before. We'd had no sense that anything was missing in our lives until we realized how complete we felt now with our daughter. As a couple, we didn't need a lot from the outside world. As a family, we needed even less.

Caroline started off in the bassinet next to our bed, but she never made it to her crib. She was nursing every two or three hours and soon just fell asleep in bed with me and stayed there. Co-sleeping has its critics, but it was a gentle and tender way for us to be. Caroline snuggled in beside us and awakened to coo and cuddle with her dad. Ron didn't know any lullabies or melodies, so all he ever sang to her in the wee hours of the morning was the "Happy Birthday" song. I hope those melodies linger somewhere inside of her. It was as if he were singing his heart out for all the birthdays he was destined to miss.

But life, to paraphrase Kierkegaard, must be lived forward even as it is understood backwards. We were happily immersed in living our lives. All we knew about our future was that we wanted four children, each three years apart. Ron was a money manager for what in the financial world are called high-net-worth investors. That translated into individuals who might give Ron $20 million to invest. Ron was paid on performance, a percentage of how his portfolios performed. He had no mechanical or common sense, and he never learned how to empty the Diaper Genie (which was maddening to me), but he excelled at managing stock portfolios and always beat the market by a number of percentage points, something that is exceedingly hard to do over time. Ron's idol, god, and oracle was the

financier Warren Buffett—whom I'd never heard of. My Buffett
was the Jimmy of "Margaritaville" and my sybaritic summers at
the Jersey Shore. One of the high points of Ron's life was when
he wrote to Warren Buffett and then received a handwritten letter in return, thanking him for the suggestion Ron had made.
(That year's annual report from Buffett's company, Berkshire
Hathaway, contained the quote Ron had suggested. Ron
couldn't believe it.)

Ron's brilliance at the office soon became eclipsed by his
new exuberance for being a dad. While he was home from
work, we became a threesome effortlessly. Caroline was cheerful and content. She rarely slept in the daytime, but the pedi-
atrician assured me that some babies didn't need as much
sleep as others, and if she wasn't irritable there was no reason
for concern. And Caroline was far from irritable. In fact, to this
day she has never really thrown a temper tantrum. She has always been upbeat, cheerful, and extremely easygoing. Just like
her dad.

Our daily life remained the same except that Caroline was
inextricably part of it. We never had babysitters, not because of
any philosophical opposition to them, but because we enjoyed
taking Caroline everywhere with us. And as she grew older, she
became accustomed to being out in public—whether that
meant fancy restaurants or long car rides. The everyday delight
we found in one another made us inseparable.

Ron was usually out the door by 6:30 A.M. to take the fast
ferry to Wall Street. He'd call me when he got to his desk at
Fiduciary Trust and we'd run through our day and remind each
other of our love. Caroline and I did errands, shopped, and gar-
dened. I made her a child's garden with berry brambles, straw-
berry patches, and cherry trees. There was a hidden area for tea
with a tiny chair. And there were tree stumps and bark houses

that made the perfect hideout for elves, gnomes, and fairies of the forest. I wanted the garden to be an adventure for my little girl. I wanted her to explore and to use her imagination. Our lives felt, if not magical, then at least delightful.

Ron was home by 5:30 every evening, and after he changed clothes, we'd hike as always, but with Caroline in a carrier on my chest and Sam rocketing alongside us. We would hike up to the clearing and watch the light change and the clouds shift as day gave way to twilight. Ron would show Caroline all the things I'd shown him. The intricacies of leaves, the moss on a rock, a squirrel's nest in a tree.

On Saturday mornings we'd drive to the beach at Spring Lake and take the four-mile walk along an old wooden board-walk that sits between the bluffs and the beach. The morning light sparkled on the ocean and the surf fishermen would be casting into the waves. Sam raced ahead of us, reckless in his exuberance, practically taunting Ron when he refused to come when called or to stop chewing on a dead horseshoe crab. At the end of our walk we'd stop in a small café for banana-nut pancakes and coffee. Caroline was known by all there as Smi-ley because she was always, always smiling, giggling, and bounding with happiness.

If your mother has had breast cancer, the recommendation is that you have your first mammogram when you are ten years younger than she was when diagnosed. My mom was thirty-six when she received her diagnosis. When I was twenty-six, I was pregnant, and then I nursed Caroline for eighteen months. I finally, reluctantly made an appointment for my first mammo-gram in the summer of 2001. I was no longer nursing, and Ron and I were thinking of trying to get pregnant with our second child. I knew I couldn't postpone the mammogram any longer.

After the first set of pictures was done I knew something

was wrong. I could just sense it in the air. My ob-gyn was called for a referral for an ultrasound. The nurse in the radiological suite explained it away as something that was needed to establish a baseline mammogram. Within an hour, I had the ultrasound. And then I needed to have more films done of my right breast. By this point I had noticed that many women had come and gone and I was still sitting there in my pathetic paper-thin gown.

After the second and then third set of films were taken, I was called in by the radiologist, who flipped on the light, pointed to the image on the film, and said, "See that right there? That's a tumor." I said, "Really? What am I supposed to do?" In a matter-of-fact way that was unsettling he said, "Find yourself a surgeon."

I found my cell phone and called Ron. When I heard his voice I managed to say, "Oh, my God." He asked what was wrong. "This is so bad. I have a tumor." When I went home and looked at Caroline, I felt a chokehold of fear and too many what-ifs. I shut them off because each was too dire to contemplate.

Ron was worried. He was optimistic, as always, but we were both on edge. I bought *Dr. Susan Love's Breast Book* and read as much as I could find about treatment options. I wanted the most aggressive option available, even if it meant removing both breasts. Ron agreed. He kept saying to me, "Sweets, you're not going anywhere. You're not leaving us."

Caroline turned two and a half that September and we enrolled her in a cute little nursery school down the street from our home for three mornings a week. Her speech was somewhat delayed, and we thought putting her in nursery school surrounded by other children would be just the sort of stimulation she needed. Her first day of nursery school was September 10. We were supposed to be on vacation that week, but we pushed it up by two weeks so we could all spend time together before Caroline's days were interrupted by nursery school.

We decided to stay local and do day trips. We went to the Bronx and Philadelphia Zoos and the Baltimore Aquarium. But our favorite place was the beach. We went there over and over, splashing and playing in the water still warmed by the summer sun. We were there on Sunday, September 9. I have a picture of Ron holding Caroline at the water's edge. As I wrangled Sam and steadied the camera, Ron pointed out toward the Twin Towers and said, "See those big buildings, sweetheart? That's where Daddy works."

It's one of the last pictures I have of him. Ron had thirty-seven hours to live.

CHAPTER TWO

———— ⚬⚬⚬ ————

From Wife to Widow

RON WAS RUNNING LATE on the last morning of his life. He didn't take the time to put his coffee cup and breakfast things in the dishwasher. He was trying to catch the 6:30 ferry that got him to his desk on the ninety-fourth floor of the World Trade Center shortly after 7:00 A.M.

I was half awake in bed, listening to the familiar morning sounds that filled our home. Ron running the shower, dressing, brushing his teeth, making coffee, opening the refrigerator door and pouring himself a glass of orange juice. He usually ate a bowl of granola with bananas for breakfast, and that Tuesday morning was no different. As always, he left a note for me on the bathroom mirror—*Smile, Sweets* with a big broad smiley face underneath. He had also gingerly placed a wad of toothpaste on my toothbrush; it was his way of kindly reminding me to brush my teeth and letting me know he was thinking of me.

As he found my warm body buried beneath the beige duvet and the piles of big pillows, he kissed me on the cheek and whispered his apology for running late and leaving his dishes in the sink. I rolled over, opened my eyes, and kissed him on the lips, saying, "That's okay, I love you. Have a good day." He then walked over to the other side of the bed, where he found Caroline at the top of the bed and Sam sleeping at the foot of the bed. He kissed Caroline on the forehead and whispered, "Good luck at school today, my little bug." He turned to Sam, who had opened his eyes but left his head buried in the covers. Sam performed a thump wag—a slow, persistent wag of the tail—on the bed. Ron kissed Sam on the nose—he always kissed him on the nose—and gave his orders, "Okay, little boy, you take care of our girls. You're the man of the house when I'm gone. Be a good boy." Sam raised his head, licked Ron's face, and jumped clumsily off the bed to follow Ron to the back door.

I slept another fifteen minutes or so, finally getting out of bed after hearing Sam's relentless scratching at the back door so he could get outside to take his morning stroll around the garden. Ron called me at 8:30 from his desk at Fiduciary Trust. It was the first of our daily telephone calls. He was having his second cup of coffee, I my first. I told him I was taking Caroline to the speech therapist at 9:15 and then to her second day of nursery school. The yellow Post-it note from Ron the day before still hung on the cabinet. It said, *Good luck to my little girl on her first day of school.*

Glancing at the clock and realizing that I, too, was running late, I told Ron I needed to get going. "I love you, Sweets." "I love you, too."

We had talked for roughly ten minutes. Six minutes later, American Airlines Fight 11 slammed into the North Tower of the World Trade Center. It was 8:46 A.M.

The speech therapist was fifteen minutes away and I was cutting it close by still being home at 8:50. I was rushing back into the bedroom to brush my teeth. The phone rang. It was Ron. I was standing between the doorway of our bedroom and the hallway. He blurted breathlessly, "Sweets, I'm okay, I'm okay. Don't worry, I'm okay." I said, "Sweets, what are you talking about?" He said, "Don't you know? Turn on the TV. The building next to mine exploded. It's unbelievable. Turn on the TV, Sweets." I ran into the kitchen and flipped on the small TV on the counter. I gasped. "Holy shit, it's really bad." Ron responded, "That's why I am calling you. I didn't want you to worry. I'm fine. I'm okay. Sweetheart, it's not my building."

Ron's voice cracked. "But, Sweets, you don't understand. It is really bad. I am sitting here looking and people are jumping out of the windows. It is really bad. They are jumping out of the windows. Right across from me. I can see them. And they are just jumping. I'm okay, though, Sweets. I'm okay."

"Oh, my God, honey. Are you okay? What happened?" He said he wasn't sure. He said that he had been sitting at his desk working when suddenly his cheek got warm. He looked up and saw a huge fireball erupt from the North Tower.

I began to grow scared. Nervous energy started vibrating through my body. Caroline was holding on to my leg. Sam was jumping up at my side—I was still holding my handbag and keys and Sam was excited about going for a ride in the car. I jostled loose from both of them and steadied the phone. "Oh, my God, sweetheart. It looks really bad. Please be careful. Just be safe. I love you. But just be careful."

"I will. They told us to stay in the building. I've got to go. We're going to go watch it on the trading floor. They have TVs on the trading floor. I'll call you back. Sweets, I'm safe. I'm okay. Don't worry. But I have to go. I love you."

I immediately called the speech therapist and said we would not make it because my husband was in the World Trade Center. She didn't know what had happened. I quickly explained to her that there was apparently some explosion in one of the World Trade Center buildings and that I knew we'd be getting calls all morning from people who weren't sure which building Ron worked in, wanting to know if he was okay. I remember telling her that I knew it sounded stupid, but that I just wanted to stay home.

I hung up and continued watching the television. I was watching NBC. Suddenly an enormous red fireball rocketed out of the side of *Ron's* building. I never saw the second plane slice into his building—I just saw the huge fireball shoot out from the side of his building, the building he'd called me from just moments before. It was 9:03. The flames roared from the building and licked up the sides of the steel frame and windows.

I stood there absolutely stunned. My body—my eyes and ears—continued to take in the scene and send those bits of information to my brain, but my brain couldn't seem to process what was being sent. It was if my brain just suspended itself for those brief initial moments, struggling to compute, to make sense of, what my eyes and ears had just witnessed. And then my body too began to try to understand what was happening. I felt dizzy and nauseated. I remember shaking my head, trying to steady the world that seemed to be spinning out of control. I continued shaking my head, trying to fix my eyes on the television. Then I began hurriedly to count the floors of the building from top to bottom. I remember placing my finger on the small screen and trying to count the floors from the television screen. It was useless. I remembered that Ron had said that he was heading to the trading floor. My mind frenzied itself with questions: Where was the trading floor? Was it on the same floor as his desk? Was it near the windows? Where the hell was he? Was he okay? Alive? Maybe—maybe he was alive.

Terror had slammed into the morning like a torpedo. A

serene kitchen, filled with the slant of morning light and the day's possibility: coffee cup with half-and-half and way too much sugar, card from the day before wishing Caroline good luck at school, pictures from our two-week vacation hanging on the cabinet fronts. Smiles. Life. All of it now suspended in a moment of holding, holding in abeyance what was to become. The storm of disbelief began to grow, and it grew in violent degree. It soon enveloped me in a dizzying and sickening chaos. The walls, the sky, the ceiling, everything was inside out and upside down. My brain seemed to shut down, ejecting itself from my body to spare me from the horrendous, gut-wrenching pain of this new, unthinkable reality. But my heart immediately knew what my brain would not accept.

Ron was dead.

My husband was dead. Ron was dead. My Sweets was dead. Gone. Forever. My legs struggled to support me and I was bracing myself on the kitchen counter. Caroline was confused and grabbing onto me. Sam was circling me, periodically jumping up and knocking Caroline down in the process. I would scoop her up and hold her on my hip, still stumbling and staggering around the kitchen. A terrifying primordial scream unleashed itself, pouring out of my lungs. "Noooooooo, nooooooo, nooooo."

The phone rang. I grabbed it, thinking it was Ron. A wave of sheer delight and relief barreled through my body like a freight train. He was safe! He was alive! *It's him.* I fumbled for the phone, hitting the button to talk, wiping the tears from my face. "Ron! Ron! Sweets, is it you? Hello? Sweets, is it you?"

But it was Jill from across the street. She was desperate and screaming, "Have you heard from Ron? Have you heard from him? I haven't heard from Donald. Oh, my God, what if they aren't alive? Where are they, Kris? Where are they? Oh, my God, they have to be safe. They have to be safe. What are we going to do?" Jill's call-waiting clicked in. She hung up.

My head continued to ignore what my heart already knew. My brain was lured by the rush of possibility and hope delivered by the simple ring of the phone. Part of me began to think Ron might be alive. Maybe, just maybe, he had survived. Maybe he had decided to leave the building—to get the hell outta there—right after he got off the phone with me. Bloodied, beleaguered, breathless from escaping death; I envisioned him walking up our driveway and through our back door like a dazed and defeated soldier, but *alive*.

The phone rang again. I lunged. "Hello, hello? Ron, is it you? Hello, hello? Ron, if it's you I love you." Silence. Maybe he was trapped, trying to let me know he was still alive. "Sweets, can you hear me? I love you, Sweets—Sweets?" I was pacing back and forth in the living room, shouting into the phone. Tears were streaming down my face. My hands were shaking. I was barely standing. I couldn't feel my legs. I was blowing my nose on the sleeve of my shirt. Wiping my eyes, periodically stumbling to the floor. Caroline was still clinging to me. Sam was still jumping and circling around me, nervous and anxious. I continued to talk into the phone. The severity of the situation was settling in. I wept into the phone. I was trying to be strong and positive, hoping that Ron was on the other end clinging to my voice. Horrible images streamed through my head: Ron unable to speak, trapped, in pain, facing imminent death. "We're home, waiting for you, Sweets. Please come home. We love you, sweetheart. Caroline is here and Sam is here and we want you to come home. Please come home, Sweets, just come home. Sweets, can you hear me? I love you, Sweets, I love you."

Call-waiting clicked. I got angry. Who was calling? What if

it was Ron? Maybe the phone line I was talking into was disconnected and I was talking to dead air and Ron had actually
called back on the other line. Before hitting the call-waiting
button I sheepishly and nervously said, "Sweets, maybe that is
you on the other line, calling to tell me you are alive. Sweetheart, can you hear me? I'm going to click over to see if it is
you. I'll be right back, Sweets. I will be right back." I clicked
over.

The caller was Ron's friend Brett. "Have you heard from
Ron? Has he called?" Brett quickly told me he'd been talking to
Ron on the phone when the plane must have hit Ron's building. Brett had been home watching television and called Ron
to find out what was going on. Ron and Brett were talking
when, mid-sentence, Ron said, "Oh, my God." Brett heard a
rumbling and then a rushing sound. And then the phone simply went dead. Brett said that Ron didn't scream or sound
afraid. He just plainly and flatly said, "Oh, my God."

Brett asked if I'd heard from Ron. I barked back, "No! I
haven't heard from him, and what the hell were you doing calling him anyway? If he hadn't been talking to you on the phone
he might have been getting the hell out of the building. What
the fuck were you thinking, calling him? Don't you *ever* fucking call this home again." I clicked back over to the other line,
but the line was dead. I cursed.

The phone rang again. The roller coaster continued. It was
Jill calling back to see if I had heard anything. We both continued to cry hysterically into the phone, sobbing while intermittently trying to appease our small children and fend off the
awful, awful thoughts of the reality that was coming to be. By
this point, the Pentagon had been hit by Flight 77. It seemed
that our entire world was coming to an end. Thoughts that we
were all going to die started to permeate my mind. Jill and I

kept talking and crying hysterically to each other, trying to hold on to something—anything—because it seemed like our world was spinning so totally and utterly out of control.

Jill was watching CNN and I was watching NBC when Tower Two, Ron's building, collapsed at 9:59 A.M. Jill knew immediately because CNN showed a different vantage point and reported the tower as collapsing. But NBC, filming from another angle, initially reported the collapse as another building exploding. I first said, "Shit, another building just exploded." Jill said, "No, honey, it's his building. His building collapsed." I countered, "No, it is another building. Another building just exploded. Look at all the smoke." I walked up to the television and tried to clear the smoke that was blocking the view. A vain attempt, but I had to see. At that exact moment, NBC switched to the on-street reporter, who reported that Tower Two had just collapsed. I gasped, "Oh, my God. He is gone." Jill was silent on the phone. She then whispered, "Honey, I am so sorry. I am so sorry." Having nothing left to say because there were no words that could be said, she hung up. (Jill's husband ultimately survived.)

I dropped the phone. It crashed onto the floor as I fell right along with it.

First, everything went black. Sight and sound stopped. Caroline was there, but I don't remember what she did or what she was saying. Sam kept licking my face and jumping about. I felt violently bewildered, numb, and dead. I screamed and rolled around on the kitchen floor, lurching and contorted and screaming, "No, no, no . . ." until the words weakened and fell flat. For a time I remember looking down on the pathetic scene from a tranquil, peaceful, and safe place above. And then, slowly, I returned to my body and my mind. As my awareness slowly crept back, the anguish I felt about Ron became coupled with the fear unleashed by the attack itself. What was happening to us? Were we all going to die? Was the world coming to an end?

I struggled to hold on to some sense of clarity. I consciously reminded myself to take a breath. I focused on Caroline. She was only two and a half. But other thoughts crowded their way in. Survivor thoughts. Someone always makes it out. Ron could, Ron would. He was strong and in great shape. He wanted to live. He loved us so much. If there were a way to manage coming home to us, he would do it. I knew that. Alive, dead, dead, alive, alive, alive, Ron had to be alive. Or had that huge fireball engulfed him and immediately turned him to ash that floated peacefully, breathlessly, and most important, painlessly up into the heavens above? No. No. He was alive. But how could he be alive? Or could he be alive? The wild roller coaster had now completely broken loose from its tracks. I was being whipped around and around. And upside down. Around and around it continued. My beautiful, safe, simple life was forever untethered from its tracks.

When I began to get my bearings, I called Ron's family. I wasn't sure they realized that Ron worked in the World Trade Center. The last few months had been especially tense among them. Ron felt his sister and mother had broken a promise to him in the preceding weeks; this had precipitated a heated confrontation that spread out into his entire family. It was a bitter falling-out that had left them all not speaking to one another.

Nevertheless, this was his family. And I felt obligated to call them. When his father answered the phone, I said, "Fred, It's Kristen. Listen, I don't know if you guys want to come over here and wait for Ron, but I just want you to know that you are more than welcome to do so." Ron's father barked, "What the hell are you talking about?" He handed the phone to Ron's mother and mumbled something about not knowing what the hell was wrong with me. When Ron's mother got on the phone, I had reached the end of my rope and simply shouted, "Gerry, Ron works in the World Trade Center. His building just got attacked. I haven't heard from him. I don't know if he is okay. If you want to come over, come over." Ron's mom apparently had no idea what had transpired and asked what I was talking about. I coldly shouted, "Turn the goddamn television on. Ron could be dead." I hung up the phone.

They arrived at our house with boxes of pizzas and submarine sandwiches. They sat in front of the large TV in the den. I don't remember even speaking to them, although I am sure I did. Memories of that day, those next few weeks, exist for me only in flashes, images, and bursts of conversations. I've had to rely on the memories of those who love me and stood by me for the details.

My sister, Judy, her husband, Rich, and their children, Trey and Lauren, drove straight through from Virginia shortly after they heard the news. Judy and her husband are federal agents and have badges, guns, and the ability to get through checkpoints. They were fully prepared to do whatever it would take to get to me. But Judy said that what was striking to her was that I-95 was completely empty. No one was even on the highway. At one overpass between Delaware and New Jersey, a lone couple stood on the bridge waving an American flag so large it took both of them to hold on to it. My sister looked up as she drove underneath. She felt an enormous wave of grief wash over her. She looked at her husband. She looked at her two small children in the backseat. A tear washed down her face.

Judy remembers walking into my house and being assaulted by chaos, rage, and sorrow. I was alternating between shock and a fury that knew no bounds. My father was there but found himself unsure of how to handle me. No one knew what to do. Judy's husband, Rich, took Caroline, who was still in diapers, out with Trey and Lauren to play on the swing set, walk in the woods, and visit the horses that were nearby—anything that helped keep her world far removed from the all-too-sad and violent reality that had overtaken our lives. Judy remembers that for the first few weeks, whenever Caroline would hear a car pull up the driveway, she'd run to a window and say, "Daddy! Daddy! Daddy's home!" Thankfully I have no memory of that.

The first day was endless. Waiting, hoping, questioning, imagining, fearing, realizing, grappling, recoiling, and of course, denying. There just had to be a way Ron could still walk through our back door. "Bad shit doesn't happen to me" was one of his refrains. He had fought his way through his childhood, persevered through college, and finessed his way onto Wall Street, where he had steadfastly proven that he belonged there. There wasn't a thing he couldn't do. He knew that. And I knew that. He had the confidence that came from having earned his success. But beyond that, Ron loved Caroline, Sam, and me so much that I just knew he would never give up. I knew that if there were ever a way to survive, he would find it.

But an inferno that could melt tons of metal and steel could make a mockery of muscle and bone. Awful images from that day bombarded my brain: Ron, choking with smoke, curled up in a tiny corner, gasping for air, watching the carpet burn around him, watching the dancing flames coax their way toward him. "Bad shit doesn't happen to me, Sweets." It kept ringing in my ears.

The next morning Judy and I went to pick up Ron's car at the ferry. I cut some roses from the garden, the same roses I had struggled so hard to make bloom in our shady yard. I hadn't slept. Judy was sobbing, "How could this happen? How could he be gone?" I was crying, too. Caroline sat strapped in her car seat. Sam was in the far back scratching at the windows as he always did, cluelessly happy to be along for the ride.

We drove down to the water as the sun was getting a foothold on the day. The ferry was parked at the dock, so many of its patrons dead. The cars of the dead stood like silent sentries, marking lives that had come to a halt. I remember pulling into the parking lot and seeing the faces of the policemen who were given the job of barricading off the abandoned cars. They looked at my sister and me as we eased the car past the wooden barricade. They tilted their heads and motioned. All eyes were silently fixed on us as we pulled next to Ron's car. I wasn't stupid. I knew what they were thinking. This was to be the first set of looks I would get—the look of acknowledgment that I was one of those: a 9/11 widow. It was also the first time I realized that I was going to have to share my husband's death with the rest of the world. I felt violated by the intrusion. I didn't want anyone to know my sadness. I didn't want to share it with anyone. I felt like it was mine and mine alone to keep.

I reached back in the car and gathered up the roses. I unhooked Caroline from the car seat and walked around back to let Sam out. Together my sister and I walked to the end of the dock. The fire from Ground Zero was still visible. The smell was overwhelming. The wind had carried the stench south. I will never, ever forget that smell, thick, foul, and putrid. I hobbled to the end of the dock. Hot tears streamed down my cheeks as I continued to walk. Sobbing, with Caroline walking beside me and Sam bounding ahead, we reached the end and tossed the flowers into the water. I told Caroline to say "I love you, Daddy" as she threw each of her rose petals into the water. Life being what it is, we almost lost Sam twice as he tried to jump in the water to retrieve the flowers. That made us laugh. And we wiped away the tears for a few moments. Silly, stupid dog.

The flowers floated away as if with a sense of purpose, but it was only the current, strong enough to make it seem as though they had somewhere to go. Judy was quiet now. She told me later that she'd prayed to our mother, asking her to send Ron home to Caroline and me. We walked back toward the car and I remember approaching it slowly. I lowered myself onto the seat and held the steering wheel, thinking that my hands were where his hands had been the day before. I looked around for little signs of his presence. Tears welled up inside me. When I turned over the ignition, the radio was on. I don't remember the song because I immediately turned it off. I wanted silence. I drove the short drive with tears streaming down my cheeks. Talking to myself. Talking to Ron. Begging him to come home. The world was in shock, but it still moved on. As I drove home I noticed that people were buying groceries, making left-hand turns, running errands, filling up gas tanks. But my life was different. My life would not go on. At least not in the way it used to be. I fell into an emotional coma, a deep, dark sleep.

On Thursday evening, September 13, I wrote a letter to Caroline. I wanted to unleash my feelings and memories onto a page.

*It's one o'clock in the morning now, Thursday has
begun. . . . You are lying in bed, bundled up in pillows—
sleeping horizontally—restless, so restless, Sammy is
guarding you at the door. Aunt Judy sleeps in your bed. I
have such an aching pit in my stomach. Is it because I*

haven't eaten in two days? Is it because I am on Xanax and an antibiotic or is it because I am so scared and so deeply, deeply, and profoundly wounded.

My soul is broken. I just constantly lurch forward as the tears run down my face and then my mind gives me a reprieve, it kind of shuts the thoughts out and I feel numb—like I am in an alternate place. Everywhere I look I see your dad. I turn on a light, I sit in a chair, I put on my shoes. I am the walking dead.

Honey, if you weren't here I could not go on, my soul is so wounded, my eyes are so sad . . . nothing . . . not even you . . . can make me forget. . . . I need to see that sparkle in your eye. I need to hear your infectious laugh. I need your little open arms, you running toward me, and that little tilt of your head as you touch my face and ask "Mommy, what's wrong?"

Just writing those feelings has calmed me, my God, I love you so much . . . and now you truly are my life. I am so scared for us. What will we do? How will we go on? We are really just two little girls holding hands with bonded hearts.

Oh my God, honey, why us, why you? Your daddy loved you so much. He just adored you, he just did. I thank God for every single moment we shared with him, I thank God that we were inseparable. . . .

We used to walk the woods, and I'll have you know I carried you the most, you little chunky monkey. We used to walk every day and Daddy just loved it. He loved seeing the deer and he would point them out to you and say, "Look, bug, look at the deer." He truly felt so blessed and happy. And he knew how lucky we all were to share such a beautiful life together.

You made your dad so happy and he just adored watching you do everything. He would giggle with you and tickle your belly and get thousands of bug hugs. Honey, we just never knew . . . we had no idea this was going to happen. . . . I look back and regret not having him keep a journal for you, not videotaping him more for you, not saving all of his little notes that he wrote to you. But I just didn't know.

He carried a picture of us in his wallet and a poem that I wrote to him from Winnie the Pooh, and so I know that we were with him when he died. . . . We were, honey . . . and I just know in my heart that he tried so hard to get home to us. I just know he did. But oh, my God, honey, he didn't have a chance . . .

You are so innocent, you are just a little sparkle of life. Honey, he was the best daddy in the whole world and he just adored you. . . . I just can't believe that you will never feel that or know that firsthand. . . .

I was lying in bed next to you tonight, and of course I had the heel of your warm little foot in my eye, and I just thought, who will teach her how to do things lefty? He assured me that he would teach you everything because he was lefty and now he is not here to do it. Honey, he is not here to hold your little hand, he is not here to cuddle with you, to hug you; oh, God, honey, I am so, so sorry. I would do anything to have him here for you. I would give my own life for him to be here with you.

I keep saying to people, "You know, I don't care that he is not here for me, but what about Caroline? She is just so young and innocent and she loved him so much."

He just didn't have a chance; you will see the videos someday and you will realize that if he could have been here for us, he would have. Honey, he loved all three of us so much. And as I take a deep breath, I just focus on and think about that he is an angel now . . . your angel. . . . He is going to be with you forever, and if you are quiet enough and still enough you will feel him on your shoulder, whispering into your precious little ear, saying "I love you, buggy, I love you."

You know the first night I went to put you to bed, and I thought you were pretty much asleep and all of a sudden . . . you giggled, you sat straight up and pointed to the ceiling and said, "Daddy." I whispered out to you, "Is your daddy here, honey, did he come to say good-bye? Tell him that we love him and that we'll be okay. Tell him that we are going to get through this. Do you hear me, Sweets? Ron, are you there? I love you and we'll be okay. Honey, we miss you but we are going to make it, so go on, it's okay, we love you." And with that, honey, you kept smiling and blowing raspberries up to the ceiling. I wonder . . . was your daddy there to say good-bye . . . to sing you one last birthday song? I miss him, honey. I miss him so much. But we are going to be okay. I promise.

During the day the phone rang incessantly. Friends wanted to know what we had heard. At one point early on, Fiduciary Trust called and said Ron's name was on a list of survivors. I felt a burst of hope. I was so desperate to convert my agony into joy that even the hint of such a possibility pried my heart wide open. There were three calls from people who said he was possibly alive in a burn ward. But that person was only five feet ten inches tall, and he was blond with burns over 90 percent of his body. I would have taken him that way. Hell, I would have taken him any way, just so long as he came home.

I realized, though, that none of the burn victims could have been Ron. But still, there was a moment of hope when I thought if his hair was burned off, maybe what was left might be mistaken for blond. Maybe it had been hard to measure his height and it was off by a few inches . . . maybe, maybe, maybe—but of course it never was.

There was the report of a man who rode the rubble down atop a steel beam. One of Ron's co-workers called to say she was sure it was Ron. She confided in me that she just knew he had to be alive. "He loved you and Caroline too much to leave you. He just can't be dead. It doesn't make any sense. He loved you too much."

Judy took charge of all the immediate needs with supreme skill and called all the 800 numbers that had been set up to provide information. We had to get a photo of Ron so a "missing" poster could be made and put up in the subway stations, at the bus stops, and on all the "missing" boards that popped up around the city. DNA samples had to be collected and given to police. I gave them his razor, his contact lenses, and his comb. I refused to give them his toothbrush.

The night of the eleventh, prior to going to bed, I walked into our bathroom and placed some toothpaste on Ron's toothbrush. I did it as a way of symbolizing that I believed that he was going to come home. I remember looking in the mirror as I squeezed out the toothpaste and saying out loud, "Okay, Sweets, your toothbrush is waiting. You have to come home now so you can brush your teeth." I explained to a police officer that I had done this and therefore damaged Ron's fresh DNA by placing the toothpaste on his toothbrush. The officer just sort of looked at me. How could he understand something so illogical? I didn't care. It was a routine of my life with Ron. And it made me feel hopeful and safe. So I was going to follow that routine until the bitter end. (The toothbrush stayed on the counter for many months waiting for Ron to come home.)

The police officer continued with his report. Did Ron have any identifying marks? Yes, he had a scar on his left abdomen but no tattoos. The police needed to know every detail, right down to the labels in the clothes Ron was wearing that day. That was easy, since I put out Ron's clothes every night. I knew he had been wearing Calvin Klein boxer briefs, size 34. I knew he had on Ralph Lauren beige linen pants, with a 34 waist, and a brown Cole Haan belt. He had brown suede Cole Haan shoes, size 10, a brown Ralph Lauren sweater vest, and a beige linen dress shirt. I found the serial number for Ron's big Breitling aviator's watch. He was also wearing his wedding band. Our dentist made a copy of his dental records. The police also needed any photos that showed identifiable body parts. I found a picture from our wedding album that showed the scar that Ron had on his stomach. The police took the picture as well, promising to give it all back to me.

It felt like the end of the world. It was terrible, surreal, and gruesome. What did I hope for now? A body? A piece of him? Knowledge of how he died? Was that what I wanted? What if I found out he had jumped? What if, God forbid, he became one of those people whose fate he had chillingly told to me in our last phone conversation: the jumpers? Had he seen what his own death would be? I shut those thoughts out of my head immediately. What if someone saw him trapped and screaming under rubble, unable to move?

What if he'd been hit on the head and was sitting in some hospital ward with amnesia? What if he was only injured? I would love him without legs. What if he had only one arm? Well, then he would master doing everything with the other one. What if his body were covered with burns? We could handle that. We could handle anything together. But we would first have to find him.

I didn't sleep. Judy and I would stay up most of the night. I don't remember what we talked or cried about. I never saw my sister cry during the day. She would go on long walks with Sam and shed her tears alone. I do remember one day when we were out walking in the woods. The sky was so crystal blue and amazing. The sun was shining absolutely brilliantly overhead. And she just looked up and started crying. She turned to me and said, "I don't understand. I don't understand how God could give us such a beautiful day and yet do such horrible things. How can the sun still shine? How can the sky be so blue? How can it be beautiful outside when all of this horror has happened? I just don't understand it, Kris. I just don't understand." I didn't answer her because I too was wondering how the sky could still be so blue and beautiful. It felt like the sky should have fallen dark and gray and remained that way forever. I wanted the outside to feel like I did on the inside. I felt that nature was betraying me.

Sam would get on Judy's nerves. The two of them would sleep in the living room on the sofa bed. Sam would be all cuddled up, edging Judy off the couch. And Sam would also jump all over Judy when she would try to fix dinner or eat a sandwich. Judy believed in discipline, and Sam was not an example of anything remotely akin to discipline or order. He was wild. And Ron and I, well, we liked him just like that. It worked for us. So Judy and Sam worked out a deal. He spent most of the day outside chasing squirrels and chipmunks while she manned the phones and took care of Caroline.

Judy was my pillar of strength and order. She bought the diapers and the food and whatever else Caroline and Sam needed to survive those first few weeks. Judy, attempting to add some normalcy to Caroline's life, even tried to get her back into nursery school. It didn't matter to me. Nothing much mattered to me. I couldn't even begin to think about the magnitude of my daughter's loss, so what was the point of taking her to nursery school? I wanted her home. I wanted her close to me. I wanted to make sure she was safe.

Because I had the breast biopsy coming up and needed to be under general anesthesia, I had to write a will and do it immediately. Judy took me to the lawyer's office and we sat there figuring out a plan for Caroline in case something happened to me on the operating table. The thought of Caroline being left an orphan was a little too much for me to handle. I kept wondering how I'd gotten where I was. I kept saying repeatedly, "How did I get here? How did this happen? What happened?" The poor lawyer didn't know what to say to my sister or me. He just sat there stunned. Shuffling the papers. Pointing out the spots I needed to sign. Everything was still a big blur to me. Confusion. A sense of other-worldliness. Thank God Judy was rational, because I certainly was not. In fact, I specifically wrote a section for Sam's custody. I even left a trust fund for his care. I remember the lawyer saying that if the will was ever contested, the fact that I was cognizant enough to put in a passage about the family dog leaned toward the fact that I was clear-headed and of sound mind. That was refreshing because at that point in time I didn't quite care whether I was alive or dead, let alone of sound mind.

I kept trying to call Ron on his cell phone for days. It rang endlessly. I didn't expect him to answer, but I wanted to keep alive the possibility that he might. Judy and I drove to Radio Shack to buy a small tape recorder so I could record Ron's last message from the answering machine. I wanted to hold on to every single little bit of him. I even tape-recorded Caroline running around the house saying Ron's name. In my desperate mind I thought it would mean something to her one day when she could hear her own voice saying her father's name when she still knew what it meant to have a daddy. Our romantic and silly Post-its around the kitchen and throughout the house now seemed to mock the absolute happiness we once had.

I remember one day I opened the pantry door and saw the large container of peanuts Ron had purchased from Costco the week before he was killed. He had been in the aisle and seen the peanuts and turned to me and said, "Sweets, do you like peanuts?" At the time, I looked at him and said, "Sweets, everybody loves peanuts. Nobody eats them because they are bad for you. They are arguably one of the worst nuts you can eat. No, you can't buy them." He looked so forlorn and sad that I finally relented and let him buy the restaurant-sized container of peanuts. Now, after he was killed, I laughed out loud. What the hell did it matter that he ate half the container of those stupid nuts? He was dead. High cholesterol or no high cholesterol, it didn't matter. Stupid peanuts. So many things that had mattered. So many things that I had cared about. Now none of it mattered. It all was senseless, meaningless, and useless.

Once we had delivered all of the information about Ron to the appropriate authorities, I had to engage with the bureaucracy of death. There was money from the Red Cross if you filled out these forms. There was money from the United Way, but you had to go to Catholic Charities first, and in order to do that, you had to sit down with a nun and talk to the nun before you got your check. And frankly, at that point the last person I wanted to talk to was a nun. I was angry with God—if there even was a God. All of this took hours, endless hours, of standing in line, waiting, answering questions, providing documentation, and mapping out the perimeters of this alien world where thousands of good people had been slaughtered in a wholesale massacre that had seemingly defied our capacity even to imagine it.

I had a passport into a world I never wanted to enter, where I certainly didn't belong, and from which it felt as if there were no escape. Every time I opened my back door the putrid stench of death was there. Even though our home was forty-some miles south of Manhattan, the way the wind blew down the coast somehow pushed the smell of incinerated flesh and ruin into my backyard.

My sister remembers my rage in those early weeks; I would throw and smash things. Cancer killed my mother. Terrorists murdered my husband. Had it not been for Caroline, I might have opted out of the rest of my life. Instead, Judy and I went to Barnes & Noble and I bought every book I could find about grief and explaining loss to a child. As if there were any answers to be found. I called a couple of therapists who explained to me that for a child Caroline's age, the sense of losing her father was akin to losing a favorite toy. They actually told me that losing her father would feel like she had simply "misplaced her favorite toy" and that in time the feeling would pass altogether as she began "forgetting about her father entirely." She was too young to participate in art therapy or play therapy. They just told me to give her a reassuring environment and consistency. Basically, none of the therapists knew what to say to any of us. Nothing of this magnitude had ever happened in America before. We were on our own.

My breast biopsy had been scheduled for September 21. I was so numb and shut down that the procedure no longer carried the fear and enormity it had when Ron was alive. I can still hear his sure voice: "You're not going anywhere and I'm not going anywhere."

My dad took me to the surgery. Judy stayed with Caroline. When we got to the hospital, the television in the preoperative waiting room was turned on and the images of the smoky ruins made me cry. I huddled in a corner, sitting on the floor with my knees up protecting me, and my face covered in my hands. My dad explained that I had lost my husband and then everyone stared at me, at a loss for what to say. I felt like I was doing okay—and I was—until my father lost it when he saw me on the gurney, waiting to go into surgery. He started to cry and said how unfair it was that I had lost Ron and was going through this now. Then he started to talk about my mom and draw analogies about what my mother had gone through.

I realized at this point that the last time my dad had been in the hospital was with my mother when she was battling cancer. He really started to lose it, and I felt compelled to do something. I looked over at the anesthesiologist who was hooking me up and joked that perhaps my dad could use the sedative more than I could. That broke the sadness and my dad smiled and laughed. He said that I had a lot on my plate and that he just felt so helpless. I told my dad I would be fine. Not to worry. I wasn't worried. I was confident. It was all going to be okay. I then cracked my last joke, saying, "Look, Dad, if you think I am going to die and leave Caroline and Sam to Judy and Rich, you've got to be kidding me. Judy would kill Sam. And that would not be a good thing." My dad laughed and watched the surgeon wheel me down the hallway.

My final words to the surgeon before they put me under were an apology for anything I might say while under the sedative. I was worried that all of my latent fears, worries, and anger would manifest themselves once I was anesthetized. The surgeon smiled and told me that there was nothing I could say that would shock him. He told me to close my eyes and go to sleep.

The truth was, I really didn't care if I lived or died. I knew that was heresy for a mother with a young child, but at some level it was the plain truth.

When I came out of surgery, the news was tentative but good. My surgeon said he could not be absolutely sure until the lab work came back, but based on what he had seen, and what he knew, he was confident that my tumor was benign. About ten days later, I found out he was right. Ron and I would have celebrated. I was clearly relieved, but that was about it.

Early in October, I made my first trip to Ground Zero. It wasn't important for me to go there, but I felt that I should. I resisted for weeks because I kept thinking Ron would come home. But at some point it felt respectful, even appropriate. I knew I should go bear witness. I went to Ground Zero with my best friend, Paul, the same stalwart friend from law school who had once walked me home from a beach bar to get away from Ron when he was pestering me for a date. Paul wrapped his arms around me, gave me a hug, and somehow carried me through the day.

I knew I wouldn't feel close to Ron at Ground Zero. I never would. He wasn't there. It was Ron's life that meant everything to me, not the place where he was murdered. That place meant nothing to me. It was, for me, aptly named "the Pit." If Paul and I talked, I don't remember what we said. When family members arrived at the site there was a hush in the immediate area; people stared at us with sorrow and respect. I remember looking across the vast, smoldering ruin, whispering something privately to Ron, turning to Paul and saying, "Okay, I want to leave now." Paul looked at me, bewildered. He wanted to be sure I was really ready to go so he made an entreaty to stay a bit longer. "Are you sure you want to leave?" I tucked my arm around his, grabbed him tight, and said, "Yup, let's get the hell out of here." I held my head up, threw my shoulders back, put my hard hat back on my head, grabbed the teddy bear handed out to every family member tightly under my other arm, and walked toward the ferry that had shuttled us over, leaving the other family members to continue their reverence.

I survived for at least the first month on chicken soup my neighbor brought over to me in big, steaming pots. I couldn't eat solid food. My teeth were incapable of chewing whole foods. My mouth didn't work. Sipping soup was all I could muster, and even that I didn't want. I barely had any appetite at all, but I knew I had to make some effort. I cooked for Caroline; at least I must have, although I don't remember doing so.

I was so paralyzed by fear when I first went out of the house. I remember going to the grocery store, walking down the aisles and thinking that all the food had been poisoned. The first anthrax attack involved our main postal processing facility, so I started opening my mail with gloves. I developed a serious phobia of everything. I trusted no one and nothing. My world, my reality, my logic had betrayed me. And now nothing was to be taken for granted, assumed, or trusted. I was paranoid.

In those early weeks, I spent a lot of time outdoors with Caroline. The woods around our home were gorgeous in the fall. It was gentle and pure beauty, and I imagined that the glimmer of the sunlight filtering through the leaves was Ron's love embracing us. It made me feel safe in a way that nothing else possibly could. One day a neighbor came by while we were out in the brilliant sunshine. She asked how I was doing and I remember saying to her: "I'm surviving because of this. Every single bit of sparkle in these woods is Ron's love surrounding us." I felt a deep and powerful connection to him in the tranquility and beauty of those woods. But then one day it was gone. Over. I didn't want to be in my garden, nor did I want to hike with Caroline and Sam on our old familiar paths through the forest. Something snapped, and what once gave me solace became as desolate as a vacant crypt.

I had just put Caroline to bed one night in mid-October when there was a knock at the back door. Sam began barking. It seemed strange that someone would come at nine-thirty at night. As I neared the back door, I saw two somewhat pathetic-looking policemen standing there with long, very sad faces. As soon as I opened the door I started crying. My heart sank. I lived in the middle of the woods. They certainly weren't coming out at nine-thirty at night to make solicitations for the policemen's charity. Before they could open their mouths, I held up my hand, motioning them to stop. I found the phone and called Paul.

One of the policemen began giving his speech. When I heard the word "remains" I screamed until he stopped. "I don't want to know, I don't want to know. Just stop. Please. Just stop!" I shoved the phone into his hands and made him talk to Paul.

I walked out onto the deck and looked up into the cold night air. I took a deep breath of that awful, acrid smell that still drifted over from Ground Zero. It was so sad. For days and weeks I had kept hoping. It was just the smallest, tiniest corner of my brain that wanted so desperately to believe that Ron could still be alive. Like a pilot light of hope, there was a faint flicker of my love that couldn't let Ron go.

As I stood alone outside looking through the windows of my once happy and life-filled kitchen, I could see the two policemen taking out their paperwork, shuffling through their stupid, insipid forms. I looked up to the night sky one last time, took a deep breath, and walked through the door to face my new concrete reality. I had confirmation now. Ron's death was a fact.

It would be a year before I felt able to ask Paul what parts of Ron had been found. But, in the meantime, Paul had told me that they had identified Ron through his fingerprints and that they had recovered his wedding band from Ground Zero. Paul's uncle was a funeral home director. Fortunately for me, Paul was able to give the police all the information they needed as to where to send Ron's body parts. Paul saved me from that horror.

But I still needed to pick up Ron's ring. Initially I fought with Paul, arguing that there must have been some mistake. That it couldn't be Ron or his ring because Ron's ring wasn't engraved. Paul finally blurted out that the ring *was* engraved and had my name and the date we got engaged on it. I continued to fight with him, denying that Ron's ring was ever engraved. Paul finally just said, "Honey, it's him. I am so sorry, but it is him. He is dead, sweetheart. He is dead. Sweetheart, it is a fingerprint match and the ring was still on his finger when they found his hand."

While the police were still on the phone with Paul, I left and ran over to my neighbor's house. I knew she smoked. I asked for a cigarette and started smoking. I was furious at Ron. He detested the fact that I smoked when we first met. I laughed through my tears and said, "If this doesn't bring him back, I don't know what will." People looked at me in a strange way when I told them that. No one knew what to do or say, and everyone seemed to be waiting for me to fall apart. I was, in fact, more dangerous than that. I could pretend to be fine while actually being unraveled inside. Not sleeping, not eating, and hardly drinking anything. I stumbled through days and hours that somehow lined up into weeks and then months.

Early in November, one of my other neighbor's sons, Chris Tucker, approached me and asked me to attend a lawyer's meeting. He had lost his brother, Michael, on 9/11 and was trying to help his sister-in-law, Mary Beth, who had four young daughters, as much as he could. Chris knew about a meeting that was going to be held to help explain the legalities of the Victims' Compensation Fund. Chris knew I was a lawyer and thought I might want to go. Besides that, he just thought it was time for me to get out of the house.

I disagreed. I had no interest in engaging in anything remotely connected to the broader issues of 9/11. My husband was dead. I still hadn't mustered the courage to go pick up his gold wedding band, which was sitting in the funeral director's office. I couldn't absorb anything more, and especially not something focused on legal issues and victims' rights. I was still not really accepting that I was even a widow—let alone a victim. But Chris was persistent. I didn't have the energy to keep saying no, so I went. I was wearing baggy cargo pants, a baseball cap on backwards, a black turtleneck, and hiking boots. In retrospect, it was quite a disrespectful look, but certainly indicative of the huge chip I had on my shoulder. What the hell could any of those lawyers say to me in some stupid meeting that would make a difference in my life? How were they going to help me? They were all useless and clueless.

The meeting was held at a law firm with some personal injury lawyers who were briefing a group of family members about the proposed Victims' Compensation Fund. The lawyers felt families needed to clearly understand what rights they were relinquishing if they opted to participate in the fund. At first I sat there listening politely, but clearly not very engaged or interested in the topic at hand. I noticed in particular that some of the widows were very forthright; they were fighters.

As I listened, my brain began to engage. Tentatively, I asked a few questions and then a few more. My questions started to get more pointed and more probing. Some of the lawyers didn't quite know the answers to my more pointed questions. My attitude became "Well, then go find the goddamn answers." I wanted to understand the implications of the choices we all had to make. I wanted to know whose idea this Victims' Compensation Fund was and why it was being thrust upon us so hastily. My brain began to reorganize itself. I would never have admitted it then, but I think at that point I began to care. But that certainly did not manifest itself into any overt commitment or sustained interest. To me, at the time, it just felt good to rattle some lawyers' cages.

As I left the meeting, a petite intense-looking woman approached me. Sheila Martello's husband, James, had worked at Cantor Fitzgerald. She grabbed me and said she needed me to speak at a symposium for victims' families in a few weeks. "You're a lawyer and you understand all this. You need to give a speech explaining this stuff to the other families." I told her flatly that I couldn't do such a thing. I didn't bother explaining to her how shy I was and that the mere thought of addressing a room of people, let alone a symposium of people, was not happening. I just thanked her and said I couldn't do it. But Sheila was not going to take no for an answer. She persisted. "Give me your number and I'll call you tomorrow." I gave her my number mostly because I just wanted to go home. I figured if she called I would blow her off by not taking the call.

But Sheila called. And called. And called. And finally she came over to my house and cornered me. "Did you write your speech yet?" I tried to charm my way around her, and finally I confessed to her that I was painfully shy and that there was simply no way I could give a speech. Sheila flat-out told me she didn't care. She told me, "Listen, Kristen, these people, these families, they need help. They don't know any of this stuff. And you do. You became a lawyer to help people. And you have to do this. You have to do it. I am sorry, but you do. So get over your shyness or whatever your problem is and write your speech, because I am picking you up and we are going to this symposium."

A few weeks later, I showed up at a law firm in North Jersey on a cold November night. I had made a few notes and put together an outline of what I planned to say. I didn't want to say anything; I was terrified of facing 600 people. But Sheila would not let me back out no matter how hard I tried.

I went into the ladies' room and looked in the mirror. I took a deep breath and said, "You can do this, you can do this." I rolled my head around on my shoulders, trying to loosen some of the tension in my neck. I thought of Ron in the last moments of his life, what he had faced. I will never know if he was alive long enough to be afraid. But he and thousands had faced real fear. I took a long, deep breath and walked onstage.

I spoke off the cuff, barely looking at my notes. The thrust of what I said was "Look, folks, no one is looking out for our rights. I know we are all going through a terrible time, but if we don't stand up now and fight for our rights, rights that we are all entitled to under the laws of this country, we are short-changing our future and our children's futures. We have to rise up—and find our strength, first as individuals, and then collectively . . ."

People started asking questions and I answered them as best as I could. There was an energy and a momentum in the room.

This meeting was the first time I met a 9/11 widow with whom I had been talking on the phone regularly. Patty Casazza had a wicked sense of humor from the very start and a sort of insightful understanding of what was going on around us. We would talk for hours at a time, discussing our new lives. At our more introspective moments, Patty and I would convince ourselves that we would have two lives: a waking state and a sleeping state. While awake we would trek through our days, miserable and missing our husbands. At night we would delightfully sleep and dream about our husbands, who would come to visit us. Totally illogical, but Patty and I were convinced (after reading some books on death and dying) that our husbands would come back to us in our dreams. We were quite content to live out the rest of our lives in this split capacity. We truly believed that it could happen. (Years later, Patty and I continue to joke that we are still waiting for our husbands to show up. Truth is, they never have. But Patty and I are still waiting!)

I walked up to Patty and gave her a hug. The voice that had grown to become a lifeline for me matched the person exactly. Patty was immaculately dressed, had beautiful auburn hair, Irish freckles dancing across her face, and a warm smile. Patty and I were immediate sisters. She got it. She knew what our new lives were like and she knew the only way we were going to survive it all was through friendship and laughter.

Patty took me over to meet two other widows with whom she had been corresponding: Mindy Kleinberg and Lorie Van Auken. I shook their hands and made some small talk, having no idea that our futures would be bound together for the rest of our lives. Like Patty, they too would become sisters to me, my new family.

Mindy and Lorie had that same shell-shocked look on their

faces that all of us had, the deer-in-the-headlights look. The look that said, "Okay, I am here now, but how the hell did I get here? Oh, that's right, my husband's dead. He was murdered by terrorists. That's right. That is how I got here. Okay, now I need to put one foot in front of the other and somehow get through the next minute and then the next hour of this day."

But what brought Mindy, Lorie, Patty, and me together was that, in addition to the look of shock, we also shared another look that few family members had at this point in time. It was the look that said, "We are going to get to the bottom of this and we are going to make sure someone is held responsible so that nobody else *ever* has to walk in our shoes."

We were devastated by the loss of our husbands, but we were fueled by our anger and fear, and our belief that our husbands did not have to die. We understood that there was a difference between victims and survivors. Our husbands had become senseless victims. We were going to be survivors. Bin Laden had murdered 3,000 victims, four of whom were our husbands. We were not going to rest until we knew that something like 9/11 would never happen again.

CHAPTER THREE

⊷

The Widowmobile

BEFORE IT BECAME the Widowmobile it was simply my dark green SUV I nicknamed Texas Tommy because it was proudly made in Texas. It was a monster on the road and a major-league gas guzzler. But I didn't care. What I cared about at the time was ensuring that if Caroline, Sam, and I were in a car accident, we would survive. I also wanted a car that could drive 500 miles on one tank of gas and hold enough food, water, and clothing if in an emergency I needed to gather all the things that mattered most and get the hell outta Dodge.

I figured that if New York City were attacked again, I would load the car up with survival essentials and drive west. With 500 miles of driving range, I knew I could reach the center of Pennsylvania before having to refuel. It sounds stupid right now, but I truly felt safer having such a large, hardy vehicle at my disposal. I knew that no matter what happened I would be prepared. I could drive through the woods, through the snow, and over any road barriers to protect my daughter and myself. It was both a maternal and a survival instinct.

I suppose it was the first sign after 9/11 that I had become a new person. It was the first purchase I made without my husband standing at my side—and that was a scary notion. It was also a major departure from the car I was driving at the time, a brand-new silver Mercedes wagon. Clearly, when I walked into the car dealership I looked like a lamb being led to the slaughter. I was a young woman who had no idea what mattered in purchasing an SUV; I just knew I wanted the largest, sturdiest car available. The salesman asked me why I was interested in purchasing an SUV and questioned me about what needs I had: children, pets, hauling capacity, etc.

He began to show me smaller-sized SUVs, since he was concerned about me switching from driving a Mercedes wagon to a large SUV. I kept thinking about the many things I would need to fit in the car in the event of another attack. Of course I didn't share any of these paranoid thoughts with the salesman because he would have thought I was nuts. I just kept my mouth shut, nodded, and then walked over to the largest SUV on the lot and told him that I wanted to purchase it that day. Within a few hours, I was driving, and rather cautiously at that, out of the dealership with Texas Tommy, who looked (and drove) pretty tough.

Texas Tommy remained in the garage for my first trip to Washington. Prior to 9/11, I wasn't much of a car-trip person. I hated being in the car for long drives and felt anxious and unable to sit still. Besides that, the concept of driving all the way to Washington, an unfamiliar place, intimidated me, since I didn't know my way around the city streets. So I took the train the first time I visited Washington to meet with congressional leaders to discuss tax relief for the 9/11 families.

One of the 9/11 widows from my area, Ginny Bauer, had learned through a friend that soldiers who were killed in the line of duty were given tax forgiveness for the years before and after their death. She thought that such tax relief for the 9/11 families could offer financial support, since many of the people killed on 9/11 had worked on Wall Street and made big salaries that translated into large tax burdens. Ginny figured that if the 9/11 families could receive a tax break, it would mean one less bill to pay in the upcoming months.

One of the arguments Ginny made was that the 9/11 victims were killed in the line of duty. In other words, the 9/11 attacks were an act of war and our husbands should be given the same benefits soldiers receive when they are killed in battle. Ginny's argument made me uncomfortable. I remember raising my concerns about likening our husbands to soldiers. They were not soldiers. They were civilians who went to work and were murdered at their desks. It just didn't seem appropriate to me. Soldiers were men and women who knowingly joined the military and assumed a risk in making that decision. They signed up to serve their country knowing that their lives were being put at risk and they planned their lives accordingly.

When I met my husband he was not a soldier, or even a fireman or policeman. If he had been, I might have thought twice about marrying him. I might have decided not to raise a family with him, knowing that one day he could be killed on the job. If I did marry him and raise a family, it would have been an informed decision. I would have knowingly chosen to have children, realizing that one day I might end up raising those children alone if my husband was killed in the line of duty. I would have knowingly purchased a home recognizing the possibility that one day I might be solely responsible for taking care of that home if my husband was killed on the job.

My husband and the thousands of others in the World Trade Center never signed on the dotted line for a job that placed their lives at risk. They were people who wore business suits to work, sat at desks, and picked investments—certainly not anything like men and women who fought on the battlefield. I could never have imagined on the morning of September 11 that my husband would be killed while sitting at his desk on the ninety-fourth floor of the WTC while drinking his morning cup of coffee and waiting for the stock market to open.

Nevertheless, I joined the other widows because they asked for my help. At the time, few 9/11 widows were functioning. Many were still in their beds, immobilized by their sadness. Others were isolating themselves out of fear. And then there were some who simply had no interest in anything related to 9/11 and just wanted to move on and away from it. They swallowed their fate, picked up the pieces of their lives, and decided to just accept what happened. But Ginny knew that there was power in numbers, and she needed widows to make the trip. She asked me to go, so I went.

We took the Amtrak Acela train for the trip, and being on mass transportation made me extremely anxious. Our time on the train was spent sharing photos of our kids and husbands and venting about the massive amounts of paperwork and filing that had consumed our lives since we became 9/11 widows. We found navigating the maze of forms and mountains of applications confusing, frustrating, and bewildering. Many of us just finally gave up on the whole process.

In order to receive charity money from the Red Cross, for example, we had to hand over all of our financial documents. This included our tax returns, mortgage statements, utility bills, car payments, private school payments, and our bank statements. Additionally, we had to give them our Social Security numbers and credit card statements. For many of us, this seemed like an incredible invasion of privacy, since the Red Cross was not staffed by professionals. Its staff was comprised of volunteers who rotated in and out of working there on a daily, weekly, or monthly basis.

Many times we would be handing over these sensitive documents to complete strangers who would be volunteering at the Red Cross for only two weeks. We didn't know these people, and frankly, neither did the Red Cross, who seemed to conduct only cursory background checks on its volunteers. Inevitably, after jumping through all the hoops—certifying letters, notarizing papers, and photocopying originals—we would learn that we were being reassigned to yet another new volunteer who needed additional new documentation because the prior set had been lost. Obviously, it was unsettling to think that our financial papers, Social Security numbers, credit card statements, and mortgage statements were continuously being lost and/or passed on to another set of total strangers. My paperwork was lost three times. Finally I gave up and refused to send any further documents to the Red Cross.

Because there were no bodies to confirm the manner of death, legally proving our husbands' deaths also required paperwork. The death certificates were issued to us only after our husbands' companies signed affidavits. The affidavits confirmed that our husbands were last seen in the World Trade Center on the morning of 9/11. We also had to sign affidavits stating that the last time we saw our husbands was when they were heading to work at the World Trade Center. At the time it seemed crazy to need an affidavit to prove that my husband was killed at Ground Zero. Who would want to lie about something like that? It was bad enough witnessing Ron's death on television, let alone having to *swear* to it in a legal document.

It was shocking to finally receive Ron's death certificate; the manner of death is listed as a homicide. For some reason, just seeing that on my husband's death certificate was shocking beyond words. How could someone I loved be killed in a homicide? How could my daughter's dad have been *murdered*? Who could imagine such a horrible thing?

But we needed the death certificates to collect life insurance policy payments and to close out bank accounts, stock accounts, retirement accounts, credit card accounts, and the lease agreements for our vehicles. Because Caroline is a minor, every time I fly on a plane, I need a copy of Ron's death certificate. That was a tough lesson to learn. Often widows would show up at the airport planning to go on a desperately needed vacation (simply to escape the painful memories of what used to be), only to find out that they couldn't board the plane without a letter from their spouse granting permission to fly on a plane with their minor children. Clearly, that was impossible since their husbands were dead; but they had to prove that death via the death certificate.

These widows simply wanted to run away from the reality of their husband's murder—they just wanted to forget about their sadness for a few days—and in order to do that they first had to *prove legally* that their husbands were actually dead by showing the death certificate to the airlines. Widows would stand there thinking to themselves, Do you really think I would look like this, be doing this, and be saying that my husband was killed on 9/11 and lie about something as awful as that? Why do you think I need to get away? Yes, my husband is dead. Here is his death certificate. Here is my sad son. I am a sad, pathetic widow. And we just want to go away and forget about our lives for a few days. Now can we get on the plane? Needless to say, many of us have now learned to carry a death certificate with us wherever we go—as if we need yet another daily reminder in our handbags that our husbands are really dead!

The widows and I discussed all of these things on the train ride down to Washington. We also discussed the morbid topic of the body parts that had started coming back from Ground Zero. One of my friends received a whole, intact body back, minus all fingers and toes. Another friend received just part of a thigh; another, a torso and a foot. And of course I shared that I had received my husband's wedding band. This made some of the women envious. They interpreted it as a sign that my husband had sent to me symbolizing the depth of our love for each other. They wanted a sign from their husbands, too. They told me how lucky I was to receive Ron's ring.

Arriving at Union Station in Washington, D.C., we were immediately struck by how drastically our country had changed. There were soldiers dressed in fatigues and carrying machine guns. There were bomb-sniffing dogs and huge cement barricades everywhere. Checkpoints were placed at all corners. Police cars with their lights on sat alongside the sidewalks. The sound of sirens seemed to permeate the air constantly. The streets looked like those of a ghost town because there were no tourists walking around. In fact, other than the uniformed soldiers, there were no people on the streets at all, and that left us feeling eerily isolated.

As we walked toward the Capitol, we noticed air-to-surface missiles placed in strategic spots throughout the city so as to provide better defense in the event of another terrorist attack. One of us wondered where those missiles had been on 9/11. We walked on in silence, wondering once again how different our lives might be if more had been done to prevent an attack like the one that had shattered our lives.

Other than feeling terribly unsafe and dazed by the slate of meetings scheduled for the day with leaders of both the House and Senate, I don't remember much of my first visit to Washington as a 9/11 widow. I don't remember what I was wearing, what I ate for lunch, or what elected officials I actually met with that day. It was a lot of handshaking, hugs, and promises of support. Looking back from where I stand now, I realize that it was a typical dog-and-pony show, complete with the requisite photo ops for all the elected officials. They were all jockeying to shake hands and hug the real live 9/11 widows.

We were so naïve in the early days—at least I was. We just sort of shuffled around, being led from office to office. We looked up at all the flashing bulbs and heard the constant buzz of the cameras winding film and clicking photos of us as we sat in the offices of these very important people we barely knew. Prior to each meeting, the press was ushered in to ask questions for a short period of time and then escorted out so the 9/11 widows could have some "private time" with whatever elected official we were meeting with for that particular fifteen minutes. As I said, I was naïve. I had not yet learned the power of using the press to persuade or "inspire" elected officials to do something they didn't necessarily want to do. So I asked and answered few questions during this maiden voyage to Washington. For the most part, I sat silently and observed.

I don't know how it happened, but the tax relief legislation miraculously passed by the end of Christmas week 2001. I don't remember lobbying for it or doing any interviews. I might have made a few phone calls to my elected officials, but for the most part the tax legislation was not much of a battle. It just seemed to get done on its own, with no outside effort.

Looking back now, I realize why it wasn't a battle. We handed Congress exactly what they wanted and needed from us. When we requested that they treat us like military families by giving us similar tax forgiveness, it paved the way for the manner in which Congress had planned to value a life in the

9/11 Victims' Compensation Fund. And that value of a life was based on federal guidelines applied to soldiers who were killed in the line of duty—not wrongful death in tort guidelines applied to innocent civilians killed by negligence or accident.

The 9/11 Victims' Compensation Fund (VCF) was created by Congress in the days immediately after 9/11. In essence, the airline lobbyists worrying about their profits descended upon Washington, D.C., and requested a bailout bill to keep them out of bankruptcy. Of course it was sold to the American public as a dire and necessary step to keep the American economy afloat after the devastating attacks. Recall that we were told that the airlines were a cornerstone of the United States economy and if the airlines went bankrupt, so too would our entire economy. It was all nonsense in my mind, since the airlines were always going bankrupt—I had learned something from my husband the investment manager.

Nevertheless, the airlines were quite successful in their lobbying effort and were handed $15 billion from Congress. I guess it didn't hurt that one of the airline lobbyists was Linda Daschle, whose husband was a very influential person: the Senate majority leader, Tom Daschle. The money was supposed to be paid to the airlines only after they met certain requirements; in other words, there were certain strings attached to the funds. Strings such as locking cockpit doors on all flights. Even four years later, the airlines still haven't met all their requirements, but they have collected all of their monies. How's that for congressional oversight?

In the early morning hours during the all-night heated debate surrounding the Airline Bailout Bill, someone on the floor of Congress realized that it would be political suicide to bail out the airlines while giving nothing to the 9/11 families who had lost loved ones in the attacks. It was rumored to have been

Hillary Clinton or one of her staffers. So, in a very hasty manner, the VCF was born. Whether the VCF was meant to be a form of tort reform from its very inception or not, it clearly ended up being tort reform. And in the longer term, I think most Americans will realize that the VCF set an extremely dangerous precedent.

The VCF was a program that was set up to compensate the 9/11 victims with a monetary award for their losses—losses that were both economic and noneconomic in nature. And it set a cap on the total final award that a decedent's family could receive. The cap was why the VCF was a form of tort reform.

Not providing fair compensation to the families meant that they were not compensated at a level that would have allowed them to maintain their pre-9/11 standard of living, a standard of living that would have been met had the 9/11 families been able to sue negligent or criminal entities in court. For example, instead of recovering 100 percent of their economic loss (a figure calculated with the use of a set formula), families of high-net-worth victims were given only a small fraction of that number—in some cases around ten cents to the dollar—as compared to what they would have recovered in a court of law if they were able to pursue a wrongful death lawsuit. Before my husband died, he wasn't allowed to pay only one-tenth of his income tax burden each year, so why was it okay for the government to compensate people like him for only one-tenth of the value of their economic worth when they were wrongfully murdered? It would be one thing if the VCF were a charity or welfare program. But it was not. And it would be another thing if the government actually had one thing to show for itself in even attempting to prevent or defend itself against the attacks that took place on 9/11. (Anyone who thinks that the VCF was born out of Congress's goodwill should consider the level of our government's contributory negligence and residual guilt toward 9/11.)

The VCF was paid exclusively through taxpayer dollars; because of that, I hoped that the taxpayers would have understood how the program was so terribly against public policy. But people didn't really get it. What happened was a backlash against the 9/11 families. Labels of "greedy widows" who felt "entitled" were strewn about in newspaper articles and letters to the editor. At the time I was so caught up in fighting for fairness for all the 9/11 families in the VCF calculation analysis and also arguing against the dangerous precedent it set (i.e., tort reform) that I ignored most of the venom being spewed at us. But still, some of the things that were said were very nasty and hurtful.

What I had hoped was that people, instead of feeling anger toward the 9/11 widows, would have aimed their anger at those who were responsible for creating the VCF: Congress. More than that, I also felt the people should have been angry at our government for failing to prevent 9/11 and needing the VCF in the first place. If the government had done its job prior to 9/11, the VCF would not have been needed or created. Citizens pay taxes to our government, in part, to keep us safe. The government utterly failed to do that on 9/11. As a result, thousands were killed and injured. And the government created the VCF to "pay off" those victims with what some would call blood money—in some cases, discounted blood money. As taxpayers, why didn't people turn their outrage toward Congress's "misuse" of taxpayer dollars (in not adequately funding intelligence agencies and carrying out effective oversight of those intelligence agencies, which would have gone a long way toward preventing 9/11) and toward our government? Why did they blame the victims? We did nothing wrong. We never asked for the VCF. In fact, it was shoved down our throats while our constitutional rights to hold anyone accountable in a court of law were ripped from our hands.

Conveniently for the government, which had an awful lot to hide when it came to 9/11, the avenue of legal redress for the 9/11 victims was slammed shut when the VCF was created. This was the first problem with the VCF. Our legal system was set up for a reason. It serves to hold people accountable not just by jury verdicts when people are found liable, but also by evidence revealed to the American public during open court proceedings.

Because the 9/11 victims were not able to pursue any legal remedies in a court of law, we did not benefit from any judicial process that would have permitted evidence, subpoenas, discovery, and witness testimony. As the special master of the VCF, Kenneth Feinberg, said over and over again, the 9/11 families couldn't sue anyone in court; the VCF "was the only game in town." Whenever Feinberg used that term *game* I wanted to wring his neck—as did every other 9/11 family member, who knew that the murder of our loved ones was not a game.

What Feinberg meant was that upon signing up for the VCF, you had to relinquish your right to sue anyone other than the "co-conspirators of the terrorists who carried out the 9/11 attacks." Incidentally, as time has passed, it seems to me that such a list of co-conspirators is a bit more lengthy and all-inclusive than anyone might have ever imagined. For example, can you be a member of a conspiracy if, after the crime has been committed, you help fly certain individuals out of the country and away from the scene of the crime? Is that not aiding and abetting? Would that mean, therefore, that anyone in our government, past or present, who arranged for certain bin Laden family members to flee the country immediately after the

9/11 attacks would be a co-conspirator? Better yet, how about an individual who purposely withheld vital information that undoubtedly would have prevented the 9/11 attacks had it been shared with the appropriate authorities? Is someone like that a co-conspirator?

Our nation was founded upon the rule of law. According to that rule of law, when a law is breached or an individual is negligent, the victims of that negligence or breach of law are entitled to seek redress in a court of law. This provides a check and balance against the wrongful/criminal entity; it provides justice. The VCF did not provide any degree of justice to the 9/11 families. It set up a system of no-fault government. In other words, no matter how unconscionably and abysmally the president, Congress, FBI, CIA, NSA, Defense Department, airlines, INS, and local authorities failed to do their jobs prior to, on, and even in the years following 9/11, none of these individuals, agencies, and entities were to be held accountable. (The only people who were held responsible for 9/11 were the American taxpayers, who were required by Congress to foot the bill of the VCF.)

While it wasn't entirely impossible for 9/11 families to sue in a court of law, very few lawyers were willing to take such cases. In fact, personal injury lawyers felt enormous pressure from higher-ups (for example, American Bar Association presidents) to persuade most people (i.e., anyone who lost a loved one on the ground on 9/11—in other words, non–airline passenger victims) to enter into the VCF. The lawyers were interested only in the airline victims because they knew that was where the big and easy money was to be found. Each passenger plane is insured for millions of dollars. With a limited passenger load, the lawyers knew those millions would be divided by only a few. That meant big money. The lawyers also knew that, as with most aviation litigation, the airlines always settled. That meant easy money. Not so for the ground victims, because those victims numbered in the thousands and would require those millions to be divided by those same thousands. Therefore, it played out that people whose loved ones were killed on the planes were able to pursue civil litigation, while the rest of us were relegated to the VCF.

The trial lawyers saw an opportunity to better their bad reputations and decided to create an organization called TLC, Trial Lawyers That Care. Any lawyer in TLC provided their legal services pro bono, for free. The hitch was that they would represent you for free only if you entered the VCF. I initially hired one of these lawyers. He was a close family friend from a large, prestigious law firm in New York City, and I felt relieved and fortunate that he offered to handle my VCF claim pro bono. Unfortunately, soon after accepting my case, his firm was approached by some Saudi clients who needed representation in other 9/11-related litigation. Since my lawyer was a partner at this firm, I got dumped for the Saudis. How is that for justice? Or patriotism, for that matter?

Along with justice, our Constitution entitles citizens to fairness—equality—under the laws. The VCF used "federal" guidelines to define its value of a life. Many of the men and women who died on 9/11 were earning very high salaries. And their lifestyles reflected that salary. But the VCF penalized 9/11 families with life insurance and pension plans by deducting the value of such policies and plans from the final award number. This kind of deduction is never done in court because it runs so strongly against public policy—the government should want to encourage people to plan for the future by taking out life insurance policies and pension plans, not discourage them from doing so by using such plans as dollar-for-dollar deductions in a federal wrongful-death compensation program.

The VCF also punished people for having numerous young children. When a child's parent dies, the child receives Social Security benefits until that child's age of maturity. Obviously, the younger the child when the parent dies, the more money he or she will receive in Social Security benefits. Necessarily, then, the more children you have, the more Social Security checks you will receive for your children's support. (Realize that the Social Security benefits being paid to these children are funded from the same Social Security program their deceased parent paid into for the many years he or she was earning a very high salary and being taxed by Social Security accordingly.) The VCF deducted all Social Security payments made to each household from the final award number. Therefore, the greater the number of children and the younger the children in your household, the more Social Security monies were deducted from your final award.

Thus, a thirty-year-old widow with no children whose husband died at the age of thirty-nine, making $250,000 a year with no life insurance, was awarded more money in the VCF than a thirty-year-old widow with a set of three-year-old triplets whose husband died at the age of thirty-nine, making $250,000 a year with a $1 million life insurance policy. To me that made no sense. But according to the VCF, that was the law.

The largest flaw of the VCF, however, was that it set a known dollar amount for the noneconomic damages in a wrongful death or injury claim. The pain and suffering, or noneconomic, number is the one that most juries have been known to run away with by awarding millions and millions of dollars to someone who spills hot coffee on his lap. While some of these verdicts are indeed ridiculous, they never actually play out because most judges in such cases typically lower the jury award to a much more reasonable amount. Unfortunately, the media reports only that initial astounding verdict, neglecting to do the follow-up story of how the trial judge lowered the final noneconomic award to a more reasonable number.

These jury awards serve a very powerful deterrence factor by holding individuals and corporations accountable when they wrongfully harm or injure another person. And specifically because of these jury awards, the noneconomic value of a human life in wrongful injury or death cases was always a variable—sometimes in the multimillions. Out of fear of being sued for millions and millions of dollars, corporate America felt compelled to keep their products reasonably safe for consumers. Such corporate behavior serves public policy.

Unfortunately, with the VCF, a precedent assigning a finite value to the pain and suffering of any victim was set. So now that corporations know the noneconomic value of a human life ($250,000), they are able to conduct a very cold calculation by asking a simple question: Is it cheaper to overhaul our product to make it safer for the public at large or is it just cheaper to pay for the injured or dead consumers who might be maimed or killed by it?

This sort of cold calculation happens every day. Just look at the airlines. Ask yourself why cockpit doors were not retrofitted years ago so they could be locked in flight. Cockpit doors were not locked because the airlines determined that there were only a certain number of passengers on any given plane and the cost of that plane blowing up in the sky and the airlines having to pay for the finite number of dead passengers was far cheaper than overhauling an entire fleet of planes. Such a calculation is called a cost-benefit analysis. The dead passengers are called collateral damage. Imagine if those cockpit doors had been secured years ago. Nine-eleven would not have happened and thousands of innocent lives (more collateral damage) would have been saved.

Unfortunately, both Congress and the court's treatment of the airlines industry before and after 9/11 has not had much impact on the airlines' bottom-line cost-benefit analysis. For example, one legal question that spun out of the 9/11 attacks was whether the airlines were responsible for any of the damage that occurred on the ground during the 9/11 attacks. If the courts had decided that they were, this would have meant billions of dollars in liability for the airlines, since they could have been found partially liable for all loss of life and property in both the World Trade Center and the Pentagon. In the longer term, it would have forced the airlines to make their planes safer from mid-flight attack. Why? Because after conducting a cost-benefit analysis and realizing the billions of dollars in liability an airline might face after a mid-flight bombing over a densely populated area, the airlines would have realized that securing their planes from bombings or hijackings would be far cheaper than the cost of lost life and property damage incurred when a plane falls out of the sky.

But, unfortunately, the courts held that the airlines were not responsible for any damage on the ground on 9/11. For the airlines this meant that their cost-benefit analysis could remain the same: Their greatest liability is determined solely by the relatively small number of passengers on any particular flight. Because this is a finite and relatively small number, the airlines have almost no impetus to make their planes safer from attack. In short, negligence is cheaper.

Most chillingly, the VCF also set the precedent of this very same cost-benefit analysis for our government when it comes to homeland security. People wonder why so little has been done with regard to securing our infrastructure from terrorist attack since 9/11. The answer, again, is simple: Negligence is cheaper.

Recently, the New York City subway system was a target of terrorist threat. When presented with the problem of making the subways as safe as humanly possible from terrorist attack, what did the government do? They ran a cost-benefit analysis and determined that it paid to put some cops with dogs down in the subways (mostly to provide a false sense of security) but that it didn't pay to do much more than that, since a subway bombing would result in the loss of only a handful of lives. In a cost-benefit analysis, a handful of lives is worth losing when you consider that the city would have spent billions making the subways as safe as they could be from terrorist bombings.

It should be noted, however, that immediately after 9/11 New York City in particular was given absolute immunity by Congress for any prior and/or future terrorist attacks. In other words, even if New York City is found to be 100 percent negligent in preparing for and preventing another terrorist attack, it is not liable for any loss of life or property that may occur as a result of that attack. So if New York City has no liability, where exactly is the impetus for it to do everything it needs to do to make the city as safe as it can be? Should we simply hope for the best and assume New York City is doing its job? I learned the pain of that lesson on 9/11. And now that I am collateral damage, I no longer assume with blind faith that my government is doing everything it can to protect me. I now know better than that.

Unfortunately, cost-benefit analyses don't stop at the subway system in New York City. Our government is running similar calculations for security at nuclear power plants, chemical

plants, ports, and railway stations, and for everything else that
goes hand-in-hand with keeping us safe in the homeland. Most
likely that's why so very little has been done to shore up our
homeland infrastructure against terrorist attack post-9/11: because our government recognizes that it is just cheaper to pay
for the dead and injured than to make us safer. Again, negligence is cheaper. Too few Americans are aware of this cold calculation. And such ignorance leaves the public vulnerable and
terribly unsafe.

When faced with the revelation that we, the 9/11 families,
were never going to have our day in court to hold people accountable and to gain valuable information, the widows and I
decided to shift gears and fight for a 9/11 commission. Because,
more than any financial recovery, we wanted access to information so we could learn valuable lessons from that dreadful
day and ultimately become less vulnerable to future terrorist attacks. Our attitude was that if the government took away our
right to sue and hold people accountable in a court of law, then
we wanted accountability through an exhaustive investigation
into 9/11 to be conducted by a nonpolitical independent blue-
ribbon panel.

Mindy, Lorie, Patty, and I first met during the informational
forum held at the law firm in northern New Jersey where I reluctantly gave my speech on the 9/11 Victims' Compensation
Fund. After that first meeting, we all became better acquainted.
Since none of us was able to sleep, we would spend countless
hours late at night on the phone with one another. The night
we figured out how to conference-call was a transforming moment for us. We called it patching, and we would joke many
months later that we were like a spaceship that could function
at optimal level only when all four pods (or widows) were con-
necting. We would be on the phone and suddenly say, "Hey,

we are missing a pod. Where is pod four? We must patch immediately." The phone was our monkey rope, the lifeline that kept us tethered to something real and solid—the friendship we shared together—while our other world continued to spiral, spin, and disintegrate.

As the battle for a 9/11 commission began, we gathered mountains of information while patched together on the phone each night. In the midst of conversation, one of us would shout out some new tidbit of information, which would then lead to all of us researching that particular topic over the Internet for hours, sometimes days, at a time.

Eventually we would e-mail the documents to one another and print out hard copies for ourselves. And when the piles of papers grew too high, we began "binderizing" them. Each of us had her own set of neatly organized and indexed binders. The topics included such things as U.S. foreign dependency on oil, U.S. foreign policy in the Middle East, the Afghanistan pipeline, the Carlyle Group, Osama bin Laden, the CIA, the FBI, tort reform, airline security, NORAD protocols, skyscraper safety, the Port Authority, and the INS, among many, many others.

We carried our set of five two-inch binders everywhere. During meetings, we would enter the room with our binders, plunk them down on the table, thumb through them, open to a page, and start the meeting armed with every bit of information known to man on that particular topic. Our tactic was extremely successful. When we met with an elected official or staffer who disagreed with our position, we simply went to the binders and pointed out that particular congressman's statement in the press, or that particular agency's public admission that proved our point. If our point was countered by them, we went back to the binders to cull more information and we continued to do so until the elected official, agency official, or staffer was backed up against the wall and given no other choice but to agree with our position. Frankly, I think we were able to disarm them so easily because they had such low expectations of us; we were underestimated by all of them.

Our long conversations during the wee hours of the night and morning were how we educated ourselves about the myriad issues linked to national security. They also provided a healthy distraction from the sadness of our new lives. We were still trying so hard to keep our feet balanced on the ground, trying not to stumble as we walked through the minutes, hours, and days of this new life we were trying to live. It was a life we had not chosen. A life we had not signed up for. It had been jammed down our throats, and it tasted awful. It made us choke and vomit—literally. Our brains and hearts couldn't stomach the reality of how bad this new life was. So we kept ourselves busy, like gerbils running wildly on a spinning wheel. We were frenetic.

We desperately tried to hold on to the remnants and routines of our prior lives, but somehow those shards and schedules of the past no longer fit. There were no more family meals, holiday celebrations, or birthday joys. All of those things stung painfully, making us acutely aware of what was lacking in our lives: our husbands and the fathers of our children.

Unlike so many in the rest of the world who are accustomed to living with fear, terror, and violence on a regular basis, we were newcomers. The privilege and perfection of our lives had been revoked—and revoked abruptly. And that scared us just as much as it depressed us. It made us want to scream, stomp our feet, pull our hair out, smash things, and ultimately end up curled in a tight little ball, crying and sobbing for hours. But we had children to raise, so that never happened. Our kids looked to us for their security and love. Mom suffering a total mental breakdown—staying in bed all day, crying her eyes out, not showering—wasn't an option because Mom had breakfast to make, lunches to pack, bills to pay, leaves to rake, laundry to wash, and hundreds of other errands to run.

We valiantly tried not to cry in front of our kids because we knew it completely unraveled them. So we waited. Once they were tucked safely into bed and sound asleep, we would release our crying jags. And after we were done crying privately, we would quickly get on the phone and talk it out with one another.

We found that when four women get on the phone and cry together, the crying soon turns into anger, which then turns into humor, which then ends up in distraction and major productivity—i.e., manic major midnight Google cramming sessions that went on for hours, days, and weeks at a time. And that is how we learned so much in such a short amount of time. It was a heck of a lot easier to sit on the computer and learn about security screening at airports or INS protocols than it was to feel sorry for ourselves, because we all knew that feeling sorry for ourselves wasn't going to make our children any safer—nor was it going to bring our dead husbands home.

We weren't sure if we would even make an impact by going to Washington, but we knew we had to try. We weren't determined to change the world. We were widows. We had children. We needed answers. We wanted to be able to tell our kids the truth when they asked us if bad men were going to blow them up, too. We had seven children among us. My daughter, Caroline, was the youngest; Lorie's son, Matt, the oldest, was fourteen.

Our children had lost their fathers, their sense of security, their confidence in their futures, their faith in even *having* a future. We wanted to be able to reassure them by saying that they would be protected, that everything was being done to keep them safe. And we knew that having blind faith in our government to provide that safety and security was foolish—the murder of our husbands by nineteen hijackers had proven that.

The answers we needed for our children were answers we needed for ourselves, too. But our kids provided the urgency, the passion that drove us never to quit. Our children gave us a reason to try. With their dads no longer around, they needed us to make them feel protected and safe. We just had no idea where to begin.

We had no agenda, structure, or plan. We had our collective insomnia, the Internet, and one another. In our former professional lives, Mindy had been an accountant; Lorie, a graphic designer; Patty had studied nursing; and I had worked as a judicial clerk for a year and then in a law firm for three days.

Our bubbles had burst. Our husbands were dead. And now it was left to us to carry on.

Patty's husband, John Casazza, had been trapped in the North Tower and had called home. He and Patty had talked for fifteen minutes. He knew he could not escape. Patty kept saying over and over, "John, you're a good man, we love you."

Lorie had been exercising and missed her husband's call. Kenneth Van Auken worked on the 105th floor of Tower One. He'd left a message on their answering machine, sounding like he was deliberately trying to be calm. "I love you. I'm in the World Trade Center building that was hit by something. I don't know if I'm going to get out, but I love you very much. I hope I'll see you later. Bye."

Mindy has no idea how her husband, Alan Kleinberg, died. Like Kenny and John, Alan also worked for Cantor Fitzgerald, the bond trading company that occupied four of the top floors—from the 101st to the 105th—in Tower One. But there was no phone call from him.

I became the driver of the Widowmobile on our many trips to Washington by default. Patty drove too slowly. That made us crazy. Lorie didn't drive at all, and Mindy was the worst. She never wore a seat belt, which angered all of us since she had three children at home and no backup (i.e., a husband) if something happened to her. For Mindy, there was always some sort of crisis going on at home with her three children. Mindy would be talking on her cell phone, smoking a cigarette, with her sunglasses falling low on the bridge of her nose and her jacket draping elegantly off her shoulders, trying to resolve whatever dilemma the kids faced, while intermittently changing lanes and sometimes driving completely off the road onto the shoulder. So even though I drove much too fast, I became the designated driver.

I'd set my alarm for 4:00 A.M. I'd shower, dress, and fasten my sleepy daughter into her car seat. By five I'd be at Mindy's house, where I would put Caroline back into bed. Mindy would be dressed and tottering around on her wedgies, totally put together. My style was a lack of one. My unruly hair was wild and bouncy, with curls that had air-dried on the way to Mindy's. My jeans were frayed and well-worn Levi 501s, and I always wore the same thing on top: in winter, a black turtleneck; in summer, a white T-shirt.

Mindy would climb into Texas Tommy and immediately light a Marlboro Red 100 cigarette. I, of course, was always trying to quit, so I would quickly light a Marlboro Ultra Light—as if that made a difference. We smoked and talked as we headed to Dunkin' Donuts to get bagels, doughnuts, muffins, and coffee. I always held out for Starbucks, but Mindy, Patty, and Lorie were fans of Dunkin' Donuts coffee, something I've never been able to appreciate. It had nothing to do with snobbery; it was really about efficiency. For me to enjoy Dunkin' Donuts coffee I needed to put at least twenty packets of sugar in a large coffee. Opening twenty packets of sugar takes a lot of time. It was much easier to just order a venti double shot mocha from Starbucks.

For me, it was always too early in the morning for real food. I always preferred the manager's special at Dunkin' Donuts. This was a glazed coffee bun with chocolate icing and colored sprinkles. It was delicious. Not for Lorie, though, who showed up like a yenta with bottles of water for everyone, fruit that was going bad in her house, some sort of nuts, and, of course, hard candy in very bad flavors. Lorie is notorious for carrying around French candies that are lavender flavored. We hate them. Even when faced with starvation we would never eat them. They taste like soap.

The seating arrangement was always the same in the Widowmobile. I drove. Mindy rode shotgun. Lorie rode in the back right and Patty in the back left. This configuration was initially demanded because Mindy and I were the smokers and we needed to sit in the front of the car for cigarette drafting purposes. But when Mindy lit the car on fire with a cigarette ash and singed Lorie's hair in the process, we finally agreed not to smoke in the car.

Another rule for the Widowmobile was that one person had to stay awake to talk to the driver while we made the long drive home. Patty was always the first to fall asleep. She would curl up in a ball, looking like a little girl—except for the dainty snoring. Lorie would be next, and that was perfect for Mindy and me, since once those two fell asleep we had a chance to smoke. Unfortunately, almost every time we would light up,

Lorie would wake up and yell at us. It probably didn't help that we smoked with the windows cracked open, and the blast of cold air at eighty-five miles an hour woke poor Lorie out of her peaceful slumber.

The ride home was also always consumed with cell-phone interviews with print journalists who wanted to catch up on our progress from a long day's worth of meetings. We would also frequently do live radio interviews. Radio interviews were always dangerous, since there were four of us in the car and our alertness after a grueling day of meetings was always somewhat lacking. Besides that, we were always extremely punchy. So when one of us was tired of answering questions we would just pass the phone to somebody else. We never told the interviewer we were doing this and we always wondered whether the radio audience noticed the change in voice on the line. Finally, we would check in with the kids. We always waited until we were fairly close to home before calling them, so that when they asked if we were close to home we could answer truthfully that we were almost there and would see them soon.

We talked to reporters so often from the car that many of them requested an opportunity to ride along with us. We were stunned by the intrusive request. The first time we were asked, we responded, "You want to ride in the Widowmobile? Well, you can't because you aren't a widow. No offense, but we have rules." Suddenly the word got out that we called Texas Tommy the Widowmobile. And then everybody wanted to take a ride in the infamous Jersey Girl Widowmobile. All requests were denied except one. And that one was a big mistake.

One journalist was writing a book about 9/11 and was rather pushy. Somehow she wheedled her way into the Widowmobile. It was negotiated that she could ride with us for only a small part of the trip: about fifty miles. While we drove, she asked why Lorie was not in the car with us that day. Feeling too relaxed in the Widowmobile and not being in proper widow form, I quipped back jokingly that Lorie was on sabbatical. Unfortunately, the journalist took it seriously and didn't check with Lorie; she wrote the following week that Lorie had taken a leave for a "much-needed sabbatical." Lorie was really hurt. And I learned a valuable lesson about being a wiseass in front of a journalist. Reporters were never again permitted in the Widowmobile.

(I am still apologizing to Lorie, who received many e-mails from people concerned that she had suffered a mental breakdown.)

Driving to Washington was time outside of time. The Widowmobile was the one place we could be ourselves. I was a tomboy as a child, and my closest friends had always been boys, which remained true through law school. Then I married Ron and he became my best friend. I never understood the power of female friendships. Patty, Lorie, and Mindy became closer to me than anyone except Ron, and that's been a revelation. Without them, I would never have left my house. With them, I found courage within myself I never knew I had.

Trenton, Philadelphia, Wilmington, Baltimore—as we flew down I-95 there wasn't a vulnerability we couldn't share. We didn't have to be model 9/11 widows with one another, putting on brave faces for the world and valiantly carrying on. Our lives were tragic and often tragically absurd, and we could laugh about that without being judged. Exiled from our former lives, we were rebellious, raunchy, and sometimes just ridiculous in the car. But as we got closer to Washington, we would settle down and start focusing on our talking points and the schedule of meetings we had for that day.

When we first went to Washington, we didn't even have

business cards. We thought we might make a few trips there over the next few months, but we had no intention of doing anything in a more formal or organized way. Statements? Press releases? News conferences? Please. We were moms first and foremost. With our cell phones, our kids and baby-sitters could always reach us. "Where are the cleats for my soccer shoes?" "The dog ate a chipmunk and is throwing up." "I have a report due tomorrow on Belgium."

I drove fast; at eighty-five miles an hour we were easily in D.C. by 8:00 A.M. We listened to the same music every time we headed into town: Diana Ross singing "Ain't No Mountain High Enough." It became our anthem. Mindy sang lead vocals complete with flourishing hand movements, Lorie and Patty sang backup, and I just laughed. We always parked in the Rayburn Building, compliments of our local congressman, Chris Smith, who arranged for us to get a parking pass. We would pull up to the armed guards around the cement barricades and flash our driver's licenses, they would sweep the car inside and out for bombs, and we would finally pull into the garage with the music still blasting.

The guards in the garage were so used to seeing me that they often mistook me for an employee who absentmindedly always left her government identification badge at home. I would always laugh at them and say that if I had been a federal employee I certainly wouldn't be there as much as I was, since federal employees and particularly members of Congress didn't work as hard as I did. And I wasn't really joking.

After parking the Widowmobile, we changed our clothes. At first we changed in the car with the doors closed, but as the months wore on we became bolder and didn't try to camouflage what we were doing. Eventually we just parked, got out of the car with the music still playing, stood up in the garage, which was usually almost empty at that early hour, and changed clothes. Running shoes were tossed back into the Widowmobile and black heels were pulled on.

Our personalities meshed well for our meetings in this new foreign world. Patty would start things off with pictures of handsome men in the fullness of their lives, with strong bodies and sure smiles, playing tennis or basketball or frolicking in a swimming pool with their children the weeks before 9/11. Patty would pass the pictures around the room and say, "All of these men playing volleyball in the pool are dead. See these guys on the tennis court? They are all dead. And those dads playing basketball with their sons? Dead. All of them. Those guys eating at the barbecue? All dead." Patty would establish the emotional connection between us and whomever we were meeting. She never failed. It was heartfelt and genuine time after time.

Once Patty had touched them emotionally, I'd go in with the laundry list of things that needed to be done and highlight the points they needed to understand to support the legislation or policy change we needed. We were not too aggressive, but firm, clear, and tough.

I would answer questions and sense how things were going and flowing during the conversation. If there seemed to be any hesitation, I'd say something like "We have a reporter following us around today from the AP, and after this meeting we have interviews set up at three, four, and five with local and national media. We'd be more than happy to share the fact that you are supporting us on this position. If not, we'll make it abundantly clear to your constituents that national security is not a top priority for you." That usually got their attention.

Mindy would soften that a bit, coaxing people into being their best selves. Mindy was also really good at dumbing down highbrow arguments. She would always tell us to dumb it down more—make it simple, stupid, so people can understand. We used to call this Mindy's dumb blond routine, a routine because Mindy was far from dumb. Lorie was frenetic, curt, and assertive. She's more circumspect and would often throw a rogue point into the mix. Sometimes we'd have to rein her in or balance what she said, but for the most part her points were strong, solid, and undeniable. Then we'd tie up our key arguments again and Patty would throw in an anecdote or two that typically left us all crying.

We hadn't intentionally orchestrated the meetings along these lines—our natural personalities just created a dynamic that quickly became effective. After some time we could say things like "Kristen, enough with the legalese," or "Lorie, enough with the theories," or "Hey, Min, we need the charm of the dumb blond."

The widows also learned that after not eating all day, I needed a hit of sugar around four o'clock. On days when we'd be in back-to-back meetings all afternoon, they'd notice that my energy would start to wane from three o'clock onwards. Mindy would usually be the first to notice and lead the charge to get me a candy bar and a Coke; usually those brought me back to life. If they didn't, we were in for trouble, because once one widow was down, so too were all the widows.

During meetings, the girls always knew when it was time to go in for the kill with an argument. In leading up to leveling someone, we would always start out by saying "respectfully," "frankly," or "with all due respect." Patty joked that whenever the widows heard me start a sentence with one of those three expressions, they would all look at one another, get prepared, and think to themselves, "Incoming! Hit the deck!" because they knew I was about to launch an attack and verbally destroy the individual; and they of course needed to be prepared to soften the blow and pick up the pieces. Years later, the three expressions have lost their bite and become a sort of joke among us. In fact, when any of us gets interviewed on television we can barely use those words without breaking into a smile. It is one of our many inside jokes.

I always changed clothes for the ride back home, and that included throwing on a baseball cap backwards. Lorie would typically change clothes, too. Mindy and Patty stayed dressed in their widow-wear. "Widow-wear" was another expression we coined while trying to figure out what we should wear for a particular day's meetings. The phone calls would circulate the day before and the questions would be "What should we wear to meet the director of the FBI?" or "What should we wear to the White House meeting?" or "What should we wear to testify?"

The print media always noted that "the 9/11 widows were severely dressed in their black pantsuits" (even though mine was blue). We never quite understood why it was necessary to comment on our clothing—or our widow-wear—so we joked about it. What did it matter what we wore to hearings or television interviews? Did journalists ever report what men wore to hearings or meetings? And frankly, we were women from New York. We always wore black—even before our husbands were killed—because it is slimming and sophisticated.

We also had a rule that if one of us missed the trip to Washington, it was not okay to call and ask for a rehash of the day. At first we did, but it would take us until Baltimore to get off the phone. It was too tiring. And we had another rule. Whenever anyone called us and asked where we were on the road, we always said that we were "just outside of Baltimore." Whether we were in southern New Jersey or in northern Maryland didn't matter to us, because in our new lives it seemed that we lived on I-95 and were always somewhere just outside of Baltimore, heading either south to Washington or north back home to New Jersey.

We usually didn't have time to eat during the day. So we'd always try to gas up in D.C. and then get out of town fast enough to make it to the rest stop in Maryland where we could buy TCBY yogurt. But more often than not we'd roll in just as the place was closing up. It was maddening. We were left to get a bad hamburger and an even worse cup of coffee.

It was at this same rest stop that we once encountered a man who looked very much like George Tenet heading home. While standing in line for coffee, the widows and I made sure to make a few choice comments in loud voices for all to hear— including the personal bodyguards who were relegated to getting their boss some lousy coffee. Needless to say, former DCI Tenet was not our favorite person in the world. He had made many mistakes that had cost our husbands their lives, and we wanted people like him to be held accountable, not heralded as heroes. As things turned out, George Tenet became one of the biggest reasons—although there were plenty of others—we fought so hard for a 9/11 independent commission.

CHAPTER FOUR

The Fight for the Commission

THE NIGHT BEFORE my first congressional testimony on September 18, 2002, was nerve-racking. I'd spent three grueling weeks in total isolation, preparing and writing what I wanted to say to the Joint Intelligence Committee of Congress. I rarely answered the phone. I saw no one. When I wasn't caring for Caroline, I was obsessed with meticulously sifting through all of my research: all of the files, newspapers, and documentation that had been carefully binderized, highlighted, and annotated. It was intense, but I was utterly focused and in total control.

Now it was the night before and I was frozen with fear and anticipation. The stakes were high. This was make-it-or-break-it time. The Joint Intelligence Committee had been authorized only to look into the nation's intelligence failures on 9/11. For months the widows and I had been arguing that an independent commission was needed because it was the only way all of the other systemic failures that occurred on 9/11 (airlines security, national air defense, immigration, local response, and foreign policy) could be fully examined and addressed. Now was our opportunity to state our case publicly.

We all understood that the odds were not in our favor. The White House was determined to block every attempt we made for an independent commission. True, as 9/11 family members our goal of a 9/11 commission was undeniable. But time was not on our side. We knew we could not sustain the public interest for a 9/11 commission and the media's focus on national security indefinitely.

In watching our loved ones die on television over and over again, we knew what our pain was: It was understandable, explainable, and definable. And we knew why we felt our pain: Our husbands had been brutally murdered. But the facts that lay behind our husbands' murders were different. The facts were not so understandable, definable, or explainable. We didn't know why our nation had been so vulnerable on the morning of the attacks. Why jets were not scrambled on time to intercept the four hijacked airliners. Why evacuation protocols in the Twin Towers were not followed. Why the hijackers were able to carry illegal weapons like box cutters and Mace onto the planes. Why al Qaeda terrorists planning an attack and under our intelligence community's surveillance were not stopped.

Indeed, the many failures that occurred on 9/11 gnawed at us because they were neither explainable nor understandable. Too many failures had occurred for no good reason. And, more pointedly, nobody seemed to be doing anything to address those failures—that was the fact that scared us the most. How was it possible that no one wanted to investigate and fix the problems? Why weren't people worried about our country's still being so vulnerable to further terrorist attacks? Didn't people realize what it felt like to lose a loved one in a brutal terrorist attack that didn't have to happen? Didn't they want to fix the problems so that fewer lives would be lost in the next attack?

We didn't want empathy; we wanted action in fixing the gaping holes left in our national security. The only way to get that action was to build, support, and argue the most compelling case we could for a 9/11 independent commission.

A failure to connect the dots—that was the intelligence community's lame excuse for not preventing the 9/11 attacks. Evidence showed that all the information needed to thwart the attacks was in their possession, but no one had bothered to connect those pieces of information—or dots—together in time to stop the attacks from happening. And those dots were damning.

I knew that I could string together the facts of how 9/11 happened into a persuasive argument that we should have expected and received better results from our country in defending itself against those nineteen hijackers on the morning of 9/11. But I also knew that the failures were so many in form and so complex in nature that it was overwhelming to grasp. It needed to be woven into a story.

Certain failures riled me with their sheer incomprehensibility—for example, the fact that NORAD, our national air defense squadron, was unable to get F-16s off the ground in time to intercept any of the hijacked planes. I knew that the 9/11 attacks took almost two full hours to carry out; what I didn't know was why we stood utterly defenseless in the air for those two whole hours. How was it possible for one of the hijacked planes to fly loop-de-loops over Washington, D.C., airspace? I also didn't comprehend why people like my husband were told by the New York/New Jersey Port Authority, who managed the Twin Towers, to remain at their desks and not evacuate the building immediately after the first plane sliced into Tower One. To me, having a building in such close proximity and a fire so high up in Tower One would seem to warrant the evacuation of all surrounding areas, including the tower standing immediately next to the one in flames. I also couldn't comprehend how the hijackers managed to board the four hijacked planes with Mace, pepper spray, masks, and box cutters. But what disturbed me the most was the information surrounding two of the hijackers, who actually lived with an FBI informant in San Diego. I knew after only meager research that the nineteen hijackers were not a rogue group of unknown actors who lived and plotted beneath the radar of our intelligence agencies. Some of them were known al Qaeda operatives under active surveillance. Yet our government was telling us that these hijackers had lived, trained, and plotted in this country for nearly two years before 9/11 and went wholly undetected by our intelligence agencies. I couldn't understand why our intelligence agencies and our government were leading us to believe such a clearly bogus story. I wanted the rest of the world to know what I knew and to ask similar questions. But I was scared—little-kid kind of scared.

The night before testifying I had a dress rehearsal with a Senate staffer who walked me through what I'd be actually doing the following day. I would enter the hearing room through a back door because of the hordes of media that were expected. I would sit at the huge table in the front of the room, and the congressmen and senators would be on raised platforms in front of me. The widows would be sitting directly behind me, and a copy of my submitted testimony would be on the table, waiting for me. The microphone was on the table, and I was told how to move and adjust it. When finished testifying, I had the option of either leaving the hearing room by a side exit to avoid the media or walking out toward them to answer questions. I was also told that once I passed through security and entered the hearing room, there would be no bath-room breaks. It all felt intimidating.

My guide pointed to some panels that would slide out of the wall and explained that there would be television cameras behind them. The hearing was going to be televised live on C-SPAN and cable TV. The networks would cover it for their evening newscasts. The room would be air conditioned and there would be a glass of water ready for me. There was some-thing in the precision of the planning and all the details that was unsettling. It was well organized to the point of being cho-reographed. I knew that for something as formal as a congres-sional hearing such orchestration was necessary, but it still put me on edge. It seemed that even the slightest misstep on my part might derail the entire process. Not logical, but then nei-ther were my fears.

While normal people have gradations in their levels of fear, I go from zero to a hundred almost instantly. If there is a traf-fic jam in the tunnel, I immediately look for smoke and expect the problem to be an explosion. If my plane is delayed, I un-controllably envision the plane blowing up in midair and start scanning the other passengers onboard, sure I will find the sui-cide terrorist among them. Again, it's not logical; it's just 9/11 residue. So while I stood in the hearing room envisioning the day ahead, I pictured myself having a complete meltdown and losing my marbles. It is the sort of illogical daydream many people have, like imagining yourself sitting in a movie theater and wondering what would happen if you just stood up and started screaming, or sitting in church and wondering what would happen if you just jumped up out of your seat and started reciting the Pledge of Allegiance. Silly thoughts, irra-tional thoughts, but still thoughts that were running through my mind. I also envisioned a terrorist attack occurring during the middle of my testimony. I scanned for the exits and put a plan in my head as to what I would do. That was my life post-9/11—always planning for the worst-case scenario.

Shortly after waking up the next morning, I went down to the hotel room Lorie and Patty shared. We were staying at the Hamilton Crowne Plaza on the corner of Fourteenth and K Streets. Though not centrally located near the Capitol or the White House, we liked the hotel's plush duvets and big breakfasts, since breakfast was usually the only meal we'd eat all day. I was too nervous to eat that morning. I thumbed through the papers quickly and then decided to go for a walk to the nearest Starbucks a few blocks away. Mindy had been unable to make this trip, and I was really missing her no-nonsense attitude.

Mindy was always really good at sensing when I was becoming anxiety ridden. She would then nip it in the bud by looking me squarely in the eyes and saying, "Hey! Snap outta it! Knock it off! Now get ahold of yourself. Focus. You can do this." She would then inevitably make some funny remark about needing to find a cup of coffee for herself or needing to smoke a cigarette, wishing me luck and sauntering away with a final one-liner like "And don't worry if you fuck it up, it's *only* live national television." She would then add, "We'll still love you . . . at least Patty and I will still love you. Lorie is another story. But we will deal with Lorie when it happens. Now, good luck!"

It was funny. It was our routine. And, most important, it relaxed me. Whenever I was about to go on the air for a tough interview or head into a contentious meeting, Mindy was always there to bolster my courage. And she was there for me that morning, just not in person. So I decided to call her on my cell phone as I walked the damp streets. True to form, Mindy gave me her usual pep talk and told me she would be watching from her television set at home.

Returning to Patty and Lorie's room, I found them both fully ensconced in their morning rituals. I have no complicated morning routine. I don't wear makeup and I don't blow-dry my hair. I shower, wash my face, and tie my hair back. Done. But that gave me a lot of time while the others were getting ready.

Both Lorie and Patty enjoy real food for breakfast. The maxim that breakfast is the most important meal of the day is not lost on either of them and they lecture about it relentlessly. Looking at their gooey french toast and crisp sausage made me want to vomit. Patty encouraged me to eat one of her muffins or a piece of her fruit. The widows were always trying to make me eat fruit. But that wasn't even in the realm of possibility. I shuffled through the newspapers some more and mentioned that I might run to Starbucks a second time. My nervousness was palpable. Patty looked at me: "Are you okay, girlfriend?"

I said I thought I was. "Are you sure?" I told her how shaky I felt. But then, who wouldn't be? Patty said, "I don't know how you're going to do it. But, Kristen, your testimony is amazing. Only you can do it. Don't worry, if you screw it up or have a panic attack, Lorie and I are going to be right behind you and ready to jump on deck." Frankly, at that moment, I wasn't sure I could pull it off. I finally voiced what I'd been thinking repeatedly: "All I can think of is Ron. Sitting in the corner of his office, watching the carpet melt in front of him, waiting to die, knowing his skin is going to melt like that carpet. Patty, if he could withstand that, if they all could go through that horror, then this is nothing." And with that thought constantly running through my head like a grainy movie reel ever since 9/11, I had been able to do a lot of things I never thought I could do. Looking back, testifying before the Joint Inquiry of Congress was just one step in a long post-9/11 marathon that, sadly, I continue to run today.

I knew my testimony was extremely pointed—it was going to push the envelope—and I knew that was going to be an unwelcome surprise for the congressmen and senators who were anticipating something more emotional and tame. When news of 9/11 family members being invited to testify before the intelligence committee leaked out to the press, *USA TODAY* ran an article that quoted an intelligence official saying that Oprah must be in charge of the hearings. If *Oprah* was what they were expecting, I knew *60 Minutes* was what they were going to get. At least I had that in my back pocket.

I hadn't planned on incorporating much of my own personal story into my testimony. I never spoke about my emotions or my love for Ron to anyone. It just wasn't me. Out of the four widows, I was not known as the warm, cuddly one. My reputation was that of the coldhearted, detached widow. It wasn't that I didn't have those feelings about Ron and didn't yearn to shout from the rooftops how in love and happy I had been, it was just that I viewed my pre-9/11 world as intensely private and mine alone. I didn't want to share it with anyone. And, probably more to the point, I never wanted to show any signs of weakness or vulnerability—ever. No tears on camera and no breakdowns in meetings. The only way I was able to carry that off was by not mentioning, talking, thinking, or dreaming about or longing for Ron in public.

After my testimony was presubmitted to the intelligence committees for their review, I was urged to make it more emotional. Apparently, my testimony needed to be softer and more Oprah-like. I reluctantly added a few paragraphs about Ron and the return of his wedding ring. I knew it was a mistake to do so, because I knew talking about it in public would emotionally unravel me and make me lose focus. And as it turned out, it did. Throughout the entire testimony my face exhibited a very visible nervous tic where I dropped my jaw to the right repeatedly—it was my body's response to holding back tears and steeling my nerves.

After picking aimlessly at Patty's and Lorie's breakfasts and flipping channels on the television (all of which talked about the upcoming hearing), I went back down the hall to my room and got dressed. I wore a white dress shirt and my navy pantsuit, basic and appropriate. I also threw on a string of heirloom pearls. The widows thought the pearls would be a nice touch symbolizing our purity of mission; they were always accessorizing me.

As I entered the hearing room, cameras began clicking and flashbulbs snapping. It was mortifying. Once I was seated, the photographers crouched down in front of me, still clicking away furiously. It was loud and distracting. I immediately noticed the nameplate placed in front of the microphone that said MS. KRISTEN BREITWEISER. My heart sank; I felt like it was a personal dig. I didn't want to be a "Ms." I showed it to the girls, who were seated behind me. Lorie jumped out of her seat, pen in hand, and immediately added an "r," saying with a wry smile and a wink, "Now that's better." I relaxed. All of us hated being called widows. We still wanted to feel like wives. I still felt married to Ron, even if he was dead. Lorie then gave me a box of Dots candy to remind me that my mission was to connect the dots. I giggled, placed the box of Dots on the table in front of me, and took a deep breath. The final thought that ran through my head was "Sweets, this one's for you."

Senator Bob Graham, a Democrat from Florida, opened the hearing and began talking about the pursuit of truth in the aftermath of 9/11. I blanked out on the rest, and when my moment came, I took a deep breath and began. My voice felt startling, unfamiliar, and altogether strange. It was weak and quivering.

"I would like to thank the families of the three thousand victims for allowing me to represent them here, today, before the Joint Intelligence Committee. It is a tremendous honor. Testifying before this committee is a privilege and an enormous responsibility that I do not take lightly. I will do my best not to disappoint the families or the memories of their loved ones.

"Toward that end, I ask the members here today to find in my voice the voices of all the family members of the three thousand victims of September eleventh. I would also ask for you to see in my eyes the eyes of the more than ten thousand children who are now forced to grow up without the love, affection, and guidance of a mother, father, grandparent, aunt, or uncle who was tragically killed on September eleventh."

I then became more personal. "My three-year-old daughter's most enduring memory of her father will be placing flowers on his empty grave. My most enduring memory of my husband, Ronald Breitweiser, will be his final words to me: 'Sweets, I'm fine, I don't want you to worry, I love you.' Ron uttered those words while he was watching men and women jump to their deaths from the top of Tower One. Four minutes later, his tower was hit by United Flight 175. I never spoke to my husband, Ron, again."

The room was still. I'd adjusted the microphone and felt as though I was indistinguishable from the words I'd so carefully prepared.

"I don't really know what happened to him. I don't know whether he jumped or he choked to death on smoke. I don't know whether he sat curled up in a corner watching the carpet melt in front of him, knowing that his own death was soon to come, or if he was alive long enough to be crushed by the buildings when they ultimately collapsed. These are the images that haunt me at night when I put my head to rest on his pillow."

I finished the most personal part of my testimony this way: "I do know that the dream I had envisioned, that I so desperately needed to believe—that he was immediately turned to ash that floated up to the heavens—was simply not his fate. I know this because his wedding band was recovered from Ground Zero with a part of his left arm. The wedding band is charred and scratched, but perfectly round and fully intact. I wear it on my right hand, and it will remain there until the day I die."

I could feel the power in the silence. I could hear sniffles being choked back and people wiping away tears. But, being past the emotional piece of my testimony, I was now much more comfortable to move into the cold, hard facts I could spit out of my head like a laundry list of damning items. I quickly found my cadence and moved into the core of my testimony, the "catalogue of failures" that doomed our loved ones to their deaths. I was now comfortably ensconced in my own world of facts, and I let it rip.

"Our intelligence agencies suffered an utter collapse in their duties and responsibilities leading up to and on September eleventh. But their negligence does not stand alone. Agencies like the Port Authority, the City of New York, the FAA, the INS, the Secret Service, NORAD, the air force, and the airlines all failed our nation that morning. Perhaps said more cogently, one singular agency's failures does not eclipse another's.

"An independent blue-ribbon panel would be the most appropriate means to achieve such a thorough and expansive examination, in large part, because it would not be limited in scope or hindered by time limits. An independent blue-ribbon panel would provide the comprehensive, unbiased, and definitive report that the devastation of September eleventh demands."

What came next was an invaluable lesson I'd learned from my invaluable political tutor: Mary Noonan. Mary worked for New Jersey congressman Christopher Smith for over twenty years. Mary was savvy in the ways of Washington and sympathetic to our pursuits. She had grown to be a close friend. She said to me early on, "Always give people the room to do the right thing. Always leave the door open." In other words, create the space for a political U-turn—or the political cover for an about-face.

Here's where I used her advice. "Soon after the attacks, President Bush stated that there would come a time to look back and examine our nation's failures, but that such an undertaking was inappropriate while the nation was still in shock. I would respectfully suggest to President Bush and to our Congress that now, a full year later, it is time to look back and investigate our failures as a nation. A hallmark of democratic government is a willingness to admit to, analyze from, and learn from our past mistakes."

I had such hope and faith when I wrote those words. I wholeheartedly believed that genuine accountability would flow from an independent commission. How could it not?

I knew when I crafted my testimony that the only hope I had for creating serious momentum was in laying out the facts in a sequential story-like manner. Facts were power. I could make the most emotional appeal possible and people might be touched, but what would move their conscience to act? My only hope—and I knew this—was to set out a case that was so factual and damning that it would be impossible to refute and utterly unconscionable to ignore.

I first took aim at Condoleezza Rice, who was at that time the national security adviser—responsible for coordinating, planning, and evaluating the defense policy of the United States and for overseeing the CIA—by reminding my audience what Rice had said on May 17, 2002:

" 'I don't think anybody could have predicted that these people would take an airplane and slam it into the World Trade Center . . . that they would try to use an airplane as a missile, a hijacked airplane as a missile.' "

But I challenged that by saying, "The historical facts illustrate differently." I then listed seven specific instances when the government was aware of plots and attempts to utilize airplanes as weapons. One of the most dramatic was the 1995 plot disrupted by Philippine authorities. It was called Project Bojinka. Islamic terrorists plotted to blow up eleven commercial airliners over the Pacific; and in an alternative plan, U.S. planes were to be hijacked. Quoting from the report, I said, "Among the targets mentioned were CIA headquarters, the World Trade Center, the Sears Tower, and the White House."

To underscore and further support my case, I pointed out that in 1997, this plot resurfaced again during the trial of Ramzi Yousef, the mastermind behind the 1993 bombings of the World Trade Center. During his trial, FBI agents testified that "the plan targeted not only the CIA, but other U.S. government buildings in Washington, including the Pentagon."

I continued, "Two years later, in 1999, a report prepared for U.S. intelligence said suicide bombers linked to al Qaeda 'could crash-land an aircraft packed with high explosives (C-4 and Semtex) into the Pentagon, the headquarters of the CIA, or the White House.' "

In a similar way, with an inventory of facts, I took apart

At a Manasquan High School football game, 1987.
I am in the middle row, far left.

Enjoying Europe on a break
from law school.

With my best friend Paul, summer 1995.

My friends from law school.

Our wedding, January 1997, on Petit St. Vincent in the Caribbean.

Ron on our wedding night, standing behind our wedding cake and champagne. I gave this photo to the authorities to help them identify Ron's body after 9/11 because the scar on his stomach was visible.

My favorite photo of Ron, Caroline, and Sam.

From the start, Ron was a doting dad.

Most nights Ron, Caroline, Sam, and I would hike in the woods behind our home.

My mother with Kip.

Caroline and my grandmother.

My sister, Judy, at the beach with Caroline, summer 2001.

My dad with our family dog Kip.

On Saturday mornings, we would head to the beach at Spring Lake.

One of the last pictures I have of Ron and Caroline together at the beach.

Caroline in one of the Gap sweatshirts I frantically rescued from the Dumpster after emptying our house in New Jersey.

With Caroline, my sunshine. This photo was taken by Ron on September 9.

Caroline with Sara, my best "non-widow" friend.

Caroline celebrating her sixth birthday in Disney World.

My autographed copy of
The 9/11 Commission Report.

Lorie, Patty, Mindy, and I with Dean Pat Hobbs from Seton Hall Law School.

I discovered that campaigning involves a lot of sitting around in airports.

Campaigning in Colorado with former New Hampshire Lieutenant Governor Jeanne Shaheen.

Talking with a Bush supporter in Colorado Springs, with Monica Gabrielle.

With Monica at a traveling memorial for those who have died in the Iraq War. Every pair of shoes symbolizes a life lost.

With John Kerry.

Our last campaign rally was in Cleveland and it featured another New Jersey native—Bruce Springsteen. He dedicated a song to "four true Jersey Girls."

With Larry and Laurie David in Cleveland.

In our New York City apartment, shortly before Sam's death.

Our new puppy
Cooper.

One of my favorite photos of
Caroline and me, 2002.

A more recent photo of us in 2006. Still smiling and doing okay.

statements by the director of the CIA, George Tenet, and the FBI director, Robert Mueller.

Tenet had said on March 11, 2002, "We knew in broad terms last summer that terrorists might be planning major operations in the United States. But we never had the texture, meaning enough information, to stop what happened."

Two months later, on May 8, 2002, the director of the FBI had said, "There was nothing the agency could have done to anticipate and prevent the attacks."

In my testimony I then rebutted Tenet and Mueller's claims with specific warnings issued by the FAA and Rice's own statement on June 28, 2001, that "it is highly likely that a significant al Qaeda attack is in the near future, within several weeks."

I then segued into the failure to investigate and share information, beginning with a statement on July 5, 2001, from Richard Clarke, at that time the government's top counterterrorism official, who said, "Something really spectacular is going to happen here and it's going to happen soon." Clarke directed every counterterrorist office to "cancel vacations, defer non-vital travel, put off scheduled exercises, and place domestic rapid response teams on much shorter alert." For six weeks that summer, the nation was at its "highest possible state of readiness and anxiety against imminent terrorist attack."

People seemed spellbound in the hearing room. By this point in my testimony, members of the Joint Intelligence Committee—the congressmen whose job it is to conduct and carry out effective oversight for the intelligence community—were visibly squirming in their seats, paging anxiously through their copies of my submitted testimony, and growing more nervous by the minute. This information was all in the public domain. I certainly didn't have the benefit of any security clearance or subpoena power. But I had meticulously and diligently organized it into a narrative, a comprehensible story, paving the way for two of the more damning incidents known at the time. Little did I know at the time, some people were alarmed with how Eleanor Hill's staff statement and my testimony so closely dovetailed. Some were even raising the possibility of collusion.

The first was the Phoenix memo, written on July 10, 2001, by a prescient FBI agent who urged the FBI to investigate whether al Qaeda operatives were training at U.S. flight schools. Agent Kenneth Williams suggested that followers of bin Laden might be trying to infiltrate the civil aviation system as pilots. Williams's memo was written two months before 9/11, but it was mostly ignored, in some cases not even read, and clearly not shown to other intelligence agencies. I asked why in my testimony.

Equally disturbing was the information reported to the FBI on August 15, 2001. A civilian flight instructor at a Minnesota flight school called the local FBI with this question: "Do you realize that a 747 loaded with fuel can be a bomb?" The next day, Zacarias Moussaoui was arrested. Investigators learned he wanted to fly big jets, even though he didn't have a license to fly a Cessna. He was also interested in flight patterns around New York City. By early September 2001, an FBI agent had written a memo analyzing the Moussaoui case, theorizing that he could fly a plane into the World Trade Center. There was also information that could have exposed key elements of the plot that would unfold in less than a month and turn out to be the attacks that occurred on 9/11. But none of it was discovered in time.

Why? Because the local FBI office in Minnesota was rebuffed when it tried to get a FISA (Foreign Intelligence Surveillance Act) warrant to investigate Moussaoui more thoroughly. Had that happened, pivotal elements in the 9/11 plot would have been revealed prior to the attacks, and in all likelihood the attacks would have been prevented.

I then explained to the rapt spectators in the hearing room the upsurge in trading on the Chicago Exchange Board and overseas markets. Our intelligence agencies routinely monitor sudden shifts in trading patterns with Promis software, which gives intelligence agencies the valuable ability to track and analyze market indicators that might hint at possible worldwide events and planned terrorist acts. I'd learned that in the run-up to 9/11, massive amounts of trading occurred on American Airlines and United Airlines and reinsurance companies and leaseholders in the World Trade Center. Promis software had the ability to pick up on these market aberrations. I highlighted the fact that the whole reason intelligence agencies were permitted to use such software was to get a jump on possible terrorist activities and patterns so they could prevent them from happening. And I said, "And yet concrete indicators of an impending attack and the targets of those attacks were in evidence at the FBI and CIA and nobody noticed?"

But most upsetting to me, perhaps, were the two 9/11 hijackers the CIA was trying to find in late August 2001. The two men, Khalid al Mihdhar and Nawaf al Hazmi, had been linked to the bombing of the USS *Cole*. The CIA asked Immigration to put them on a watchlist in case they tried to enter the country. When it was informed that both men were already here, the agency asked the FBI to find them. The FBI's attempt was unsuccessful despite the fact that one of them was listed in the San Diego phone book, the other had opened a bank account, and finally, they had, at one point, a roommate who'd been an FBI informant.

The catalogue of failures was building up. But I was not fin-

ished. My last line of questioning was whether or not the terrorists were already under surveillance.

On the morning of September 12, 2001, the *New York Times*
reported that FBI agents descended on flight schools, neigh-
borhoods, and restaurants in pursuit of leads. Within *hours* of
the attacks, FBI agents were at Embry-Riddle Aeronautical University seeking information. According to the *Times*, federal
agents were dispatched to a store in Bangor, Maine, again
hours after the attacks, to run down details of a phone conversation that had occurred a week prior to the attacks. Five Arab
men had tried to rent cell phones in a store in Bangor. They
were refused for lack of identification, but when $3,000 was
put on the table, the phones were theirs. How had the FBI gotten this information so fast? How were they able to know the
content of a telephone call that had transpired three weeks before 9/11, a time when, according to officials, the hijackers
were operating under the radar? Had somebody recorded the
conversation? If so, why? I asked, "Had any of the hijackers
been under active and ongoing surveillance?"

There were allegations that the hijackers ran practice runs
on the airline routes that were chosen for the September 11 attacks. I asked, "Had any intelligence agents been shadowing
the hijackers on practice runs?" I wondered whether any of our
intelligence agents were killed on the planes. Where were the
complete flight lists?

The *New York Times* also reported in that same article on
September 12 that the authorities had already identified ac-
complices in several cities who had been involved in planning
the attacks the day before. Authorities had also prepared biog-
raphies of each of the identified members of the hijacking
teams and had been tracing their recent movements.

How was all of this information produced and gathered together on such short notice? How was an FBI that was apparently so totally inept on September 10, 2001, so completely on the mark on September 12, 2001? The only logical explanation was that the hijackers were under surveillance by our intelligence community before 9/11. And if so, by whom? More important, if the hijackers had been under active intelligence community surveillance, why weren't they stopped?

Finally, in the heart of every survivor is this question: Did my loved one have to die? It was as vivid for me as if it had been in Technicolor; it was the movie that had been streaming through my mind whenever I closed my eyes and tried to find peace—so I had to pose it as one of the unanswered questions in my testimony. Why wasn't Tower Two, where Ron worked on the ninety-fourth floor, evacuated in a more timely and effective manner? The New York/New Jersey Port Authority had an open phone line with the Newark Traffic Control Center. The Port Authority was told that a second plane was bearing down on the South Tower. An express elevator at the World Trade Center could make it from the top to the bottom in a minute's time. How many lives could have been saved if an evacuation order had been immediately given after Tower One was hit? Was Ron's life one of those that could have been saved?

I was nearing the end. I had spoken for roughly thirty minutes but I wasn't tired. My nervousness had morphed into a driving intensity.

I wasn't interested in blame or politics. All I wanted was accountability. "We need people to be held accountable for their failures. We need leaders with the courage to take responsibility for what went wrong. Mistakes were made and too many lives were lost. We must investigate these errors so that they will never happen again. It is our responsibility as a nation to turn the dark events of September eleventh into something from which we can all learn and grow, so that we, as a nation, can look forward to a safe future.

"In closing, I would like to add one thought. Undoubtedly, each of you here today, because you live and work in Washington, D.C., must have felt that you were in the bull's-eye on September eleventh. For most of you, there was relief at the end of that day, a relief that you and your loved ones were in safe hands. You were the lucky ones. In your continuing investigation, please do not forget those of us who did not share in your good fate."

I was finished and put my testimony down on the table. For a moment, everyone was quiet. Then the room broke out in applause. I turned around and looked at Lorie, who winked at me and had a broad smile. I knew if I had Lorie's approval, I had done an okay job.

⸙

The next day, I was invited to a meeting at the White House. I met with one of the domestic policy advisers to the president, Jay Lefkowitz, and Nick Calio, who was a liaison for congressional affairs. Both had kind words for my testimony. I sliced past the niceties and got right down to it: "Why isn't the White House going to support the commission? What is the logic behind your opposition? Gentlemen, please enlighten me with your reasons, and I will tell you why you are wrong."

Both men indicated to me that it came down to the question of timing. They explained sheepishly that the White House wasn't quite ready to move ahead before, but *now* things looked different. Both Nick and Jay indicated to me that it wasn't that the White House was ever outright opposed to an independent commission, they just thought the timing wasn't

right. In short, they explained to me, the White House was opposed to the *timing* of an independent commission, not to the
commission itself. I knew, of course, that they were so totally
and utterly full of shit. The White House had opposed the commission from day one, square one. I'd been in the meetings. I'd
heard the veiled threats. They were full of it. Nevertheless, I
soared inside. I knew we were going to get our commission.

I didn't let on to Nick or Jay that I knew the commission
was a done deal. In Washington you have to play the game,
and nobody is allowed to steal the president's thunder. I just
thanked them for meeting with me and told them that I was
very hopeful that the White House would soon publicly show
its support for a 9/11 commission. The first of many lessons
Mary Noonan had taught me had been proven to be true. I had
left the door open for the White House to do the right thing,
and they'd waltzed right on through. Or so I thought.

When the Widowmobile pulled out of Washington later that
afternoon, I told Patty and Lorie that I had a good feeling. I was
pretty sure the momentum had turned in our favor. My cell
phone rang. I looked at the phone number on the caller ID and
knew that the call was not from Capitol Hill; it was the White
House. Jay was on the line, asking me where I had gotten the
quote in my testimony that alluded to President Bush saying a
year ago that it had not been the right time to probe into what
went wrong on the morning of 9/11.

My testimony had been required to be footnoted, so I knew
I had documentation, but I couldn't recall the sourcing. While
driving eighty-five miles an hour in the Widowmobile, I told Jay
that I knew exactly where it was at home. I neglected to add
that it was in a plastic laundry basket, which was where I
tossed all the footnoted documents after I'd finished writing my
testimony. But the widows and I had just set out in the car—

we were just outside of Baltimore—so I told Jay that I'd be home in five or six hours and call him with the documentation then.

Jay said he needed it immediately and that the Library of Congress was searching for it. Could I possibly remember any key words? He told me that the president wanted to refer to it in a speech, but that they needed to know exactly what he'd said and when he'd said it. I suggested they Google it instead of relying on the Library of Congress. My phone kept ringing incessantly. The president apparently wanted to use the comment. White House staff needed to find it. Mary Noonan was calling me, too, and asking me if I had made up the quote. "I didn't fucking make it up!" I told her.

As it turned out, it was Ari Fleischer, the president's spokesman, and not the president himself who'd actually said the words, which is why the Library of Congress couldn't find the quote. Of course I only realized that when I went home and rummaged through the laundry basket of papers. I immediately patched the widows and started panicking about the fact that I had testified and been mistaken. Then the lawyer in me surfaced. I argued that if Ari Fleischer had said it and he was the president's spokesperson, then it is pretty much the same as the president saying it, right? Shit. I was panicking. The widows calmed me down. "Kristen, chill out. You just hooked the president up with a way to save face. You're not getting in trouble. He probably wishes he really did say it." Lorie chimed in, "Yeah, and his sorry-ass staff wishes they thought of using it as an excuse a long time ago. Relax!"

Within a few hours it was all sorted out. On our final frenzied phone call for the day, Jay thanked me for meeting at the White House and for helping him find the quote. I told him it was no problem. I then jokingly added, "Next time I visit the

White House I want to meet on nicer terms. Next time it better be milk and cookies." At the next meeting in the West Wing, Jay made a point of having an entire plateful of delicious home-made cookies waiting, still warm from the oven. "Having milk and cookies at the White House" became a running joke with the widows when suddenly we would have to make a hasty departure from a Capitol Hill meeting.

That next week, the Senate voted 90–8 in favor of the independent commission. The president was able to say that he'd never opposed it, but that he hadn't felt the timing had been quite right. It was a complete 180-degree turnaround in a week's time. We were ecstatic. The president had clearly seen the political realities and knew it would be political suicide to continue his opposition of the commission. Dick Cheney, who had been the principal attack dog on the independent commission issue, was effectively called off. He had led the opposition to the commission with an extreme and vitriolic assault. People referred to it as a victory, which I suppose it technically was. But we never thought of this as a game.

I couldn't help but wonder what Ron would be thinking. He had venerated Dick Cheney the way he'd worshipped Warren Buffett. But Cheney had been a big fat stumbling block from day one when it came to garnering support for the commission. He would call up congressional officials and threaten them, stating flatly that there would be no 9/11 independent commission. Publicly, in his grumbling tone and with his glaring eyes that always shifted down and never made contact with anyone else's, he would ordain that the White House was opposed to any independent-style 9/11 commission because we were a nation at war and could not spare any resources. He was the puppeteer pulling the strings in the background while he placed his phone calls threatening the loss of party support for a re-election campaign, a chairmanship of a prized committee, or administration support for a pet project.

We always knew when Cheney's hand had been placed on the shoulder of an elected official. We would conduct a great meeting, make sound, effective arguments. The elected official would appear sympathetic and moved—and then merely apologize and state simply that he or she could not support a 9/11 independent commission. Representative Pete King, now chairman of the House Homeland Security Committee, and former New York City mayor Rudy Giuliani were two of these people.

Both King and Giuliani told us in meetings that they were opposed to any 9/11 independent commission. They thought that the government should investigate itself. They told us to trust the government and to stay out of areas that were better left to people who knew what they were doing. We told them flatly that we no longer trusted our government. We told them that an investigation was needed to make us safer. They told us it was none of our business, let the government handle its own investigation. We walked away thinking that both of these gentlemen must have had something to hide.

While we were never given the opportunity to meet with Vice President Cheney, we certainly had a lot of questions for him because he was the man who was calling the shots on the morning of 9/11. While President Bush sat in a classroom in Sarasota, Florida, and then hopscotched across the country on Air Force One, Cheney was in the war room making all the decisions. We wanted to know what he knew about our nation's defense failures on 9/11. We also wanted to know what he knew about New York City's abysmal emergency response and communications that day.

More important, on May 8, 2001, President Bush appointed Vice President Cheney to head the new Office of National Preparedness. In taking on this position, Cheney was responsible for overseeing a "national effort" to coordinate all federal programs for responding to domestic terrorist attacks. To wit, Cheney, in holding such a position, would necessarily be apprised of any and all national security efforts to thwart terrorist attacks. We wanted to know what Cheney did in this capacity. To us it didn't seem like he had accomplished much, given the vast devastation that occurred on 9/11. We wanted his answers as to why he failed to do his job.

Patty and I were invited to be guests on *Hardball with Chris Matthews* soon after the commission was created. During the interview Chris Matthews asked me, "Kristen, If you were sitting with Vice President Dick Cheney now, who's the real powerhouse in this administration, and could grill him and he was under sodium pentathol, what would you want to know from him?" Here is what I told him:

I would want to know exactly where he was on the morning of 9/11, at exactly what time the jets were scrambled, why was there a failure of the city of New York to effectively evacuate those buildings?

I would want to know why certain members of the bin Laden family and certain Saudi individuals were flown out of the country a few days after the attacks, prior to them being asked questions by the FBI.

I would want to know whether the FBI was, in fact, investigating any of the nineteen terrorists.

I would want to know why twenty-eight pages of the joint inquiries report are not being released to the American public.

I would want to know why the American public is not being fully informed as to what went wrong on the

morning of September 11 and why there seems to be
no sense of concern on behalf of the administration to
assure the American public that things have been fixed
and that they are safe living in this country.

Once I was finished, Chris Matthews asked, "Who is winning, Kristen? You people trying to open the files, or the people like Cheney you say are trying to keep them closed?" I
answered, "All I can say, Chris, is that we are not going away."
Matthews ended the interview shaking his head, smiling, and
saying, "How would you like to have those two coming at
you?"

I never wanted to go to war with the White House. I was
distressed by their level of opposition to an independent commission, a commission that seemed like the ultimate no-brainer
to me. Mistakes had been made. An investigation should take
place and people should be held accountable. It had nothing
to do with Republicans or Democrats. It was simply the most
logical and efficient way to make sure we were all safe. After
all, if our loved ones were killed in a drunk driving accident,
there would have been an investigation. Whenever someone is
killed there is an investigation. Three thousand people were
killed brutally on 9/11 for the world to witness, and yet the
White House didn't want to investigate that? How could anyone
oppose a commission investigating the murder of three thousand innocent people? An investigation that would go a long
way in making the nation less vulnerable on the day of the next
attack—thereby saving innocent lives.

When I first arrived in Washington, I was idealistic and sure
that people there were devoted to the common good. I was un-
prepared for the level of ego and political self-interest I found.
I wanted to witness a reverence for the legislative process. I

wanted to find well-oiled machinery bolstered by intelligent, diligent, conscientious people—people like those I had read about in my eighth-grade social studies book. Unfortunately, they don't teach you about pork-barrel politics in eighth-grade civics class, just like they don't teach you about political "cover your ass."

More often than not, a legislator is briefed by his staffer five minutes before a vote that might ratify a 1,500-page document that few, if any, have read. "How do I feel about this?" the senator or congressman asks the young staffer, who might also be covering fifteen other pieces of legislation as they both hurry down the hallway, late for the vote. Our elected officials don't write their own speeches, their comments to the press, or their talking points when they go on television. It is all orchestrated by their staff, a staff who is in constant contact with party leadership and who makes sure that their boss does not fall out of line.

The thought, care, and attention you hope would be there often just isn't. Sentences that have nothing to do with homeland security but everything to do with pork-barrel politics get more attention than the sentences needed in those legislative bills to save lives. If all the pork and self-interest were stripped out of homeland security legislation—the voluminous authorization and appropriations bills—they would be half their onerous size. And we'd be a hell of a lot safer. But the system doesn't work that way. In my naïveté, I thought the government was making choices based on caring, concern, and safety. Maybe that's true in other areas, but from my experience it is sadly most often not the case when it comes to homeland security.

I was becoming more frightened that the people we were meeting with didn't seem to know what they should have known. They were glibly going about their business while still very much in danger. During one of the meetings when we were trying to build support for the commission, I looked at one young staffer and smiled. "I was just like you once. Young, innocent, ignorant of what kind of bad things could happen to my perfect little world. I know what you are thinking right now. You're thinking that what happened to me could never happen to you. Well, wake up! Because you are sitting here and working in the bull's-eye. You are a target, whether you realize it or not. We are all targets of terrorism. And trust me, it will find you. And it will find your loved ones. Which is why you should get off your sanctimonious high horse and support us in the need for this commission. This commission is about making us all safer."

When we left the meeting, Patty looked at me and laughed nervously. We both knew that I had scared the hell out of that young staffer. And truth be told, scared Patty and me too.

We felt euphoric when the White House finally agreed to support the independent commission. I understood the political reality: The White House had no other choice once the Senate voted 90–8 in favor of it. But I was still too inexperienced, and not jaded enough yet by the system, to realize that it was entirely possible and in fact often expected that you say one thing and do another; in essence not to walk your talk. Within days I began to realize that to this administration, "support" and "subvert" were almost synonymous. It was the dawn of my political awakening.

It also proved the brilliant political wisdom of Senator John McCain, who had said to the 9/11 families early on, "Washington is a town filled with bad people. If you want a friend in Washington, buy a dog. No one in this town likes independent commissions. They've got a bad name. It will be one heck of a fight—the fight of a lifetime. But I'm up for the fight if you are."

His candor was bracing. But we knew he was telling us the truth, and there were times when he stuck his neck out for us even though there were stiff political consequences. One time he held up an entire transportation bill that involved every trucker across the country being in a work stoppage. That means that all goods across the country—food, clothing, commodities, etc.—were grounded. McCain threatened to delay the bill until the White House agreed to a much-needed extension of time for the commission. McCain meant business—he always did. We liked that about him. The widows and I used to joke about whom we would follow out of a building if there was a terrorist attack in D.C. Hands down, it was McCain. When the shit hit the fan and the chips were down, we were following McCain because he'd know exactly where to go and what to do. John Lehman, the former secretary of the navy, was another one of those guys. You've got to love a guy in his sixties who carries a backpack. We'd follow the guys in Rockport shoes and backpacks, not the ones whose staffers carry their Gucci bags.

The two immediate issues vis-à-vis the independent commission were naming the chairman and subpoena power. The White House was determined to control both, which would safely take the "independent" out of the commission. Subpoenas meant that the commission could legally require anyone to testify who might otherwise refuse. It also meant free access to all documents relevant to 9/11. Without subpoena power the commission would be a waste of time, since it would have no legal way to enforce the production of evidence in the form of witnesses or documents. Subpoena power would give the commission the teeth it needed to conduct its mandated sweeping, comprehensive investigation. So, too, would the use of co-

chairs to run the commission. The White House was opposed
to this as well. They wanted to appoint the chairman and then
have a vice-chairman with less authority.

What the White House wanted was control, control over a
more sweeping and damning account of 9/11; they wanted to
turn that factual account into a shortened, distilled, and less
damning fairy tale. The only type of sweeping the White House
wanted was a sweeping under the rug to avoid their political
embarrassment. They wanted to decide who could be forced to
testify and who could not, which documents would be seen
and which documents would be withheld, all the while maintaining their creative control over the course of the commission
and its final result.

The struggle that took place over the minute language of the
commission legislation—how the commissioners would be
picked and how they were going to vote, funding, and the time
frame the commission would require to do its work—all needed
our closest attention. From September 20, 2002, all the way
through the twenty-eighth of November, I spent almost three
days a week in Washington, often driving down and back the
same day. It was exhausting. But we knew that this was too important not to engage with directly. And we didn't trust anyone
other than ourselves to represent us. There were times when
we'd be battling over specific sentence structures and commas
that would shift from one draft to another. Each revision had to
be carefully monitored, and every word had to be passionately
fought for.

As October grew to a close, with the fall recess looming,
there was a final push to resolve the snags in the commission
legislation. The leading representatives of the House and Senate intelligence committees had worked out what seemed to be
a fair compromise. It was going to be announced from the Sen-

ate television gallery. We had what we felt was a done deal. We had checked in with each of the leaders: Everyone said it was a go.

When the press conference was held, one of the principals, Porter Goss, the Republican congressman from Florida, was missing. We weren't initially worried because we knew he was onboard. He had given us his word. But then Goss burst into the room with bad news. The deal was not satisfactory to the White House. Cheney, at the eleventh hour, moments before the announcement was to be made, had phoned Goss and encouraged him to drag his feet. The White House wanted Goss to keep negotiating, to hold firm to what was the initial White House position: control over subpoena power and the right to name the chairman. Goss, clearly having no angst about being the lackey for Cheney, exited the room with no apologies. The next morning Goss acknowledged in the *New York Times*, "It was very clear there was still angst at the White House."

The deal was unraveling. The clock was ticking. If the congressional recess started, we would have to return to the new Congress in January and start all over again. We were shocked. We were pissed. We wanted answers as to why the deal was sunk. But we continued to leave the door open. Words like "dismayed" and "disheartened" flowed out of our mouths in lieu of "heartened" and "hopeful." What we really wanted to say was that we were outraged and appalled. McCain was able to be more blunt. He knew why every bureaucracy feared where a truly independent investigation might lead. "Remember, no one has really been held accountable. No one has lost their job, no one has been even reprimanded, nothing has happened as a result of September eleventh. Unless responsibility is assigned, then we can't cure the problem."

This became a particularly frenzied period of time. Once

Goss walked out of the meeting and blamed it on Cheney and the White House, the battle lines were drawn. The press knew the whole story. They knew the White House was stonewalling the creation of the commission. We were in the center of an all-out battle with the White House. And it was becoming even clearer that we were becoming a real threat to the Washington establishment.

Reporters were now calling us constantly. There was not a time when our phones were not held up to our ears. From eight in the morning until ten at night. We had become the outsiders who had forced their way inside. We were slowly losing the label of underdogs who were constantly being underestimated even by ourselves. And now we were thrust into the venue of hardball politics. The *Washington Post* and CNN were calling us "political players" or labeling us as having the "political play of the week." Our lives became even more surreal than they already were.

We would be carrying out our motherly duties and errands and suddenly our phones would ring. It would be the White House, a senator, or a congressman. Or it could be a journalist looking for either a tidbit against the White House or some inside knowledge as to what was going on behind the scenes. In the beginning the journalists loved us because we were so wet behind the ears. We didn't realize that we were supposed to be playing by the rules—which meant no divulging behind-the-scenes antics and no badmouthing. Everything had to be minced, parsed, and hedged. The novices that we were, we didn't get that. We spoke freely and from the heart. If the White House was blocking, we said so in plain English. If we had difficulties with a House Republican, we named the name and then detailed the poor behavior and indifference he or she exhibited in a meeting. We were not in this process to make friends. We didn't need any favors. We weren't running for re-election. We were random and passionate and not bought by the system. And that scared Washington—a lot. Simply put, we were neither containable nor controllable.

But during the final weeks of the fall of 2002, my phone was most often ringing with inside calls, the elected officials themselves who wanted to check in. One time I was in the food store loading up on groceries—mostly "heatables," those high-calorie, low-nutrition staples of people who have busy lives and don't care much about eating—when my phone rang. The person on the other end said, "Kristen? It's Tom Daschle. Can we talk for a few minutes?" I didn't expect it to actually be Senator Daschle. In the past, when a senator or a high-ranking official from the White House called, you always got the heads-up call beforehand letting you know to expect the call and to be prepared. I hadn't received such a call from Daschle's office. So I thought it was some of my law school buddies playing a joke.

I answered, "Sure, Tom. This is Kristen. What can I do for you?" Daschle stammered a bit; he was put off by my tone. I then chimed in, "Okay, who is this? Murph? Paul? I know it's not fucking Tom Daschle, so who is it? Which one of you wiseasses is pulling this prank?" Daschle then said, "Kristen, this really is Tom Daschle. If you don't believe me, you can call the office and they will put you right through." I was mortified. I apologized profusely. The checkout girl's face was stunned and confused as she witnessed me faltering in my speech and bright red in the face, constantly saying, "Senator, I am so so so so sorry. I really thought it was a practical joke" as I hurriedly threw my groceries in the bags, swiped my credit card through for payment, and rushed out of the store—still carrying on a conversation with the man who was at the time the most powerful Democrat in Congress.

Realizing that something drastic needed to be done to force the hand of the White House, we had the idea of holding a candlelight vigil outside the White House front steps. I wasn't sure I wanted to go; my paranoia was still fairly acute, and the fact that a sniper was running loose in D.C. made me a little edgy about driving through town, never mind the fear I had about standing in the dark in front of the White House with a candle. Talk about a target. But we went. And we stood vigil. And it was very, very cold.

The vigil was poorly attended. In the end a group of about twelve of us actually showed up. But the good news was that it was a slow news cycle that day and we received media coverage. It looked like we had a thousand people standing with us. The front page of the newspaper showed just one of us holding a candle with the White House illuminated in the background. Off to the side was a picture of our loved ones with brilliant smiles that conveyed the big question: Why? Why did they have to die? It was effective. We were growing closer to resolution.

The moment of truth came on October 16. It was a Wednesday, and all the key players met in Senator Joseph Lieberman's office. After spending weeks of our time plodding from office to office and always hearing the same thing and always receiving the same result—the runaround—we decided that the next logical step had to be getting everyone in one room and forcing a deal before anybody was allowed to leave. Of course this sort of thing is never requested or done in Washington. It is far too effective. You never put every single person involved in a deal in the same room because you might actually have to agree to something. The meeting was called for and coordinated by Lieberman. And everyone showed. Including the White House.

All along, the obstruction had come from the White House, which was represented in this meeting by Jay Lefkowitz and Nick Calio. With everyone else in the room in agreement, we finally looked at Jay and Nick and said, "Well, it looks like we have a deal. Everyone is in agreement. What do you say?" At that point, Jay imparted that he and Nick were unable to commit to anything on behalf of the White House. That they did not have the authority to do so. That they were merely attending the meeting as an "information-gathering event."

There were twelve 9/11 family members in the room. We were the core group of people who fought for the creation of the 9/11 Commission. We called ourselves the Family Steering Committee for the 9/11 Independent Commission. Early on, we had approached the ten other 9/11 family groups we knew about and received their permission to lobby on their behalf for the independent commission. The other family groups were busy fighting for fairness in the Victims' Compensation Fund, a proper burial site at Ground Zero, and other 9/11 victims' issues. They were more than happy to have us representing them with regard to the fight for a 9/11 commission.

And now we were in the room with all of our elected officials and close to compromise. Yet the White House was about to kill it. The twelve of us hit the roof. We were enraged. We were tired. We started screaming and yelling as we jumped out of our seats and surrounded the other officials. At one point, Alabama Senator Dick Shelby interrupted Mindy by saying, "Will the gentlelady from New Jersey please yield the floor to me for a moment?" We looked at Shelby. Would the gentlelady from New Jersey please yield the floor to him? What? Was he kidding? We were not politicians. We were victims. And we had

had enough. We were all steadfastly supporting the legislators who were clearly supporting the legislation. We had everyone in agreement for a second time, and yet for a second time the White House was going to blow it up. We felt we had gone far enough. This—a deal at that moment—was non-negotiable. We wanted an independent commission. And we weren't taking no for an answer.

There was talk about discussing this in a subsequent meeting. The families refused. We were all sitting just a few feet away from Lefkowitz and Calio. We were exasperated. "Why can't we get this done today? Why can't you just say yes?"

The two men looked visibly upset. Our pure passion had knocked them off their game. We were demanding an answer and we were not budging. Only the White House opposed keeping the committee completely independent and bipartisan. We threatened to take off the kid gloves and openly tell the American public just how difficult the White House was being with regard to the creation of the commission. We mentioned there were journalists right outside the door who were literally chomping on their pens after hearing the screaming and yelling taking place in our meeting. Jay and Nick left promising to be back in touch with us.

Three weeks went by. No answer. Some of us on the Family Steering Committee changed our tack. The widows and I were quoted as saying, "While initially dismayed, we are growing more hopeful each day that the White House will see fit to passing this desperately needed legislation." Just as Mary Noonan had advised, we were trying to create the space for the politicians to do the right thing. However, another 9/11 family member on the Family Steering Committee, Stephen Push, took another approach. Steve let it rip in the press. He railed against the White House, saying things like "The White House is trying to kill this deal."

The announcement finally came after the midterm elections on November 15. A compromise had been reached. The White House gave in on one of the most crucial points: subpoena power. The compromise? There would be no co-chairs of equal authority running the commission. The president would be entitled to appoint the chairman and the Democrats got to pick the vice-chairman. The remaining eight commissioners would be equally selected by each party's congressional leadership: four Democratic picks and four Republican picks. But Senator McCain did not walk away empty handed. In agreeing to the compromise, he was given the right to appoint one of the commissioners. That commissioner, incidentally, turned out to be John Lehman. The commission would have a run of eighteen months. As the *New York Times* reported, it "is intended to be unflinching in assigning blame for specific government failures."

Unflinching.

Thanksgiving was two days away and I was out doing my shopping and errands. Since the anniversary of my mother's death is the day before Thanksgiving, it's become a day when I try to remain quiet and reflective.

Jay Lefkowitz could never have known that from my wiseass attitude when he called to invite me to Washington the following day to witness the bill being signed by the president. I told Jay I was home cooking turkey and I didn't relish the idea of making another trip to Washington that week, especially on the most traveled day of the year. Jay said he had really hoped I would be there. I cracked back, "Sure, if you want to send a car for me, or how about Air Force One?"

More than grieving over my husband and my mom, cooking the Thanksgiving turkey, or having to drive in crazy traffic,

I had no intention of being used as a prop for a photo op. It was not lost on me that the administration my husband had so passionately and ardently supported had been trying for months to thwart an independent investigation into the facts of his own death and that of 3,996 others on the morning of September 11.

CHAPTER FIVE

The Commission

HENRY KISSINGER: I knew he was a serious guy. Who hadn't heard of Henry Kissinger? But the minute he was named as chairman of the independent commission on November 27, 2002, for some undefinable reason, I felt uneasy.

The widows and I developed a running joke whenever Kissinger's name came up in our conversations. Once it was mentioned, one of us would punch in, "Henry Kissinger? Do you mean everyone's favorite war criminal?" Yes, just what we wanted: everyone's favorite war criminal running the investigation into 9/11.

For the two weeks after he was appointed, I concentrated on researching every aspect of Kissinger's career. I was specifically interested in any potential conflicts of interest that might exist between his prestigious lobbying firm, Kissinger and Associates, and the commission's work, particularly as it pertained to the Saudis and their funding of al Qaeda.

Immediately after Kissinger was appointed chairman, we set up a meeting with him in his New York office. During the meeting we were very frank. We wanted to know whether he had any clients who had either benefited from or been involved in the 9/11 attacks.

We sat in his overheated office, which felt like a balmy ninety-five degrees in the middle of a frigidly cold winter day. Sweating profusely in our turtlenecks and jackets, we noticed the many photos of Kissinger with his prestigious friends displayed throughout his office. Lorie quickly scanned them all, searching for any sign of him with diplomats and clients from the Middle East. When she was finished, she scurried over to us and whispered, "The photos are clean. No shots of him and bin Laden." Chuckling, she settled into her chair.

We sat in a semicircle with our notes and questions in our laps. As we began shedding layers of clothing, Patty finally asked Kissinger if it would be possible to crack a window. Kissinger reluctantly obliged. I think he liked seeing us sweat.

Coffee and cookies were set out on a coffee table in front of us. The meeting started in a congenial spirit. We went around the room and introduced ourselves and explained what had happened to our husbands on September 11. Once that was finished, Kissinger gave a short speech about how honored he was to be appointed chairman to such a prestigious commission. Kissinger said he felt as if he were being asked to serve the highest duty to his country. He told us that he considered the chairmanship of the commission to be the most important appointment of his lifetime.

We told him that we were very happy to hear that, but nevertheless, we needed to ask him some questions about his business ties. Kissinger encouraged us to do so, and we did.

I don't think Dr. Kissinger was quite prepared for what came next. Politely and with all due deference, we told him that we needed access to his client list. He declined, saying he wanted to protect his clients' privacy. He became a bit agitated and voiced his displeasure at our raising such an improper and, in his opinion, rude request. We of course didn't see the harm in his showing us his client list. We just wanted assurances that there would be no conflicts of interest. Kissinger told us to trust him. We told him we couldn't.

The problem with Dr. Kissinger was that he'd been insulated from accountability for most of his life. It was a rare day when someone stood up to him and questioned his integrity face-to-face. Here we were, a motley group of 9/11 victims, cross-examining him, asking to see his list of clients. Kissinger seemed stunned. I imagine he must have been thinking, Who in the hell do you people think you are? I am Henry Kissinger. How dare you come into my office and question me?

Kissinger told us he would be happy to answer any questions about his clients, but he would not release his client list to the public. He raised the possibility of releasing the information to an attorney, but he wasn't even so sure about that. We asked, "An attorney?" He answered by saying that he would release the list to an attorney agreed upon by both the 9/11 families and himself. At that point, one of the widows pointed out that I was an attorney and we would be happy if I reviewed the list.

Kissinger nearly died. He backed off that idea and gingerly tried to shift gears, asking why we didn't trust him. He didn't understand the fuss about his client list. They were all reputable people. He assured us that there were no conflicts. We just needed to trust him.

Lorie finally broke in. "Dr. Kissinger . . . the kind of thing that . . . you know, we are worried about is whether you might ever have had a member of the bin Laden family as a client?" All eyes bored into Kissinger. Some uncomfortable chuckles were muffled. We softened it: "It would be our hope that no client like that would be found on your client list, Dr. Kissinger. We are sure they wouldn't be, but nevertheless, we have an obligation to ask."

Kissinger seemed stricken and became unsteady. In reaching for his cup of coffee he bobbled, knocked the pot, spilled his own cup, and nearly fell off the couch—while awkwardly insisting that his fake eye threw off his depth perception. Fake eye? What? Moms to the core, we hurriedly cleaned up the mess and gave him some napkins. As he mopped up, we all looked at each other, relaying a sense of "What the hell was that?"

Kissinger never answered the question. He didn't have to. The next day it was reported in the press that Kissinger had resigned. Oh, well. So much for his higher calling and honorbound duty to his country. In the end, protecting one's clients came before serving his country and protecting its citizens.

A few days later, the *New York Post* wrote an editorial claiming that the 9/11 families wielded too much power and blamed us for Kissinger's hasty and premature departure. The editorial in the conservative *Post* praised Kissinger as a true American and said that the 9/11 families were wrong in kicking him off the commission. "Equally disturbing is the notion that the victims' families are calling the shots for this commission. It was their complaints that prompted Kissinger's resignation."

After the meeting, we had all agreed not to speak with the press about anything discussed in the meeting; it was off the record. And now it was being reported that we had forced Kissinger to resign. We never asked Kissinger to resign. We only asked him a question about the bin Ladens being clients. In fact, we were just as surprised as everyone else when we learned about his resignation. We felt we knew why he resigned, but we had not expected it to happen.

Mindy was incensed when she read the *Post* editorial. How could the *New York Post* accuse us of forcing Kissinger's resignation? How could it speak about the details of a meeting it had not attended? Where was it getting its information? Mindy called the editorial office. She set up an appointment with the entire editorial board for the following week. She rearranged her children's schedules, swapping car pools, canceling therapist and tutor appointments, and arranging for backup baby-sitting. She called us and told us that we had no choice; we were all going to the meeting with the editorial board of the *New York Post*.

As we walked into the meeting, we realized that the entire editorial board was in the room. Such complete attendance was surprising; nonetheless, we were pleased to see everyone there. We wanted to set the record straight. Mindy started by saying that she was a very busy single mother of three children and that she hoped everyone realized how important this issue was, for her to take the time to trek into the city to meet with them. She cast her eyes around the room and said she had come because she was *that* upset with their editorial about Kissinger.

At that point—within the first minute of the meeting—the editor, Bob McManus, shot her a look of utter disdain. He said, "You are upset about your schedule? I don't even know who you people are, who you may *think* you are, and frankly, I don't know how you *even got in the building*. If you have a grievance with this newspaper or one of our editorials, you don't get a meeting with us, you write a letter. How did you even get this meeting?"

Mindy replied that she had called and spoken with the receptionist, who had set up the appointment for us. Feeling like we were about to get summarily kicked out of the building, I quickly chimed in, "Since we are all here together now, who in the room is responsible for the editorial about Kissinger?" Nervous looks swam back and forth. Nobody answered. I asked the question again. Still no one answered.

"Well, that is interesting. No one here is taking credit for writing an editorial that discussed a meeting and wrongly reported the details of that meeting? It's funny. I'm sitting here looking around the room and not one of you looks familiar. I don't recognize any of you from that meeting, so I'm just wondering, how did you gather the facts about the meeting if you weren't there? How were you able to blame us—the 9/11 widows—for the resignation of Kissinger if you didn't have firsthand knowledge? If you weren't in the meeting to know what happened? Isn't that slander? Or libel? Or something?"

At this point the editor piped up and acknowledged that none of them had been in the meeting but that Dr. Kissinger was a "very old personal friend" of the newspaper—and that the newspaper felt he needed to be defended. I then challenged the accuracy of the editorial. The editor seemed to be saying that editorials didn't have to be accurate. That came as a surprise. So I asked him why, if he had the power to influence, to educate, and to inform millions of people about how unsafe and vulnerable we truly are from terrorism, he didn't use that power and influence in a positive way by supporting the 9/11 Commission and the 9/11 families.

My attempt to shame him into doing the right thing was in vain. He rose from his chair and escorted us out of the office.

❧

Christmas was only a few weeks away—the second Christmas since 9/11. I had decided that Caroline and I would get away and not endure the pain of staggering through the holidays at home. Sunshine and the beach were always an irresistible combination for me. I decided we'd go to Florida, booked a flight, and made hotel reservations. I convinced myself that I was ready to confront my fear of flying, my heart-stopping, paralyzing fear of getting on a plane at a New York City airport and seeing the skyline drop away from beneath the plane's wings. Mind over matter. That was my mantra. Two years was time enough to be a prisoner of my own fears. It was silly and stupid. Mind over matter. It was completely unrealistic to think I'd never fly again for the rest of my life. I'm a pragmatic woman and this made no sense. That was as far as I got with logic.

The panic attacks started again. I'd had them intermittently in the months after 9/11. I'd hear planes fly overhead, often while driving in the car, and my heart would race and I would shudder. Sometimes I'd feel short of breath. I'd see planes exploding in my mind. I'd have flashbacks jolting me in a severe mental whiplash to the precise moment when Flight 175 had sliced into Ron's building.

As the trip to Amelia Island drew closer, I paced around the house, fending off panic attacks, hyperventilating and trying to regain control. I was having trouble sleeping. Suddenly it all seemed ridiculous. I didn't need to go to Florida that badly. What was the rush to get on an airplane, anyway?

I then looked into Amtrak. Unfortunately, all the train reservations to Florida were already booked for the holiday. I canceled the trip, eating the $4,000 and opting for a quiet Christmas alone with Caroline and Sam.

We stayed home and had our own weird little Christmas. Caroline was too young to notice its strangeness—umm, organic pizza for our Christmas feast—but I had spared her from something that could have been potentially worse: seeing her mother dissolve in panic on an airplane. I held out hope, in theory at least, that Christmas might be happy, even joyful,

again in the future. It was out there in the realm of possibility
like those monkeys that someday might type out the complete
works of Shakespeare.

Being home allowed me to get work done on the commission. After Kissinger backed out, names were being bandied
about regarding potential replacements. Every time a name surfaced, I spent at least forty-eight hours researching for potential conflicts. When Tom Kean, a Republican and former New
Jersey governor, was nominated as chairman and heartily accepted, we felt gratified. We had done our on-line detective
work and found links to Amerada Hess, an oil company, but
that conflict was nothing compared with Kissinger's connections. Kean had a solid reputation as being a decent man of
integrity.

We asked to meet with him and he agreed, which surprised
us. We'd been requesting a meeting with President Bush for
over a year, but he always refused. We also requested a meeting with Laura Bush, thinking that as a mom she might share
our goal to learn from 9/11. We were disappointed when she
never replied. It bothered us when she flew halfway around
the world to meet with women from Afghanistan. But we were
becoming increasingly used to being rebuffed.

Tom Kean was genial and open. He seemed genuinely interested in getting to know us and did not appear to be at all
on the defensive. We did not feel like another box to be
checked off on his to-do list. He told us that he was committed
to working together and wanted to turn over every rock in carrying out his investigation. He also told us that he wanted to
learn from the vast knowledge we'd already accumulated about
9/11.

We spent over four hours with Governor Kean. He had
cleared his schedule for most of the day because he was eager

to absorb what we had to share. We never felt rushed. It was more of a brainstorming session among like-minded individuals all working toward a common goal. I began to have hope. I really liked Tom. We all did. Maybe with him at the helm we would navigate the commission through the treacherous channels ahead.

The commission had ten members: five Democrats and five Republicans. Our research had led us to conclude that each of them was likely placed on the commission to protect specific, particular things.

For example, Jim Thompson's law firm represented the airlines, as did Slade Gorton's. Jamie Gorelick sat on the board of Schlumberger, a large defense contracting company, and had also served as deputy attorney general in the Clinton administration and on a CIA advisory panel. Lee Hamilton had been a congressman who served on the intelligence committee. John Lehman was a former secretary of the navy and a wealthy businessman who owned several companies that provided military components to defense contractors and/or the government. The lists of potential conflicts for the commissioners went on and on. Throughout the commission's investigation we remained vigilant and always cognizant of where each commissioner's conflicts could complicate and hinder the search for truth.

The biggest conflict of interest that compromised the breadth and integrity of the commission was to be found not among the commissioners themselves, but in the executive staff director, Philip Zelikow. I was skeptical about Zelikow from day one. I didn't like him.

Our research revealed that he was a close colleague of Condoleezza Rice and that at the specific request of Rice, he had served on the Bush administration's transition team. This meant that as the Clinton administration was leaving office and the

Bush administration was coming into office, it was Zelikow's
job to facilitate that transition.

Because Zelikow's specialty was terrorism, he was briefed
about al Qaeda and bin Laden by outgoing national security adviser Sandy Berger, counterterrorism czar Richard Clarke, and
CIA director George Tenet. These briefings took place throughout late 2000 and early 2001.

Zelikow's job was then to take that information and convey
it to the Bush national security team. Talk about a conflict! How
could Zelikow direct an investigation whose mandate was at
least in part to investigate the role Zelikow himself played in
the transition time between the Clinton and Bush administra-
tions—a transition that went to the heart of why the Bush administration underestimated the threat posed by al Qaeda and
bin Laden?

While the commissioners were the public face of the commission, the real work was carried out behind the scenes by the
staff—and there were about eighty staff members who were divided up into each of the key areas. Zelikow was in charge of
those eighty staffers and the entire course of the commission's
investigation. He would be the commission's gatekeeper; all information that ended up in the final report was there only because Zelikow thought it should be there. In essence, the story
told by the 9/11 commission became the story that Zelikow
wanted to tell. And that made me exceedingly uncomfortable
right from the beginning.

We raised our concerns about Zelikow with the commission
on numerous occasions. We were always assured that the commission had the utmost confidence in him and his ability to
carry out an impartial investigation. Zelikow himself down-
played his conflicts on a number of occasions. One time we
met him after hours at a Starbucks in Washington to discuss

some particularly disturbing information we had obtained about him. We learned that Zelikow was being interviewed by the 9/11 commission as a witness regarding his role on the Bush transition team during the fall and winter of 2000. This concerned us, since we couldn't understand how the staff director of the 9/11 Commission could interview himself impartially and effectively.

We also learned that Zelikow was one of only two people from the commission to be given what was called primary access to all executive branch documents from the Bush administration. Primary access meant that Zelikow was responsible for receiving all Bush documents that related to al Qaeda and 9/11. He decided which documents were worthy of the full commission's review. Zelikow, the gatekeeper, then provided this limited and censored group of documents to the commissioners, but only in a secure and classified location. Commissioners could take handwritten notes about these documents, but those notes could not be removed from the classified location nor used in writing the commission's final report.

The other person given primary access to the executive branch documents was Commissioner Jamie Gorelick, who, ironically, was also interviewed by the commission as a witness regarding her former position as deputy attorney general in the Clinton administration. We were furious with the patent conflict of interest exhibited by Zelikow and Gorelick, so we wrote a press release. The commission's lawyer, Dan Marcus, and Zelikow met with us to discuss our concerns.

During the meeting at Starbucks, I started badgering Zelikow and asking him why he was needed as a witness by the commission. He answered that he was being questioned about his role regarding the transition team. I asked how it was possible that he could not be creating a conflict of interest by

having primary access to the executive branch documents:
Zelikow had most likely written and designed the underlying
policy for at least some of these documents. He argued that
there was no conflict and that he was not involved in any matters that presented a conflict. He then grew beet red in the face
and threw a snit like a two-year-old, stating, "That's right, Kristen. Everything is connected. The hip bone is connected to the
thigh bone is connected to the knee bone is connected to the
ankle bone. It is all connected!" He stormed out of Starbucks.

I looked over at Dan Marcus, who explained to me, "Philip
is under a lot of stress." (Stress or not, Zelikow did his job when
it came to covering up 9/11 failures. Zelikow was rewarded
handsomely for his service. He is now counsel for Secretary of
State Rice. How's that for payback?)

Once the commission was impaneled, the first issue to
arise was receiving clearances for all of the staff and commissioners. Security clearances were necessary because much of
the commission's work centered on classified information. All
commissioners and staff needed the highest levels of clearance to access such information. Because the White House
was responsible for issuing such clearances and they were in
no hurry to get the investigation under way, the work of the
commission for the first few months was greatly hindered by
the deliberate apathy of the White House in granting clearances.

The next battle was over funding for the commission. Initially, the $3 million budget was put into the legislation as a
"placeholder." We were told at the time that the dollar amount
didn't matter, it was just a token sum that would be adjusted
later. Nearly six months later, it was time for an adjustment. The
commission needed more money to function properly. Once
again the White House balked. But a couple of things hap-

pened that worked in support of us and our push for more funding: The president gave his 2003 State of the Union Address, and then the space shuttle exploded upon re-entry to Earth.

While watching the State of the Union Address, I noticed that the president mentioned 9/11 at least eleven times. For a president who didn't seem much interested in investigating the 9/11 attacks, he sure as hell liked to drop 9/11 references profusely into his public speeches. This annoyed me, especially because we desperately needed the president's cooperation in securing funding for the commission. This was a no-brainer. Without an increased budget, there could be no real investigation.

We set up a meeting at the White House to discuss the budget increase around early February 2003. During the meeting, I mentioned that the commission needed a total budget of $15 million—that meant we needed $12 million more than we presently had.

Believe it or not, the White House wasn't too jazzed about this idea. The feeling was that an additional $12 million was excessive. This boggled our minds. Three thousand people had died and $15 million was too much to ask? Were they joking? So I said sarcastically during the meeting, "Okay, well, here's the deal. The president mentioned nine-eleven at least eleven times in his State of the Union. How about we charge him one million for each time he mentioned it? How does that sound?"

Then came the more rational argument: the space shuttle explosion and its follow-up investigation. I quietly pointed out to the White House that after the shuttle explosion, NASA got $50 million from Congress virtually overnight. My point was this: If we can spend $50 million on the space shuttle, how about $15 million on the 9/11 attacks that killed 3,000 people? That seemed reasonable to me.

This argument was a strong argument. The White House knew that. Within a week and along with much media pressure, the White House conceded on the issue. The 9/11 Commission was given a budget increase, and the final budget was set at $14 million. (It actually did work out to $1 million for each mention of 9/11 in the State of the Union Address, but I don't think it had anything to do with that!)

At about this time we had a meeting with Commission Vice-Chairman Lee Hamilton. During the meeting with Lee, we spoke to him about our fervent desire to have light shine into the darkness of the 9/11 attacks. We spoke about democracy and how accountability is its lifeblood. We thought Lee understood what we needed out of this investigation. We passionately explained how we couldn't bring our husbands back, but that if we learned lessons that would make our nation safer, it would be a life-affirming way to memorialize our dead loved ones.

During this meeting in February 2003, we mentioned to Lee that open, public hearings were essential. We told him that we wanted an open hearing on every topic covered in the commission's mandate. We told him that we wanted witnesses to be under oath. We told him that we wanted hearings to commence immediately and to be hard-hitting in nature. We told him to subpoena often and early. That was the way we believed his investigation should proceed. We wanted answers to our thousands of questions. We wanted reassurances that we had been safer than we were on September 10.

Lee questioned the need for hearings. He asked why we were so driven to have public, open hearings, complete with staff statements to keep the public abreast of the course of the investigation. We told him we knew from our past work with the Joint Inquiry of Congress that public hearings were an excellent way to get information out to the public—information that some might otherwise wish to keep concealed.

We explained that the public can learn an awful lot in such public settings, particularly when witnesses are under oath. At this point, Lee looked directly at me. I interpreted his expression to mean that he understood where we were coming from. It looked like he was taking a mental note: Remember to hold lots of public hearings—very valuable. But months later, after watching the commission delay its public-hearing schedule, fail to ask hard-hitting questions, and fail to place many people under oath, I began to think that Lee's mental note was more akin to: Remember that public hearings are very dangerous.

The first public hearing of the commission was held in New York City on March 31, 2003. Mindy was one of the first witnesses. Speaking poignantly of her husband, Alan, she was determined to set the record straight with regard to our nation's poor air defense on the morning of 9/11:

> At 6:15 A.M. on the morning of 9/11, my husband Alan left for work; he drove into New York City, and was at his desk and working at his NASDAQ Security Trading position with Cantor Fitzgerald, in Tower One of the WTC by 7:30 A.M.
>
> In contrast, on the morning of September 11, President Bush was scheduled to listen to elementary school children read. Before the President walked into the classroom NORAD had sufficient information that the plane that hit the WTC was hijacked. At that time, they also had knowledge that two other commercial airliners, in the air, were also hijacked. It would seem that a

national emergency was in progress. Yet President Bush was allowed to enter a classroom full of young children and listen to the students read.

Why didn't the Secret Service inform him of this national emergency? When is a president supposed to be notified of everything the agencies know? Why was the president permitted by the Secret Service to remain in the Sarasota elementary school? Was this Secret Service protocol? In the case of a national emergency, seconds of indecision could cost thousands of lives. . . .

That was, and still is, at the heart of all of this: the thousands of lives that were lost because of seconds—or was it years?—of indecision, bad decisions, and tragically missed opportunities. Our research had led us to a mounting catalogue of failures. Because of this, we hoped the independent commission would now finally begin to unearth the reasons so many mistakes were made and ultimately hold people accountable for those failures. We never liked the excuse that the terrorists had to get lucky only once and that our intelligence agencies needed to be lucky all the time. The more we learned, the more we concluded that the terrorists were lucky not just once but over and over again in ways that defied the law of probabilities. We felt more comfortable pinning the blame for the terrorists' spectacular success not on the terrorists' dumb luck, but rather on our government and intelligence agencies' absolute incompetence.

The first two days of testimony were strong and emotional. The commissioners were serious and engaged. The work, so long overdue, felt like it was finally under way. The media was paying attention. The nation seemed focused. If only that momentum could have been sustained.

My disillusionment grew gradually. We continued to lobby throughout the late spring and early summer of 2003 on behalf of the commission, arguing for their access to documents and witnesses, the use of their subpoena power if necessary. Yet, at the same time, we would also be fighting against the commission to use its subpoena power more liberally, to dig deeper, to ask more questions, to hold more substantive hearings. We constantly urged the commissioners to be more aggressive and more open in their work. We begged them to write more investigative staff statements, to shed light on the many dark secrets of 9/11.

At about this time, we set up a meeting with the director of the FBI, Robert Mueller. It occurred to us that the FBI was essentially our chief investigator into the crime that occurred on 9/11. More to the point, one of the excuses the FBI gave for being caught with their pants down on 9/11 was that they were an after-the-fact crime investigation group—their specialty was not preventing crime but investigating the crime once it had been committed. We decided to check in with our lead investigators to see how they were doing on the case. Had they cracked the crime?

The meeting was set up for the middle of June. There were a ton of agents waiting to meet us. In fact, each one of us was given an escort whose job it was to stay with us at all times while we were in the building. Our photo identification cards were scanned, checked, and then rechecked. I shot a look at the girls and said, "Where was all of this organization on nine-eleven? We could have used it."

We were told that the building was secure and that all cell phones had to be turned off. No reception. We then filed into an elevator and thereafter into a high-tech conference room. We settled into our very serious-looking chairs, and were treated to a PowerPoint presentation about the 9/11 attacks. Within thirty seconds, we started raising our hands and asking questions and continued to interrupt the director, questioning the veracity of the PowerPoint program. It soon became clear that the director of the FBI had lost control. The PowerPoint program was turned off, the lights were turned on, and we were given strict rules about how the meeting was to be conducted. Three FBI people, including the director, would stand at the front. We would raise our hands and ask questions one at a time. Only one FBI person was allowed to answer each question. There were to be no sidebar conversations.

First question: "So, as our lead investigators, have you solved the crime yet?" The director looked stunned. He asked, "What crime?" We then explained that we wanted to know what he knew about the hijackers and the 9/11 attacks. We also wanted to know if they had any leads on the anthrax attacks. And, while we were at it, we wanted an update on the Moussaoui trial.

The director was not pleased. His expressions spoke volumes. He looked as if he wanted to say "How dare you ask me such questions? Don't you know that I am the director of the FBI? That I have the power to ruin your lives?" That's why so many elected officials never make waves for people like Mueller who run the intelligence community. Congress fears the intelligence agencies because they think agencies like the FBI have the dirt on them. Congressional officials never cause problems for them because they worry that somewhere, hidden away, the agencies have an archive full of congressional skeletons, dirt, and proof of scandal. The problem for Mueller was that we weren't elected officials and we had no skeletons to worry about. Nobody could make our lives any worse than they already were. We knew exactly who Mueller was, and that's why we had such difficulty in garnering respect for him. He had a lot of explaining to do for his agency and its failures leading up to and after 9/11. He was in part responsible for our husbands' deaths. And we wanted him held accountable.

Nearly every question we asked was answered with one of the following: We cannot answer that because it would harm the Moussaoui prosecution. We cannot answer that because it is part of our ongoing investigation. We cannot answer that because it involves sources and methods and national security. It was a joke. Need to know about the timeline of when NORAD scrambled its jets? Sorry, no can do. It might jeopardize the Moussaoui trial. Need to know about the informant who was living in San Diego? Sorry, can't answer. National security. Need to know why the buildings weren't evacuated on time? Sorry, that would harm the Moussaoui trial. Every single question was dismissed with one of those excuses. The one used most often was the Moussaoui trial. It incensed us.

I will say this: The FBI was very accommodating. I hold no ill will toward them personally or individually—in fact, I think Director Mueller is fairly charming. I find him to be one of the best liars I have ever met. Seriously, I do believe the FBI field agents work very hard in trying to keep us safe. What I don't like about the FBI is their institutional secrecy. It's stupid and unnecessary. And as 9/11 proved, it very often costs lives.

Once the meeting disbanded, many of the 9/11 families left the conference room to speak to the media who were eagerly waiting outside the Hoover Building. I wasn't in such a rush. I wanted to mingle a bit with the agents in a more informal setting. So as the room emptied out, I started engaging in conversation. At one point, a supervisory agent heard me talking to another agent and came over to interrupt. He pulled a chair over, plunked down in it, introduced himself, and told me that

I could ask him any question I wanted: "Ask me what you want to know, and I will tell you to the best of my ability."

With Lorie, Mindy, and Patty standing close by, I began to rattle off questions. When the agent tried to answer, I would identify the failure or glaring error in his answer and push for the truth. When he was backed into the corner, I moved on to the next issue, racking up his inaccuracies left and right. By the time I had him for about the fifth time, the FBI family liaison interrupted and wanted to know what we had been so animated in conversation about. I told her that we were just getting an explanation as to how the FBI was able to gain so much information so soon after the attacks. I then got specific. I asked about the car in Boston's Logan Airport that was driven by one of the terrorists. I wanted to know how the FBI had found it so quickly. The agent looked down at the special agent in charge (SAC), trying to read his face. I told her he had already answered and that I was interested in what she had to say. I told her I wanted to know if she was going to give the same answer as the SAC. She looked nervous. She looked down again at the SAC and started slowly mouthing her answer: "It was . . . because . . . of . . . the . . . tip. Yes, that's it. It was a tip. Someone at the airport had recognized Atta from the day before and saw him in the car." I then questioned her about the tip, wondering how it was possible for someone to call in a tip identifying Atta when Atta's picture was not shown until days after the attacks. She had nothing much to say other than that there were lots of tips flowing in during that time period—even before the photos were released.

I then switched topics, baiting the hook for some more. The flight schools in Florida—how had the FBI known to go there so quickly? I mean, with the thousands of flight schools in the United States, how had they happened to go to the one exact

flight school the hijackers had visited—and get there mere
hours after the attacks? Suddenly the family coordinator's
beeper went off. She started and unhooked it from her waist-
band. She looked at it. As she was showing it to me, she said,
"That's odd—it says 911." She walked over to one of the phones
on the conference tables and called a number. When she returned she answered my prior question about Atta's car at
Logan Airport. She answered the exact same way the SAC had
answered.

At this point, I'd had enough. The point had been made.
And the message received.

As we said good-bye to our escorts, I started apologizing
for my behavior. I kept telling them that I was a nice person,
just very frustrated with all the secrets that surrounded 9/11.
The FBI guys laughed and said, "Stop it. We were sitting in the
back watching you and talking about how we'd like to take you
out drinking." That was all I needed to hear. I quipped back,
"Really? Wanna go now? I'll drink you guys under the table and
then maybe we can get some real answers and somewhere
near the truth!"

The widows dragged me away. As I stepped onto the elevator, I stuck out my head and said, "Oh, yeah! And another
thing: Knock off the listening in on my phone conversations. I
can hear you guys breathing. It's annoying." I had a smile on
my face as the doors began to close. My parting comment: "I'm
not kidding! Knock it off!" Years later, with all the allegations
swirling about domestic surveillance, maybe I wasn't just paranoid about hearing all those clicks and strange crossed phone
lines. Someday when we are old and gray and unable to remember all the things we did, the widows and I plan to file a
Freedom of Information Act claim to gain access to our FBI

files. We figure they will be quite comprehensive and enter-
taining to read, like a walk down memory lane.

⸻ ❧ ⸻

After the FBI meeting, the rest of the summer was fairly quiet
with regard to the commission's hearing schedule. We kept
getting promises that the truly hard-hitting hearings would
commence in the autumn of 2003. And then the autumn came
and went and we still hadn't seen any really substantive hearings. We were crestfallen. But still we religiously attended
every public hearing, sometimes sending our written questions
up to the commissioners while the hearing was in progress,
goading them into asking a fruitful question or making a
pointed follow-up.

    Often we would watch as the commissioners fell asleep
during open testimony, bored with their own subject matter.
Lee Hamilton and Slade Gorton were the worst. Patty's
fourteen-year-old son, John, once attended a hearing. A reporter was impressed that he had wanted to come to Washington and see what the 9/11 Commission was all about. When the
reporter asked John what he thought of the hearing that day,
John responded by detailing which commissioners had fallen
asleep and for how long. For a boy like John whose mother
had spent so many hours fighting for such a commission, it
wasn't a very impressive showing.

    When dissatisfied with the content of the hearing or the
softball questions posed by the commissioners, we would immediately leave the hearing room and hold an impromptu
press conference. At times we were their biggest adversaries,
and at other times we were their biggest advocates. It was an
odd role to play. One minute we would be arguing for their
access to the executive branch documents, and the next we

would be arguing with the commission about whom they chose to see those documents. It was a complicated, frustrating dance that even to this day we don't fully understand.

It became apparent to us by late autumn of 2003 that the questioning at the hearings was not tough enough—that the hearings themselves were not identifying specific problems and holding people accountable. Witnesses would contradict their prior testimony and the commission would fail to ask them why. One good example of this was the testimony of Federal Aviation Administration (FAA) director Jane Garvey. When she first appeared before the commission, she laid out a timeline that described when the FAA knew the airplanes on 9/11 were confirmed hijacked. This timeline is important because the FAA has clear protocols and procedures in place for hijackings. None of these protocols were followed on 9/11. None of the failures were explained. We knew Garvey wasn't being very forthcoming. The commissioners gave her the benefit of the doubt.

When she was invited back a second time, she just resubmitted a new timeline. Of course, by that time the commission had served a subpoena and found out on its own that Garvey's prior testimony was in error. Yet the commission never pressed for a specific answer as to why Garvey had lied. Just like it never got to the bottom of why it took Garvey's agency, the FAA, so long to notify NORAD on the morning of 9/11.

The widows and I would have frequent conference calls with the commission staff. But those, too, began to feel empty. Each investigative team was kept insular and was allowed to look only at its particular avenue of investigation. In other words, no one segment of the staff was seeing the entire picture of what was being investigated—it was all fractured.

Zelikow had designed it that way because the course of the

investigation was easier to contain. At least that is how it appeared to me. Ironically, the official excuse for 9/11 was that "nobody connected the dots," and yet Zelikow set up the commission's own investigation into 9/11 in such a way that no single investigator could feasibly "connect the dots" of failure that occurred on 9/11. Zelikow did the same thing when he wrote the 9/11 independent commission's final report. The book is choppy and disconnected. It is confusing, as the story line jumps back and forth through facts and history, making it very hard to keep track of the mounting failures that keep adding up.

Richard Clarke's testimony on March 24, 2004, was obviously one of the more publicized commission events, because for the first time in the nearly 1,000 days since September 11, a government official turned to the families of those killed and simply said, "Your government failed you. . . . Those entrusted with protecting you failed you. And I failed you."

Clarke's words came as a stunning surprise. We had never heard anyone say anything like that ever before, or since. It was a satisfying moment because, in my opinion, Clarke had an awful lot of explaining to do regarding his failure to prevent the 9/11 attacks. But still, it would have meant more to me if others had followed in his footsteps. Why couldn't more administration officials from both the Clinton and Bush presidencies stand up and say, "Look, we tried our damndest, worked our hearts out, but made some mistakes and should have done some things differently. But, goddamn it, let's look at what we did, examine it, and fix the problems so that next time we might save more lives." How hard would that be?

At the time when Clarke testified, Condoleezza Rice was still refusing to do so. In her place, the White House sent Deputy Secretary of State Richard Armitage. When Armitage showed up in the hearing room, the 9/11 families rose from their front-row seats and left the room. It was our silent protest. When we reached the media outside, we clearly expressed our disappointment at Rice's failure to testify. We asked what she had to hide. The White House countered those comments, saying that "it is a longstanding principle that sitting national security advisers do not testify before Congress." The names Zbigniew Brzezinski and Samuel Berger made a mockery of that.

Tom Brokaw, then the anchor of *NBC Nightly News*, did an interview with Condoleezza Rice on March 24, after Clarke's first day of testifying before the commission, and one fair and obvious question slammed into her sanctimony: "Dr. Rice, with all due respect, I think a lot of people are watching this tonight saying, 'Well, she can appear on television, write commentary, but she won't appear before the commission under oath. It just doesn't seem to make sense.'"

That same evening, at the annual Radio and Television Correspondents Dinner in Washington, President Bush appeared in a slide presentation searching in the Oval Office for weapons of mass destruction. It seemed like a perfect snapshot of the arrogance and cavalier attitude of the Bush administration. The night after one of the most riveting days of testimony before the independent commission, the president was ridiculing the reason he started a war in response to the murder of 3,000 Americans, one of whom was my husband. There has never been a shortage of outrage in me with regard to the fight for the independent commission. But March 24, 2004, was one of the days when my outrage went hand in hand with revulsion.

Clarke's testimony had a powerful impact because it laid out a one-sided damning indictment of the Bush administration. Within days the White House agreed that Condoleezza Rice, its national security adviser, would testify under oath.

Watching her raise her hand and swear to tell the truth before the commission was one of the most satisfying moments of the entire grueling four-year process. We had forced her to be in a place she did not want to be: in the seat of accountability.

An agreement was also reached that President Bush and Vice President Cheney would testify before the commission, although it would be in private and not under oath. The deal had even more strings attached: After Rice testified, she could not be called back, nor could any other top White House official. The net result of that, as some pointed out, was that discrepancies would never be resolved. So much for all the promises of the 9/11 commissioners to provide us with the most comprehensive and definitive account of 9/11.

Condoleezza Rice raised her right hand and promised to tell the truth on April 8, 2004. She looked like such a prim and proper lady that putting her under oath seemed insulting. We weren't fooled by her competent outward appearance, though. In fact, we had a nickname for Condi. We called her Condi "Kinda-lies-a-lot" Rice.

Rice had several primary objectives to achieve in her testimony. One was to take apart Richard Clarke and rebut his scathing testimony. The other was to preserve at all costs the ultimate line: "Had we thought that there was an attack coming in Washington or New York, we would have moved heaven and earth to try and stop it."

A problem for Rice was the PDB—the president's daily brief—that had been prepared for the president by the CIA a month before 9/11 and given to him while he was vacationing in Crawford, Texas, on August 6, 2001. We had known since 2002 that the memo existed, but the full details did not come out until the Rice testimony. She told us, "I believe the title was 'Bin Laden Determined to Attack Inside the United States.'"

Unfazed and seemingly indifferent, Rice stayed relentlessly on message. "It did not warn of attacks inside the United States," she said. "It was historical information based on old reporting." It was as if the PDB were called "Bin Laden Used to Be Determined to Attack Inside the United States." Lorie Van Auken brilliantly pointed this out when we all appeared on *Hardball with Chris Matthews* that evening. She got a copy of the PDB and highlighted all the language in it that used the present tense. Lorie was always good with the visuals since she had been a graphic designer in her prior life.

Democratic commissioner Bob Kerrey pointed out the section in the memo that said "the FBI indicates patterns of suspicious activity in the United States consistent with preparations for hijacking." Kerrey, in another memorable and disturbing moment, pointed out that there never had been a U.S. response to the *Cole* bombing that killed seventeen Americans in October 2000. Rice countered that the president was tired "of swatting at flies." She argued that a broad strategy needed to be applied to al Qaeda instead of reacting to each incident or attack. Her excuse sounded weak.

The commissioners wanted to know if she had conveyed any warnings to the president about al Qaeda cells operating in the United States. With matter-of-fact smugness, she said, "I don't remember the al Qaeda cells being something that we were told we needed to do something about." This contradicted Clarke's testimony. Even more alarming, though, was the notion that as national security adviser, Dr. Rice thought she needed to be instructed to do something about al Qaeda sleeper cells living and plotting attacks in the country. The concept of Rice, our national security adviser, excusing her incompetence because nobody told her to worry about al Qaeda was ludicrous—and frightening.

Rice's assertion that no one knew planes might be used as weapons and flown into buildings was also patently false. She had attended the G-8 summit meeting with the president and other world leaders a mere two months before 9/11, when the possibility of an assassination attempt on President Bush had been mentioned to the group—an assassination that would be carried out by planes. Not to mention the long and well-documented intelligence history of U.S. government awareness and preparedness regarding planes being used as weapons.

While on *Hardball with Chris Matthews* that night, I told him how disappointed I was with her testimony. "We need to get more answers from her. I would have hoped that the commissioners would have asked more pointed questions, more questions about the substance of the threats that we were facing, more about the intelligence community, what they knew and where the breakdown of the intelligence information occurred, why the national security adviser did not know that planes could be used as missiles."

Matthews asked me to sum up what I thought about Rice. I said, "She is either incompetent or a liar. Or both." It was certainly not a good way to feel about the person who was in charge of your nation's national security.

One of my most personally disheartening moments was when I cornered a commissioner and asked him why more pointed questions weren't being asked of the witnesses. "It's not the Washington way," I was told. I didn't find that acceptable then, and I never will. We fought and begged to bring this commission into being. We didn't think we would have to grovel to get answers. There were often times when solid leads were passed along and then ignored.

One of the most dramatic examples is the mystery of Richard Clarke's postmortem report. Earlier on, while preparing for my testimony before the Joint Inquiry, I had found a newspaper article that discussed a 9/11 postmortem prepared by the White House national security counterterrorism czar, Richard Clarke. Clarke was running the situation room on 9/11 and had long tried to persuade the administration to take the threat from Osama bin Laden more seriously.

The article I saw said that in the immediate aftermath of 9/11, Clarke was asked by President Bush to pull every document from every file in every government agency related to al Qaeda, bin Laden, or terrorism. The article reported that Clarke first looked back three months, then four months, and then he extended his culling of documents for the entire eighteen months prior to 9/11.

This seemed vital for a commission that was having trouble locating documents from executive branch agencies. Clarke's postmortem report seemed like a potential intelligence bonanza for the commission. I asked Roger Cressey, Clarke's assistant, to confirm the existence of the report. At first he feigned ignorance about it. I then read the newspaper article to him wherein he and Clarke were quoted discussing the postmortem. Clearly caught in a lie, Cressey then acknowledged that such a report was undertaken but that he didn't know what had happened to it. He said he would look into it and get back to me. I joked with him that when he found it, he could feel free to fax it to me at my home. By the way, I am still waiting.

This postmortem report was something I pestered Chairman Tom Kean about on at least three occasions. He agreed that it sounded vital and said he wished he had a copy. Twenty months later, on the day the commission released its final report, I cornered Kean in a vestibule and asked him if he'd ever gotten his hands on Clarke's 9/11 postmortem report. He looked blank. He said he had no idea what I was talking about.

I reminded him of the conversations we'd had about Clarke's report and the massive amount of documentation he had supporting it. Kean simply looked at me and said, "Yeah, unfortunately we were never able to track that down."

By the time it came to fight for an extension of the commission in February 2004, we knew what to expect. Nevertheless we were undaunted in going after our objective, which we were convinced was not only morally right, but required judicious action. Initially, the commission was to have an eighteen-month lifespan. In the original battle to create the commission, the 9/11 families wanted a two-year time frame. We had lost that battle: The White House didn't want the report to coincide with the election. We agreed on eighteen months. But too many of those eighteen months had been squandered and/or lost by all the foot-dragging carried out by the White House— they delayed clearances of commissioners, they delayed funding, they delayed access to individuals, they delayed access to documents—and all the while the clock was ticking and the commission was losing valuable investigative time.

Of course the White House wasn't stupid. They were running out the clock on purpose. But we weren't going to stand for it. This was our only shot to have a comprehensive investigation. To have all of our questions answered. To learn lessons. To make the nation safer. How could the White House want to frustrate those goals? We needed an extension and the White House needed to support it.

Surprisingly, the Democrats were initially the main opposition to the extension. Politically, the Democrats wanted the final report out before the election. Conversely, the Republicans had no problem with the report coming out after the election—we were talking January 2005, and they were more than happy to have built-in damage control.

My goal was not a political one. I wanted the most substantive and complete report possible. Declassifying reports
took enormous amounts of time, particularly when such declassification required visible redactions—something the 9/11
families felt passionately about being used in the 9/11 Commission's final report. Visible redactions are the black lines that
are drawn through all classified material. Seeing blacked-out
lines in a report is a chilling experience; you feel the impact of
government secrecy because you can actually see the pages
and pages of information being withheld from you.

The 9/11 families knew that feeling well after reading the
Joint Inquiry of Congress's final report, which used visible
redactions and included twenty-eight blank pages that allegedly involved Saudi financing of bin Laden and the 9/11 attacks. We fought for the 9/11 Commission because we wanted
transparency in government and national security issues. Transparency could be possible with visible redactions because
Americans would be able to see exactly how much information
was being withheld from them via the blacked-out lines in the
commission's final report.

When we were arguing for the visible redactions, the commission countered that such declassification would take too
much time. They argued that the clock had already run out on
their investigation and that there was no way they could provide visible redactions in the final report. They planned to release a final report that was written in its original form as a
declassified report. In other words, there would only be one
distilled version of the 9/11 independent commission's final
report.

This concept set it apart from the congressional Joint Inquiry's final report, which had two versions: the classified and
unclassified. The 9/11 families decided that the only way we

could beat the commission's time-constraint argument was to get an extension. Besides, we figured an extension of time meant more time to investigate and provide a more thorough, comprehensive report. We didn't care what the political ramifications were to either party. All we cared about was a solid report. We therefore aimed for January 2005.

John McCain supported the January 2005 extension. I called the speaker's office to check in to see where Dennis Hastert was on the extension. Hastert was the ranking Republican in the House, the big cheese. Quite contrary to his public assertions, he was always a problem behind the scenes when it came to facilitating the commission's work. As far as we were concerned, Hastert was synonymous with Cheney. They were one in the same. Hastert's chief of staff said that his boss supported the January 2005 deadline, but unfortunately the Democrats were against it, and that meant it really could never get done. I felt his smug smile through the phone as he blamed it on the congressional Democrats. What he failed to recognize was that contrary to popular opinion, I was not a Democratic operative. Frankly, I could have given a rat's ass who was to blame for the delay in gaining an extension for the commission. I just wanted it done. We would work with anybody in Washington who supported our cause. It wasn't our fault that the only people supporting the 9/11 Commission were largely from the Democratic party. We didn't care what party or political affiliation. We were equal opportunists on our quest for truth, justice, and a comprehensive accounting of what went wrong on 9/11.

I then asked the chief of staff what would happen if I could get the Democrats to agree to January 2005—would Hastert still support it? The chief of staff laughed heartily and said, "Yeah, sure. If you get the Democrats to agree to January 2005, then you've got yourself a deal. But they will never agree. They want to use this report as a political football against the president before the election. My boss won't hear of it."

This is how it played out: I got on the phone and called key Democrats. I said, "Guys, listen. You're missing the big picture here. Let me paint it for you. Picture high-ranking officials under oath during open, public hearings every single week leading up to the election. We need more time to ask for documents, issue supoenas, and make further inquiries."

There was a pause, a momentary reflection. "All right. We trust you on this. You'd better be right."

By three o'clock that afternoon, the Democratic caucus had agreed to support the extension. But we had resolution, and we were thrilled. I called Hastert's office. His chief of staff said, in effect, "You're full of shit. Are you telling me you got the Democratic Congress to support an '05 deadline? You are totally full of shit." I told him that the Democrats were in agreement on this and that he had said if that happened, I'd have Republican support for the January 2005 extension.

Well, not so fast. If the Democrats had coalesced around me, the Republicans wondered if they were missing something. They panicked. Apparently after a few phone calls they were able to figure out how the extension had been pitched to the Democrats. The Republicans went back on their word. There was nothing I could do about it. Their strategy was to get the report out and get it behind them. We did receive an extension of two months for the commission, but that was not enough time for visible redactions, nor was it enough time for the commission to follow up on many of its pieces of unfinished investigative work—one of which was now the special operation Able Danger.

CHAPTER SIX

⚭

The Mystery in Footnote 44

B Y THE TIME the independent commission's report was released on July 22, 2004, it was almost an anticlimax for
me. I'd been preparing in the preceding weeks by reading a
compilation of staff statements that had already been published
in another book. Each time there was a public hearing, a statement was released by the staff summarizing what its investigators had found on that topic. The book *The 9/11 Investigations*
then married those staff statements with the public testimony
from the hearing, which gave a fairly comprehensive look into
what the commission had found and would most likely ultimately release in their own final report.

I felt I needed to be as organized and as ready as possible
because I knew the media attention would be short-lived. The
report would be massive, and 9/11 family members would be
in the spotlight for a news cycle or two before interest would
dissipate. *The 9/11 Investigations* was an indispensable primer.

July 22 was a Thursday. There were no leaks as to what
was going to be unearthed in the final report. The widows and
I drove down to Washington not really knowing what to expect. The commissioners held a private briefing for 9/11 family

members that morning. There were about twenty of us invited to the briefing—more people than the usual dozen 9/11 family members who always attended every hearing and played the role of watchdog throughout the commission's history. Where the other family members came from, we didn't know or care. The more the merrier.

Each of us was given the 567-page report. I sat in the front row with Mindy, Lorie, and Patty. The eagerness and anticipation in the room was palpable. This was a milestone moment. We had all fought to bring the commission into being, and whatever the outcome, it was an achievement to see its work now completed.

I was not optimistic about finding any startling revelations in the report. We were, after all, getting a report that was written all along in a declassified manner. We'd pushed to have the classified passages redacted so the public could grasp how much information was being withheld. But that request was denied. Nevertheless, I still held out a small hope that a few nuggets of knowledge might slip through, pointing me into areas that I knew were crucial and still needed to be explored further.

After being given a book, a family member got out of her seat and walked up to the commissioners to have them sign her copy. Soon all the family members were requesting the autographs of the commissioners. This seemed odd to me. I continued to sit in my seat and thumb through the footnotes in the back of the book, ignoring all the commotion.

There was something I was looking for, but I had no idea where I would find it. I had a hunch about some vital information the CIA might have withheld from the FBI, information that, if not withheld, might have thwarted the 9/11 attacks. It had always been dismissed in the press and by the congres-

sional inquiry as being an oversight—a mistake. But I felt differently. It didn't make any sense to me. I was tired of all the
mistakes that were racking up when it came to our government
and their job to protect us on 9/11.

And then, of course, there were the several paragraphs in
one of the commission's staff statements. In essence, it spoke
about 9/11 being an "intelligence story"; it hinted that the failure to share information might have been carried out purposefully and in poor judgment. It was vague. And it was written in
an odd manner, simply thrown into the middle of a chapter that
encompassed cold hard facts about 9/11. Such a digression in
the factual history simply had no place in a 9/11 Commission
staff statement. The statement reads as follows:

> That is why we think this issue must be examined from
> a broader perspective, that of overall management of
> transnational intelligence operations. After all, why would
> the watchlisting make a difference? One purpose would
> have been to turn al Hazmi and al Mihdhar back when
> they reached Los Angeles, in effect throwing them back
> into the sea. That would have served one purpose. But
> it might not have prevented any attacks.
>
> We think it may be more interesting to consider the
> intelligence mission. The intelligence mission was why
> the suspects were tracked in Malaysia rather than being
> detained and deported. If the FBI had been given the
> opportunity to monitor al Hazmi and al Mihdhar in
> California, and had been patient for months, or a year,
> then some larger results might have been possible, even
> after al Mihdhar had left. The universe of possibilities
> expands after Hani Hanjour joined al Hazmi in Decem-
> ber 2000, after which the two of them lived in Phoenix

for several months before driving across the country and linking up with other future hijackers in Northern Virginia. Up to this point, all of the hijackers were involved in Flight 77—the plane that hit the Pentagon. But in Northern Virginia they linked up with a hijacker who would join the team assigned to Flight 175, thus creating the possibility to penetrate the other teams associated with the Hamburg cell.

These are difficult what-ifs. It is possible that the Intelligence Community might have judged that the risks of conducting such a prolonged intelligence operation were too high—the risk of losing track of potential terrorists, for example. It is possible that the pre-9/11 FBI would not have been judged capable of conducting such an operation. But surely the Intelligence Community would have preferred to have the chance to make these choices. That is why we see this as an intelligence story—and a challenge for Intelligence Community management.

The above paragraph was ringing in my head. An intelligence *story*? What story would that be? I wanted the history, not a story. I'd had the report in my hand for less than a minute when I spotted exactly what I'd been hoping to find. While rapidly flipping through the pages, my eyes glanced down at Footnote 44 on page 502. I underlined it and passed it to Mindy, Lorie, and Patty. There was a bit of commotion in the front row as the book went back and forth. The commissioners looked at us quizzically as they continued to sign copies of the report being thrust into their hands. They knew something was up. We were always their wild cards.

A horde of reporters was waiting outside the doors of the

briefing room to talk to the families. They wanted to know how we'd been briefed and what initial reactions we all had. Were there any earth-shattering revelations? What did you learn? What did they say? How do you feel finally having the report in your hands?

Footnote 44 gave me the ammunition I'd been seeking. I told reporters that it proved that the CIA deliberately withheld information from the FBI about two of the terrorists who would go on to become 9/11 hijackers. For me, Footnote 44, buried in the voluminous footnotes, all written in the tiniest of print, was the damning proof of why we needed to hold people accountable.

Several reporters were understandably suspicious and wanted to know if the report had been leaked to me in advance. How could I have nailed something so specific so fast? A footnote on page 502?

What the footnote proves is that the CIA's failure to share information with the FBI was not a mistake or an oversight. It was done on purpose. And the CIA even tried to cover up their malfeasance. If you want to know why and how 9/11 could have been prevented, your answers are rooted in Footnote 44, which is quoted below:

44. CIA cable, "Activities of Bin Laden Associate Khalid Revealed," Jan. 4, 2000. His Saudi passport—which contained a visa for travel to the United States—was photocopied and forwarded to CIA headquarters. This information was not shared with FBI headquarters until August 2001. An FBI agent detailed to the Bin Laden unit at CIA attempted to share this information with colleagues at FBI headquarters. A CIA desk officer instructed him not to send the cable with this information.

Several hours later, this same desk officer drafted a cable distributed solely within the CIA alleging that the visa documents had been shared with the FBI. She admitted that she did not personally share the information and cannot identify who told her they had been shared. We were unable to locate anyone who claimed to have shared the information. Contemporaneous documents contradict the claim that they were shared. DOJ Inspector General interview of Doug M., Feb. 12, 2004, DOJ Inspector General interview of Michael, Oct. 31, 2002, CIA cable, Jan. 5, 2000, DOJ Inspector General report, "A Review of the FBI's Handling of Intelligence Information Related to the 9/11 Attacks," July 2, 2004, p. 282.

The tale of the footnote begins at the end of 1999 and in early 2000, the period of the Millennium Alert, when the danger from al Qaeda was the number-one national security priority in the country. It was the focus of meetings held almost daily by the top officials of the U.S. government. By December 31, 1999, relevant working-level officials in the intelligence community were watching two Middle Eastern men in particular—"Khalid" and "Nawaf"—and concluded the two men might be part of an "operational cadre" and that "something nefarious might be afoot." Twenty-one months later, these two men would help fly American Airlines Flight 77 into the Pentagon.

During the first week of January 2000, the CIA tracked "Khalid" and "Nawaf" as they traveled to Kuala Lumpur, Malaysia. Three days later, the agency identified "Khalid" as Khalid al Mihdhar. Around the same time, the CIA was sent correspondence from the German intelligence services that included the name "Nawaf" and a phone number. In testifying before the Joint Inquiry, CIA director George Tenet said, "In early January 2000, we managed to obtain a photocopy of Mihdhar's passport as he traveled to Kuala Lumpur." With that passport, Tenet knew Mihdhar's full name, date and place of birth, and his passport number. Even more important, Tenet learned that Mihdhar's Saudi passport contained a U.S. visa that was good for the next four months—until April 2000. This information meant that al Mihdhar was likely to show up in the United States within the next four months.

At that point, the CIA should have given al Mihdhar's name to the State Department, which could have added Mihdhar's name to its terrorist watchlist. Adding Mihdhar's name to the State Department watchlist would have meant that Mihdhar's entry into the United States would be barred. However, the CIA did not give the name to the State Department. Tenet acknowledged in his testimony to the Joint Inquiry that this was deliberately not done.

"We had at that point the level of detail needed to watchlist Mihdhar—that is, to nominate him to State Department for refusal of entry into the U.S. or to deny him another visa. Our officers remained focused on the surveillance operation and did not do so."

Mihdhar and "Nawaf" (whom the CIA had identified as Nawaf al Hazmi, a known al Qaeda killer) traveled to Kuala Lumpur in early January for a terrorist planning session. Participants in the meeting had two goals in mind: the bombing of the USS *Cole* and the 9/11 attacks. The CIA knew about this meeting and knew where it was taking place. They also knew that the participants in the meeting were major-league killers in al Qaeda and had direct connections to Osama bin Laden. For reasons that remain highly classified, the CIA did not conduct its own surveillance on the meeting. They farmed out that task to a foreign country. Unfortunately, according to the official un-classified story, that foreign country was unable to get "ears" into the terrorist meeting. In other words, they were only able to conduct video surveillance with no voice recording. Again, that is according to the official unclassified version of the story.

The two future 9/11 terrorists, al Mihdhar and al Hazmi, were initially tracked through what came to be called "the Osama switchboard." Bin Laden had used a phone in Yemen as a relay point for messages to be forwarded back and forth to him in Afghanistan. The Yemen number had been known to our CIA and NSA for several years. It was a gold mine of in-formation on al Qaeda. Some of that gold paid off when, months before the meeting in Malaysia, some messages trans-mitted through the Yemen switchboard indicated that known al Qaeda killers al Hazmi and al Mihdhar would be meeting with other al Qaeda agents in Kuala Lumpur in early January 2000 for what was deemed a terrorist summit.

Thereafter, the CIA obtained a photocopy of al Mihdhar's Saudi passport as he made his way through Dubai in the United Arab Emirates en route to the Malaysia meeting. Al Hazmi was monitored in transit as well. This was not an incidental under-taking. It was a concerted effort made on behalf of our CIA to track these two men as they made their way to the terrorist summit. By the time the two men arrived in Kuala Lumpur, the CIA knew exactly where they were headed: to a condominium complex on the outskirts of the city. A condominium complex, incidentally, that several months later would also host another al Qaeda operative: Zacarias Moussaoui.

By January 5, 2000, the case of al Mihdhar and al Hazmi was important enough that it was mentioned in the regular al Qaeda updates being given to top officials of the U.S. govern-ment. In fact, on January 3 and 5, the head of the CIA's al

Qaeda unit briefed his bosses on the developments of the operation as part of his regular daily updates. These updates were reviewed daily by CIA director George Tenet and National Security Adviser Sandy Berger.

The CIA's decision not to watchlist—add al Mihdhar and al Hazmi's names to the State Department list, thereby barring their entry into the United States—might have been discussed, debated, and decided during these meetings. But what specifically was discussed in the meetings remains highly classified. Nevertheless, Tenet's decision not to watchlist two known al Qaeda killers who were heading into this country nearly two weeks after the Millennium Alert would seem like something that would be discussed in such meetings. Unfortunately we may never know for sure. (Of course, the draft national security documents that Sandy Berger stole in October 2003 might answer some of these questions, but unfortunately Berger supposedly permanently destroyed those highly classified documents— receiving community service as his punishment.)

The Kuala Lumpur meeting took place January 5 through 8, 2000. Malaysian intelligence conducted only photographic surveillance (i.e., not listening devices) on the meeting. These surveillance photos were then transmitted back to CIA headquarters. The photos of the terrorists would prove to be invaluable in the months ahead, but tragically, they would never be capitalized upon in time to thwart the 9/11 attacks.

While testifying and being grilled about the terrorist summit in Malaysia, Tenet said that with Mihdhar's arrival at the Kuala Lumpur condo on January 5, surveillance began and "indicated that the behavior of the individuals was consistent with clandestine activity." Tenet, however, did not expand on what sort of specific behavior was carried out by the terrorists that indicated clandestine activity.

On January 5 and 6, 2000, the CIA belatedly told the FBI about their al Mihdhar and al Hazmi operation. Only the top FBI officials were briefed about the CIA's operation. The FBI officials were told that the CIA was in the lead and that the CIA "will immediately bring the FBI into the loop as soon as something concrete developed leading to the criminal arena or to known FBI cases." Notably, the CIA failed to tell the FBI officials about al Mihdhar's U.S. visa. At this point, the CIA had now failed to tell not only the State Department, who might have barred the U.S. entry of al Mihdhar and al Hazmi, but also the FBI, who might have conducted an intelligence investigation into al Mihdhar and al Hazmi once they arrived inside the United States. Once again, Tenet makes no apologies for the CIA's failure to do so.

The CIA and the FBI had a bin Laden unit at CIA headquarters in Langley, Virginia. An FBI agent who was part of the unit learned about the Malaysia meeting shortly after it ended. The FBI agent also learned that one of the participants had a U.S. visa. This FBI agent attempted to share the information with his other colleagues over at the FBI. But before the agent was able to transmit the cable to the FBI, a CIA desk officer stopped him and told him not to send it.

Thereafter, the same CIA desk officer drafted a cable that was distributed solely within the CIA that said the visa information had been shared with the FBI. In other words, the desk officer lied because she was personally responsible for ordering the FBI agent not to share the visa information with the FBI. As outlined in Footnote 44, the desk officer admitted that she lied, but she could not identify the person who had instructed her to draft the misleading cable. Purposefully withholding information from the FBI is bad enough; covering up that fact and not being able to recall who told you to do so is wholly unacceptable.

It is alarming enough that the CIA purposely failed to tell the State Department and the FBI about two known al Qaeda killers who entered this country in early January 2000. More disturbing, however, is that once the Malaysia terrorist summit ended, the CIA simply "lost track" of the terrorists in the "streets of Bangkok." And according to the unclassified story, the CIA did not pick up the trail of these two men until after the 9/11 attacks, when they were found to be aboard Flight 77, which crashed into the Pentagon.

How could the CIA inexplicably lose track of two known al Qaeda killers who were behaving in a criminal manner and headed to the United States? Recall that al Mihdhar and al Hazmi were the topic of daily meetings between Tenet and the Clinton National Security Council. The matter was being closely monitored. And the CIA just lost them? Tenet's official excuse? The CIA was busy doing other things—it had other priorities.

But according to *The 9/11 Commission Report*, Tenet seems to be lying. I say this because *The 9/11 Commission Report* details CIA cable traffic that confirmed that active CIA surveillance continued on the two men after the Malaysia terrorist summit had ended. For example, on January 12, 2000, the head of CIA's al Qaeda unit updated his supervisors in the United States that "surveillance continued" in the al Mihdhar operation. On January 14, 2000, the head of CIA's al Qaeda unit again updated his bosses that officials were "continuing to track" the suspicious individuals. Moreover, in February 2000, the CIA received a request from foreign authorities to become involved with CIA's al Mihdhar "operation." The CIA rejected the request. The CIA's reason for denying the foreign authorities' involvement? The CIA was in the midst of trying "to determine what the subject is up to." Such a statement—in February 2000—makes it hard to sustain any belief in Tenet's testimony that the CIA "lost" the suspects in the streets of Bangkok back on January 8, 2000.

What happens next with al Hazmi and al Mihdhar is important in establishing how conducting surveillance on these two known killers might have unraveled the entire 9/11 plot. Both al Mihdhar and al Hazmi would come into regular and repeated contact with all of the 9/11 hijackers for the eighteen months following their identification by the CIA. Had surveillance been undertaken, all of the hijackers' identities would have been compromised.

By March 2000, both al Mihdhar and al Hazmi had comfortably settled in San Diego using their real names to sign rental agreements and to obtain their California driver's licenses. Since the CIA never told the FBI about the U.S. presence of the two known al Qaeda killers, all of this remained a secret from the FBI. Not that the CIA's withholding of information is any excuse for the FBI, because, as it turned out, the FBI had an informant living in the very same apartment complex as al Mihdhar and al Hazmi. Nevertheless, according to the official, unclassified record, the FBI was unaware of al Mihdhar and al Hazmi and their affiliation with al Qaeda until September 11, 2001.

While the FBI was kept in the dark, the unclassified record also indicates that the CIA was given even more information about al Mihdhar and al Hazmi that they could have shared with the FBI. According to *The 9/11 Commission Report*, the National Security Agency conducted wiretaps on al Mihdhar while he was living in San Diego. The phone calls were between al Mihdhar and his cousin, who was manning the infamous Yemen switchboard.

Unfortunately, the NSA never checked to see where al

Mihdhar's calls were originating from—i.e., San Diego. The NSA's oversight in not checking to see where the phone calls were being made from seems hard to believe. Nevertheless, the NSA's negligence in this regard has been excused and overlooked. So for the nearly five months al Mihdhar was in this country and living with al Hazmi in San Diego, the NSA listened in to his phone calls back to Yemen. Notably, because NSA assumed that al Mihdhar was overseas, they passed all of their information regarding al Mihdhar solely to the CIA—not the FBI. If only the billions budgeted to NSA for intelligence had had room for caller ID. If they had just informed the FBI about the presence of al Mihdhar within our borders, the FBI would have been able to begin its investigation more than a full year before 9/11.

On June 10, 2000, al Mihdhar flew from Los Angeles to Frankfurt, Germany. If he'd ever been placed on a watchlist, he would have been nabbed as he tried to leave the country. But the CIA had purposefully chosen not to do this. Al Mihdhar apparently returned to the United States in December 2000. He turned up in New York City to get an identification card from USA ID, a company that made identification cards in New York City. This would have been the fourth time al Mihdhar could have been detained if only the CIA had shared information about al Mihdhar's U.S. visa with the State Department.

Meanwhile, al Hazmi moved to Mesa, Arizona, in late December, where he lived and took flight courses alongside Hani Hanjour, the future pilot of Flight 77. Shortly before 9/11, both al Hazmi and Hanjour traveled to Virginia, where they met up with the hijackers who would eventually fly United Airlines Flight 175 into the World Trade Center. Hanjour, a Saudi who was described as quietly submissive, already had his FAA commercial license. It had taken him a few years to pass the test because of his abysmal English and poor aviation skills.

During their nine months in Arizona, al Hazmi and Hani Hanjour did extensive flight training and communicated with several other 9/11 hijackers. During the summer of 2001, these men received wire transfers from Khalid Sheikh Mohammed, the alleged mastermind behind 9/11, and Ramzi bin al Shibh, the alleged money man behind 9/11. When they registered for their flight schools or took practice flights across the country, they did so in their own names. They also visited with individuals who were already under FBI surveillance. Some of these subjects would be mentioned in the now-famous Phoenix memo penned by FBI agent Kenneth Williams.

As outlined in the 9/11 report, Agent Williams wrote his memo in July 2001 and sent it to FBI headquarters. He also forwarded it to agents on international terrorism squads in New York City. Williams noted that there were an "inordinate number of individuals of investigative interest" who were attending Arizona flight schools. He raised the possibility that Osama bin Laden might be engaged in a coordinated effort to send students to the United States to study aviation. Williams made four recommendations to the FBI. None of his recommendations were ever acted upon by anyone.

The Joint Inquiry of Congress makes an important point about the extensive network of contacts hijackers like al Hazmi had while living in the United States for the twenty-one months prior to 9/11:

Initial reporting from observers cast the hijackers as loners who stayed aloof from those around them. While these characterizations remain an accurate appraisal of the hijackers' general orientation toward most persons they came into contact with in the United States, more intensive scrutiny reveals that the hijackers—in particular, the six leaders/facilitators—were involved with a much greater number of associates than was originally suspected. In addition to frequent and sustained interaction between and among the hijackers of the various flights before September 11, the group maintained a web of contacts both in the United States and abroad. These associates, ranging in degrees of closeness, include friends and associates from universities and flight schools, former roommates, people they knew through mosques and religious activities, and employment contacts. Other contacts provided legal, logistical, or financial assistance, facilitated U.S. entry and flight school enrollment, or were known from UBL-related activities or training.

Moreover, the Joint Inquiry of Congress found that "before September 11, hijackers al Mihdhar, al Hazmi, Hanjour, Mohammed Atta, Marwan al Shehi, and possibly others had contacts with people who had come to the FBI's attention during counterterrorism or counterintelligence inquiries or investigations. In all, some of the hijackers were in various degrees of contact with at least fourteen such persons, four of whom were the focus of active FBI investigations while the hijackers were inside the United States."

How much of this information could have been learned by the FBI if the CIA had told the FBI about al Mihdhar and al Hazmi's presence inside the United States back in January 2000? More chillingly, if the CIA was continuing its surveillance of these two men while they were inside the United States (as the record seems to indicate), how much did Tenet and the CIA know, and why would they keep that information from the FBI?

Richard Clarke summed up the FBI's chances for disrupting 9/11 when he testified before the independent commission. When asked by Commissioner Richard Ben-Veniste if Clarke had thought an attack in the homeland was possible, Clarke responded,

> The fact that we didn't have intelligence that we could point to that said it would take place in the United States wasn't significant in my view, because frankly, sir—I know how this is going to sound but I have to say it—I didn't think the FBI would know whether or not there was anything going on in the United States by al Qaeda.

Two follow-up questions Ben-Veniste could have asked were: Why wouldn't the FBI know what was going on inside the United States with regard to al Qaeda? And second, what did the CIA know about al Qaeda's presence in the United States—particularly the al Mihdhar and al Hazmi sleeper cell? These are just two of the many questions that remain unasked by the 9/11 Commission.

George Tenet is the man who knows. He was the director of the CIA on 9/11 and had served in that capacity since President Clinton appointed him to the job in 1997. He has had at least two opportunities under oath to explain why the CIA kept the State Department and the FBI in the dark about the two al Qaeda members in this country: his testimonies before the congressional Joint Inquiry and before the 9/11 Commission.

But the most Tenet has ever said publicly is "We failed to do so." Now, doesn't the obvious follow-up question seem to be "Why? Why did you fail to do so? Who was responsible? If that person was following orders, whose orders were they? If they came from the president, what was the policy or strategy behind it?"

Perhaps there are more details in the classified version of the 9/11 Commission's report. There is a good bet that there is at least a lengthier explanation in the inspector general's report, the internal report written about the CIA's failures that surround 9/11. It's a report that was supposed to be made public. On the day Porter Goss was appointed director of the CIA, he looked me in the eye and promised that the CIA IG report would be released. It never was. Chalk that up to another battle lost.

I believe that the CIA kept its own watchlist of terrorists and did not turn the information over to the FBI because it had lost faith in the efficacy of the agency. I think the CIA was conducting surveillance on al Qaeda in this country with the goal of disrupting its operations here. It's illegal for the CIA to operate domestically. But there are ways around that restriction. It can be circumvented by a presidential order—in this case that would have had to come from Clinton—or the CIA could work out a deal with a foreign intelligence agency: say, the Israelis. Israel is believed to have spies here with the tacit understanding of our government, who helps provide cover for them by placing them in businesses as legitimate employees.

What if the Israelis did some legwork on al Qaeda in this country, which is not illegal, but shared the information with the CIA? According to the Joint Inquiry of Congress, "A senior government official told the Joint Inquiry that significant information concerning al Qaeda members had been shared with foreign authorities, but that it became apparent only after September 11, 2001, that the foreign authorities had been watching some of those persons before that date."

There is important context here that explains how this

could have happened. Early in December 1999, Ahmed Ressam was arrested in Port Angeles, Washington, while trying to enter this country by ferry from British Columbia. One hundred pounds of bomb-making material were found in his car. As the investigators learned, he was headed to Los Angeles International Airport to blow it up. This breakthrough was not based on any intelligence coming from intercepted phone calls, informants, or spies, or on any dogged legwork or months of following up on a spidery web of contacts and leads.

The breakthrough came because an alert customs agent became suspicious when Ressam, who was traveling on a Canadian passport under the fake name of "Benni Noris," refused to make eye contact with the customs agent and was reluctant to respond to her questions. He seemed anxious and fidgety, and when she tried to pull him aside, he bolted from the ferry but was soon arrested.

My theory is that President Clinton went ballistic when this happened. The millennium was just weeks away, and despite an all-out effort by every intelligence agency in the country, here was a guy headed toward LAX to blow it up and nothing was known about him until an agent who was smart enough to follow her gut instincts nabbed him. He was not on anyone's radar, which could have easily infuriated a president who had made his administration security-obsessed in the run-up to the millennium.

I think it's highly plausible that a judgment call was made at that time: The CIA knew it was tracking two al Qaeda terrorists, al Hazmi and al Mihdhar. Why not run out the line on them as bait and see what operations might be rolled up or reeled in? With the president's approval, the CIA could get permission to run an operation in this country.

I think it's clear, though, that the entire 9/11 plot could have been unraveled if al Hazmi and al Mihdhar had been consistently monitored from the time of their arrival in the United States in January 2000. After the *Cole* bombing, on October 12, 2000, which killed seventeen sailors, al Mihdhar and al Hazmi should have been arrested. From June 2001 onwards, they intersected with all seventeen of the other 9/11 hijackers, and in those now infamous words of George Tenet, "The system was blinking red." Al Qaeda sources were chattering and something was brewing. But what? And, more important, when?

Those blinking lights caught the eye of a CIA officer, "John," who was part of the International Terrorist Operations Section in the FBI. He recalled the terror meeting in Malaysia in January 2000 and wondered if it had any relevance to the heightened terrorist threat now facing the United States during the summer of 2001.

John and a CIA official began to search through the agency's database. There was that old cable from January 2000 discussing al Mihdhar and al Hazmi entering the United States after attending the terrorist summit meeting. John noted al Mihdhar's U.S. visa and that he and al Hazmi had arrived in Los Angeles on January 15. But the CIA official who looked over the information with John told John to do nothing about it. Once again, the CIA had an opportunity to bring the FBI into the loop and it didn't.

John wasn't giving up yet. He spoke with a CIA analyst, "Dave," to see what insight Dave might have about the CIA cables. Dave knew that the Kuala Lumpur meeting had been a serious one—planning for the attack on the USS *Cole*—and he too felt that "something bad was definitely up." But neither man consulted nor informed the FBI about al Mihdhar and al Hazmi at this time. Another opportunity to keep the FBI in the loop, lost.

John's review of the January 2000 cables did raise the attention of "Jane," who was working at the Counterterrorist Center (CTC), which was assigned to the FBI's *Cole* investigation. Jane was an FBI analyst. While investigating the *Cole*, Jane had learned that another al Qaeda terrorist had traveled to Bangkok in January 2000.

At some point, John and Dave showed Jane the surveillance photographs from the Kuala Lumpur terror meeting; the photos were in the sole possession of the CIA and, up to that date, strictly withheld from the FBI. When shown the pictures, Jane was told only that one of the individuals in the photos was named Khalid al Mihdhar. She was not told that al Mihdhar was a known al Qaeda operative. Nor that he was present inside the United States. She was not told that the Malaysia meeting turned out to be a planning session for the USS *Cole* bombing that had occurred in the fall of 2000. She was not told why the photos were taken or why Kuala Lumpur was significant to the CIA. Most important, she was not told that Tawfiq bin Attash, or "Khallad," as he was called, was included in the photographs. The FBI was searching for Khallad as a known mastermind behind the *Cole* bombing, which Jane had been investigating for months.

Jane took the photos to a meeting in New York City about the *Cole* investigation. Beforehand, she ran her own research on al Mihdhar through the database in the intelligence community. The meeting was on June 11, 2001. Dave and another FBI analyst accompanied Jane to the meeting. She had still not been told at this point that two of the individuals in the surveillance photos, al Mihdhar and al Hazmi, had U.S. visas.

During the meeting, New York FBI agents repeatedly asked questions. They wanted to know who the subjects were in the photos, where the photos were taken, and what the significance of these men was to the CIA. Dave refused to answer any of their questions. Dave also refused to offer the FBI agents the facts that al Mihdhar, al Hazmi, and Khallad all attended a planning session for the USS *Cole* bombing in Malaysia in January 2000; that they were known major-league killers for al Qaeda who participated in the East African embassy bombings and the USS *Cole*; and perhaps most important, that al Mihdhar and al Hazmi had arrived in the United States in January 2000. All of this information was highly relevant to the FBI, which was investigating the *Cole* bombing and was in charge of domestic intelligence threats posed by any al Qaeda operatives living in the United States. But the CIA never told the FBI any of this during the meeting. The CIA simply showed the photographs and that was all the information they were willing to part with.

The mid-level FBI investigators in New York City were not the only people being kept out of the loop by the CIA. During an interview with the 9/11 Commission, acting director of the FBI Thomas Pickard stated that in the summer of 2001, executive assistant director for counterterrorism and counterintelligence for the FBI Dale Watson briefed him that the CIA was "taking a second look at the Kuala Lumpur meeting." Pickard testified that he thought that the CIA's concerns about the Malaysia meeting were the reason why the United States was at such a high threat level during the summer of 2001. Most notably, Pickard testified that Watson told him that the Kuala Lumpur information was a *"close hold."* Pickard said that he "understood this to mean that he had no authority to brief the attorney general about the meeting."

Keeping the attorney general out of the loop is particularly problematic in light of recent events discovered regarding the NSA surveillance being carried out by the Bush administration. President Bush is arguing that his illegal NSA surveillance program that carries out domestic eavesdropping on U.S. citizens is necessary because it will prevent another 9/11. Vice President Cheney has argued that had such illegal NSA surveillance been carried out on al Mihdhar and al Hazmi prior to 9/11, 9/11 would have been prevented. Recognize that in order for the president to carry out such surveillance, he needs the consent of the attorney general. Obviously, when it was determined that the information regarding al Mihdhar and al Hazmi was a "close hold" (meaning it was kept secret from Attorney General John Ashcroft), it would make it impossible to carry out surveillance—even the kind of illegal surveillance that President Bush admitted to ordering in December 2005.

While it seems that the CIA was intent on withholding information from almost all levels of our intelligence community and our government, including the attorney general, there were some CIA agents who were desperately and valiantly trying to bring at least the FBI into the loop by sharing information with them. John was one of those people. Still frustrated with the state of affairs in the CIA, John reached out to an FBI official, "Mary," who was detailed to the CIA. John hinted to Mary that she should look at the Kuala Lumpur materials "one more time." Mary had attended the New York City FBI meeting where the CIA showed the surveillance photographs but still failed to tell the FBI about Khallad, al Mihdhar, and al Hazmi. Thus, Mary knew some of the information, albeit a very limited amount, that came out of the New York City meeting. Notably, John asked Mary to conduct her research in her spare time. In other words, he did not want Mary to conduct her research during office hours.

Mary began her work on July 24, 2001. On that first day, Mary discovered the cable reporting that al Mihdhar had a visa to visit the United States. One week later, she found the cable reporting that al Mihdhar's visa application listed New York as his destination. On August 21, 2001, Mary finally located the

March 2000 cable that "noted with interest" that al Hazmi had flown to Los Angeles in January 2000.

Mary immediately grasped the significance of the information. Mary's suspicions were further aroused when she realized that al Mihdhar and al Hazmi had arrived in Los Angeles in January 2000. Had Ahmed Ressam not been arrested at the border a few weeks before, Ressam would have been in Los Angeles to conduct terrorist operations at Los Angeles Airport at the very same time.

On August 22, 2001, Mary met with some Immigration and Naturalization Service (INS) representatives at FBI headquarters. The INS told Mary that al Mihdhar had entered the United States on January 15, 2000, and again on July 4, 2001. The agent also learned that there was no record of al Hazmi ever leaving the country after his arrival on January 15, 2000.

Mary realized that both of these potentially dangerous men were in the United States during the summer of 2001, the "summer of threat" during which every FBI agent was supposed to be redoubling contacts and pulsing sources to determine what al Qaeda was planning to carry out in this country.

Earlier in August 2001, the CIA was preparing the August 6, 2001, presidential daily brief (PDB). The CIA showed a draft of the PDB to the FBI before it was delivered to the president on August 6. The draft shown to the FBI made no statement or even suggestion that the FBI was conducting any investigations into al Qaeda–related operations in this country. But prior to giving the finalized PDB to President Bush, the CIA added this sentence, unbeknownst to the FBI: "The FBI is conducting approximately 70 full field investigations throughout the US that it considers Bin Laden–related."

Why didn't the FBI know that? Why was President Bush led to believe the FBI was carrying out a significant number of investigations that it wasn't? Why would the CIA inform the president that there were ongoing field investigations into al Qaeda sleeper cells when it knew that the FBI was completely in the dark about at least one of the al Qaeda sleeper cells within the country—namely the al Mihdhar cell?

By September 4, 2001, the FBI had finally notified the State Department about the revocation status of al Mihdhar's visa. In fact, specific instructions were given to stop al Mihdhar and detain him for questioning, as he was considered armed and dangerous and participating in terrorist activities, one of which included potential hijackings. Oddly, the very next day, on September 5, 2001, the order to withhold al Mihdhar was reversed. According to the 9/11 Commission's final report, on September 5 the State Department put out a new directive regarding al Mihdhar: to let him go. Specifically, the entry reads that al Mihdhar was a potential witness in an FBI investigation and not to detain him. Quite a chilling directive given that a mere six days later he would be crashing a hijacked plane into the Pentagon. Why the State Department reversed its directive and told its agents not to detain an armed and dangerous terrorist has yet to be explained. One thing remains for sure though, Reno wall or not: apparently there was a sharing of at least some information on some levels that no one to this date is willing to acknowledge.

At that time, the system was still blinking red. But like the rest of the world, Ron and I were oblivious. That summer we went to the beach as often as we could with Caroline and Sam. We would frolic in the waves and make sandcastles. We sat on the beach in Spring Lake, New Jersey. Ironically, Ron, Caroline, Sam, and I were not the only people basking in Jersey Shore sunshine. So, too, was DCI Tenet, who had taken the month of August off to go fly-fishing down the Jersey Shore in—where else?—Spring Lake, New Jersey.

CHAPTER SEVEN

⁓⊗⊗⊙⁓

He Didn't Have Us at Hello

THE KERRY CAMPAIGN had put out feelers toward us, the Jersey widows, in the late spring of 2004, shortly before the release of the commission's report. We had always been nonpartisan and saw no reason to change. The initial overture to us had come from New Jersey senator Jon Corzine's office. Corzine had worked with us in the past on both the Victims' Compensation Fund and the 9/11 Commission. He asked if we'd be willing to meet with some people from the Kerry campaign. We declined. We felt John Kerry was not speaking out strongly enough against the war in Iraq. We knew there was never a connection between Saddam Hussein and 9/11; we knew that Iraq had no links to al Qaeda. But until John Kerry was going to make those points emphatically to the American people, we knew there was no basis for any conversation.

Once the commission's report was released in July, our strategy became clear: We had to get its recommendations turned into meaningful legislation. Whatever our disappointments with the report were, it could still have an impact if some of the more sound recommendations led to real reform—reform that would be permanently enacted into law. Accountability was important, both legally and morally. But in terms of national security, what was most essential to preventing another terrorist attack was the fundamental overhaul of our nation's intelligence system. There was only one way for that to happen: through legislation. And that meant lobbying in Washington.

The Governmental Affairs Committee had the responsibility of actually taking the commission's report and drafting the laws that would implement its recommendations. I was halfheartedly invited to testify before the committee in early August 2004; they were treating me as though I were politically radioactive. My radioactive glow was most likely acquired earlier in the year. I had received a phone call from the New York *Daily News* one afternoon asking what I thought about the campaign ads being run by the president. I hadn't seen them. The journalist then asked if she could send me an e-mail with the video footage of the commercial so I could give her a comment about it. I said sure. The campaign commercial showed footage of flag-draped body parts being recovered from the smoldering ruins of Ground Zero. Watching it first made me sick, and then it made me angry.

I was outraged because at that exact point in time, we were fighting to get the president to cooperate in testifying as a witness before the 9/11 Commission. He had wanted nothing to do with it. It made me sad because those body parts coming out of Ground Zero could have been my husband's. I didn't need any reminders of the brutal devastation of 9/11.

I wanted to know how a president who had fought against the 9/11 families for three years in our quest to learn lessons from 9/11, and was to that very day still fighting us by refusing to testify as a witness before the 9/11 Commission, could in good conscience use 9/11 body parts in a campaign commercial. I felt it was hypocritical, tasteless, and hurtful. I felt that if the president was going to speak about 9/11 in a campaign commercial, then the least he could do was also speak to the 9/11 Commission.

When the journalist called me back, I gave her my quote: "For a man who fought against the creation of the 9/11 Commission, fought against the commission gaining access to documents and individuals, and is currently refusing to testify before that same 9/11 Commission, I find it insensitive, hypocritical, and in extreme bad taste. I would respectfully suggest that prior to using 9/11 in a campaign advertisement for political gain, President Bush use 9/11 to learn lessons and to make us safer. He can do that by testifying before the 9/11 Commission and giving them more than an hour of his time. Three thousand innocent people were murdered on his watch. The least he can do is cooperate with the commission charged with investigating those murders."

When the story ran, the headline was 3,000 MURDERED ON BUSH'S WATCH. The right-wing attack machine cranked itself into motion and I was labeled: a Democratic operative and a rock star of grief. Rush Limbaugh jumped on the bandwagon, too. One of his broadcasts inspired such a vitriolic response in one of his listeners that I received an e-mail threatening the lives of both Caroline and me. That crossed the line. It scared me. It was one thing to call me names in an e-mail; it was quite another to tell me that I should have to watch my daughter be killed. So I reported it to the FBI, who tracked down the individual, warned him, and told him to leave me alone. When the FBI called me afterwards, I was promised that the individual wouldn't be bothering me again.

The *Wall Street Journal* then ran an editorial mentioning me by name—it was three-quarters of a page long. At the time, I didn't grasp the significance of being a target of the *Wall Street*

Journal's editorial page. It wasn't until journalists kept slapping me on the back and telling me that I had "finally made it in the big leagues" that I realized I had really pissed some people off with my comments in the *Daily News*. The journalists explained to me that being targeted in such a scathing editorial by the *Journal* meant that you were a real threat to the conservative right wing.

Dorothy Rabinowitz wrote the editorial, which ran on April 14, 2004, and was headlined: THE 9/11 WIDOWS; AMERICANS ARE BEGINNING TO TIRE OF THEM. Within the editorial Rabinowitz snarkily wrote: "The core group of widows, led by the foursome known as 'The Jersey Girls,' credited with bringing the 9/11 Commission into being, are by now world famous. Their already established status in the media, as a small but heroically determined band of sisters speaking truth to power, reached ever greater heights last week, when National Security Adviser Condoleezza Rice made her appearance at a commission session—an event that would not have taken place, it was understood, without the pressure from the widows."

Rabinowitz continued by detailing our appearance on *Hardball* wherein we charged that Condoleezza Rice had failed to adequately carry out her responsibilities as national security adviser, that the government had failed to provide a timely air defense, that President Bush had failed to act decisively when he remained seated reading a schoolbook during the attacks, and that our intelligence agencies had failed to connect the dots.

Then Rabinowitz posed a question: "Who, listening to them, would not be struck by the fact that all their fury and accusation is aimed not at the killers who snuffed out their husbands' and so many other lives, but at the American president, his administration, and an ever wider assortment of targets including the Air Force, the Port Authority, the City of New York? In the public pronouncements of the Jersey Girls we find, indeed, hardly a jot of accusatory rage at the perpetrators of the 9/11 attacks. We have, on the other hand, more than a few declarations like that of Ms. Breitweiser, announcing that 'President Bush and his workers . . . were the individuals that failed my husband and the 3,000 people that day.' "

Next, the editorial proceeded to question our standing and right to question our government's failure to protect its citizens during surprise attacks. Rabinowitz pondered why the victims of Oklahoma City or London during World War II did not blame their government for not keeping them safe. She went on to say, "The venerable status accorded this group of widows comes as no surprise given our times, an age quick to confer both celebrity and authority on those who have suffered. As the experience of the Jersey Girls shows, that authority isn't necessarily limited to matters moral or spiritual. All that the widows have had to say—including wisdom mind-numbingly obvious, or obviously false and irrelevant—on the failures of this or that government agency, on derelictions of duty they charged to the president, the vice president, the national security adviser, Norad and the rest, has been received by most of the media and members of Congress with utmost wonder and admiration."

Finally, she took aim at her target: our displeasure with the Bush campaign advertisements that included the body parts being removed from Ground Zero. She wrote, "Little wonder, given all this, that the 9/11 Four blossomed, under a warm media sun and the attention of legislators, into activists increasingly confident of their authority—that, with every passing month, their list of government agencies and agents guilty of dereliction of duty grew apace. So did their assurance that it had been given to them, as victims, to determine the proper standards of taste and respectfulness to be applied in everything related to Sept. 11, including, it turned out, the images of the destroyed World Trade Center in George Bush's first campaign ad, which elicited, from some of them, bitter charges of political exploitation." Rabinowitz ended her editorial by pondering when Americans would grow tired of the mouthy, entitled 9/11 widows.

After reading the editorial, I decided to write a response. Foolishly, I thought the *Wall Street Journal* was fair and balanced. When the *Journal*'s editor received my opinion piece via e-mail, he forwarded it to Dorothy Rabinowitz for her thoughts. And the story of what happened next is laid out beautifully in a column that I found on a blog while surfing the Internet: "Top 10 Conservative Idiots—How Dumb Can You Get":

How dumb can you get? Last month *Wall Street Journal* pundit Dorothy Rabinowitz wrote a scathing indictment of Kristen Breitweiser and the 9/11 widows which was published as an op-ed. This month, Breitweiser wrote an op-ed of her own and submitted it for publication in the *Journal*. Rabinowitz got wind of the op-ed and dashed off an email to deputy editorial page editor Tunku Varadaraja asking him not to publish it. She called Breitweiser's article "total and complete—not to mention repetitive—nonsense from people given endless media access to repeat the very same stupid charges." But that's not all . . . "My thoughts—we don't publish nonsensical contentions that offer no news, no insight—solely on the grounds that those who feel attacked get a chance to defend their views. For that we have the letters column." Wow. But wait a second, you're asking yourself, how do *I* know what was in the email? Simple—instead of sending it to Tunku Varadaraja, Rabinowitz accidentally sent it to Kristen Breitweiser. Shortly afterwards she sent another one: "Rabinowitz, Dorothy would like to recall the message, '9/11 Widows' Response—the 'jersey girls.'" Like I said: how dumb can you get?

Undeterred by the attacks and idiocy spewing from the right wing, I took them as a clear indication that we were making some headway with our lobbying efforts and attempts to pressure the administration into cooperating with the commission—why else would the attacks be getting so nasty? The worse they got, the more I knew we were doing a good job. While such personal attacks did hurt my feelings on some level, for the most part I ignored them.

As more stories were written, a public controversy brewed, and I started receiving phone calls from people in Washington telling me that I should not have linked the commission to the Bush campaign advertisement. They told me that I was not playing fair. Essentially I told them to shove it.

At that point in time I wanted our president to cooperate with the commission so we could have a thorough investigation and be safer as a nation. I told the people calling that it was their own fault if they didn't foresee the possibility of the campaign advertisements raising the bile of the 9/11 families.

Soon after that, President Bush decided to "meet" with the commissioners as long as Vice President Cheney was at his side. The commission met with the president, and the meeting lasted longer than an hour. While I would have preferred the president alone in the meeting and under oath, the White House

set the terms of the meeting and they were not offering anything more. We had to take what they were willing to give.

By the time the commission's report was released, it was
four months later and things had calmed down a bit. The administration knew at this point that the commission's work was
complete, they had already received their advance copies of
the report, they had made their final edits and signed off, and
they knew the president had escaped relatively unscathed.

——∞——

The next battle to be fought was over the implementation of
the commission's recommendations. That battle started in August and it centered upon the Department of Defense, which
vehemently opposed any of the commission's recommendations that meant DOD losing control over their $40 billion in-
telligence budget. DOD's staunchest ally in Congress was
Representative Duncan Hunter, chairman of the House Armed
Services Committee. He was responsible for protecting DOD's
power, turf, and money.

Hunter argued that shifting control over intelligence agencies like the NSA from DOD to that of a national intelligence
director would harm the "boots on the ground." He reminded
everyone that resources were limited and we were a nation already consumed with a war in Iraq. DOD, in his opinion, could
spare no resources or reshuffling of authority.

During an Armed Services Committee working lunch, I
countered Hunter's position by saying the following directly to
him: First, apparently, according to your Republican Congress
and president, we will be a nation at war for the next hundred
years—the War on Terror is not ending anytime soon. If we
cannot withstand a reformation of our intelligence community
now because we are a nation at war, then I guess we will have

to delay such crucial reform indefinitely—or for the next hundred years? Second, had our intelligence community been restructured three years ago in the immediate wake of 9/11, perhaps the flawed intelligence provided by the CIA regarding Iraq's WMD might not have happened, because the problems and failures in the CIA would have been fixed prior to our starting a baseless war in Iraq. And finally, Mr. Hunter, I am a single mother. I multitask all day long. I do not think it is too much for this nation to expect its Department of Defense to learn to multitask in today's post-9/11 environment. Bin Laden is able to do a hundred things at a time as he plots against us; I think it is high time that we raise our expectations of a Defense Department that employs thousands and consumes the largest segment of our nation's budget. Bin Laden proved on 9/11 that maintaining the status quo costs lives.

When I first testified before Congress in 2002 before the Joint Inquiry of Congress, there was no vetting process, no angst, and no worries that I was going to be politically radioactive against the president. If anything, my invitation to testify before Congress was seen as a soft, emotional ploy made by Congress against the intelligence agencies. However, Congress learned differently when my testimony turned out to be serious, succinct, focused, and damning to many, including the president. Maybe it was because of this that the rules were changed this go-round. Or maybe it was because we were in the midst of an election year. Or perhaps, after all of my public comments, I'd developed a reputation as someone who played hardball. Whatever the reason, this time I had to go through a vetting process unlike any I'd been through before.

I had to speak to two senators personally and answer their questions and listen to their candid warnings about turning their hearings into a "political circus." They wanted to know if

I intended to say anything bad about the administration. They grilled me with their questions and concerns. I then had to meet with their committee staffers and be questioned even further. At one point a staffer confessed that there was a "not necessarily unfounded and large concern" that I might be disrespectful to the president by embarrassing him during my testimony.

Mindy was with me in the meeting. As the hapless staffer looked on, I said to Mindy, "Do you think she Google-searched the '-en' or the '-in'?" Mindy tried unsuccessfully to suppress a laugh. Confused, the staffer asked what we meant. I told her I spelled my name two ways in the media: "When I make really hellacious comments, I spell my name Kristin. When I'm better behaved, I spell it Kristen." The staffer had a look of sheer panic on her face. Mindy, adding fuel to the fire, chirped in, "Well, you better hope she didn't Google-search Karen Breitweiser—she'll really have a heart attack." The staffer looked like she was about to cry.

Of course, it was all bullshit—I was just yanking her chain. I was outraged with the Republican senators' unapologetic attempts at censorship. I wanted to know whether other witnesses had to endure similar scrutiny. And I was hurt, too. My testimony two years prior had not been political; it was factual, hard-hitting, and pointed. It wasn't my fault if the facts made the president or his administration look bad. This was an issue of life and death for me. There was no room for political cover when it came to implementing the recommendations—for me it was about saving lives, not political hides.

But at this point it was still up in the air as to whether I would even be allowed to testify, and throwing a snit fit was certainly not going to help. We needed a plan. We decided that if I was barred from testifying I would give the whole story to the media; I cagily hinted as much to the staffers who were vetting me in the meeting. But that never needed to happen, because, after many repeated entreaties that I would not make any politically embarrassing statements about President Bush in my testimony and would submit my testimony in written form ahead of time, I received the green light to testify. To me, all that mattered was making sure the recommendations were put in place. I would have agreed to show up in my underwear if that meant I could testify toward the need for this legislation. So of course I complied. And I never told the media that part of the deal in allowing me to testify was my agreement not to say anything disparaging against the president in my written or oral testimony.

I testified on August 17, 2004. Right at the outset, I took an indirect hit at the president. I did it as payback. I wanted the senators who were giving me such a hard time about being politically radioactive to get a little nervous that I might go off the ranch during the live hearing. I said, "It has been said by some that they would have moved heaven and earth to prevent 9/11. Respectfully, three full years after 9/11, we do not need heaven and earth to move, we just need our executive and legislative branches to move so that we are in the best possible position to prevent the next attack."

I then methodically outlined the case for a national intelligence director, or NID, and then grappled with all the key areas where dramatic change was needed: intelligence, airline security, borders, the military, and diplomacy. And I closed my testimony by saying, "We ask the Congress, the White House, and all other congressional and executive branch agencies to be Americans first. Not partisan politicians with self-interests to protect. Not appointed officials with turf to protect. Not unimaginative figures unwilling to embrace change out of fear of losing the status quo. It is not sufficient to support national security on an ad hoc basis. Your support must be all-inclusive and wholehearted regardless of how it might hurt you personally or politically. We stand before you as people who have lost our loved ones. We have taken our unspeakable pain and made some good out of it by fighting for the creation of the 9/11 Commission. Today, many other families have loved ones dying on the battlefield. In the ensuing months as this language is battled out in the background, I simply, humbly and with great respect ask all of you to remember how so many of us have already learned to be Americans first. I truly hope you can do the same."

I, and others, had put a lot of effort and energy into thinking through the intelligence reform legislation, but in the subsequent weeks, prospects for its passage did not look good.

The White House was not backing the commission's recommendations. This did not come as much of a surprise, since the White House had fought the commission from the beginning anyway. We were told that the White House was setting up its own "working group" to study the report and make their own recommendations to the president. In short, as far as the White House was concerned, there would be no ringing, automatic, and full endorsement. But again, we expected this.

House Republicans, taking their cue from 1600 Pennsylvania Avenue, were being obstreperous and fighting whatever changes managed to make it to the floor for a vote. It was discouraging. The report was disappointing enough. But now to think that its more sound recommendations might go nowhere was even worse.

Then, in late August 2004, John Kerry announced that if he were president, he'd implement all of the commission's recommendations immediately. While this was a nice gesture on his

part, his immediate wholesale adoption of such recommendations made us nervous. We wondered whether he had even
read the report. Most people hadn't. There seemed to be a feeling that once he gave his endorsement, we'd jump on the
bandwagon. But we weren't so eager. To us it seemed like a
bald political move, and that did not inspire our confidence.

Then came the Republican Convention in New York City.
Reporters were calling me, asking me my reaction about the
GOP's "wrapping itself in 9/11" while not supporting the commission's recommendations. I had decided to watch the convention on television from my house on Long Island. The first
night I listened to the speeches. They seemed filled with anger
and venom. I heard the expressions "war for a lifetime" and
"9/11" repeated endlessly. I started thinking about Caroline and
her future. I started getting scared about our safety. I didn't
want to hand her a war for the next hundred years. That wasn't
my job as a mom. My job was to provide her with a safe and
happy future, not a war-torn one. I also knew that the war in
Iraq was making us all incredibly less safe than we were on
September 12, 2001.

The Republican Convention frightened me. John McCain
and Zell Miller gave speeches so militaristic in tone that I felt
like I was in Stalin's Russia. I did not believe that starting wars
like we did in Iraq was the way to control our national destiny.
McCain called the Iraq war "necessary, achievable, and noble."
He defined it as a classic battle between "right and wrong,
good and evil," and said that America had the choice of fighting the war or a graver threat. The widows and I had a term
for these scare tactics: "booga-booga." While we got along well
with John McCain on most other issues, the widows and I knew
that we would never see eye-to-eye with McCain when it came
to Iraq.

Three 9/11 family members also spoke on the opening night of the convention. One of the family members I had grown to know very well; she was often booked by the administration to oppose me in the media. So it came as no surprise when I witnessed her appearance at the convention. I always thought it was interesting that I was accused of being a Democratic operative, when in reality the Jersey Girls never operated under anyone's orders. We wrote our own press statements and editorials, created our own talking points, booked ourselves on television programs, and paid for all of it out of our own pockets. Our actions and words were backed by our own good conscience.

But it was Zell Miller's tirade of intolerance on Wednesday night that made me pick up the phone and call the widows. Miller spoke like such a zealot; he seemed like a parody of a politician. He was crazed. After his speech, I truly think his eyes rolled back in his head when he started challenging Chris Matthews of *Hardball* to a duel! It was incredible. It was scary. Miller said, "George Bush is committed to providing the kind of forces it takes to root out terrorists. No matter what spider hole they may hide in or what rock they crawl under. George Bush wants to grab terrorists by the throat and not let them go to get a better grip. From John Kerry, they get a 'yes-no-maybe' bowl of mush that can only encourage our enemies and confuse our friends."

I realized that the Republicans believed the only way to be safer post-9/11 was to blow up the rest of the world. Their tactics were no different from those of a seven-year-old bully in the schoolyard who wants to pick fights with everyone to look tough. Perhaps even more alarming to me was that after starting all these fights, Republicans weren't concerned about making our homeland safer against possible retaliation. They had zero interest in following the commission's recommendations that would have hardened our homeland defense. We had yet to witness the needed overhaul of our intelligence community. There had been no historic reorganization of our domestic security structure. Our CIA was a system that was broken and not functioning effectively. Our border security was still lacking in sufficient funds to operate satisfactorily. Our public transportation systems remained vulnerable, our local responders remained underfunded, our ports were underprotected, and our nuclear and water plants remained unguarded. We had lacked a cohesive strategy and any follow-through after 9/11 regarding our national security apparatus and its ability to fight terrorism effectively. They merely wanted to "kill 'em all"— even if starting such baseless wars made us less safe and cost thousands of innocent American lives on the battlefield overseas or here at home.

When I called the widows on Wednesday night, I said, "I know you guys are going to be really upset with me for changing my mind, but the only way we are going to get these recommendations acted upon is with a new president. The Republicans don't give a damn about sound intelligence reform or securing our homeland. They just want to start wars that have nothing to do with making us safer. I'm scared. And I want to do something about it." I had decided to campaign for John Kerry. The widows agreed to do the same.

The Family Steering Committee was upset with our decision. The committee was made up of twelve family members who lobbied and fought for the establishment of the independent commission from almost day one. They were angry because they did not want to see the recommendations politicized.

I told them the truth. I told them that after testifying before the Governmental Affairs Committee on the need for the immediate implementation of the recommendations, and after fighting over the language in the back-door meetings and hearing of the shakedown at the White House through the grapevine, I truly felt the only way we would get the recommendations implemented was with a new administration. I just wanted to be safer. I knew that we needed a new president who understood that being safer from terrorists wasn't as simple as "going overseas to kill 'em all."

I called Jon Corzine and said I thought I wanted to endorse John Kerry. I explained that it was the only way we could get anything done in terms of meaningful intelligence reform and national security improvements. I told Corzine this was a strategic and pragmatic decision on my part, not a political one. We had tried to work in a nonpartisan way throughout the life of the commission, and succeeded. But every battle we had fought had been triggered by the Republicans. For me that was a statement of fact, not partisanship.

Corzine said he would have Cam Kerry call me. Cam Kerry was John Kerry's younger brother and had worked on his campaigns since Kerry first ran for Congress in 1972. Cam called me almost immediately, and I was blunt: "I heard what your brother has to say about the recommendations of the 9/11 Commission, and I think it is great. But I have another question. I want to know what his position is on Iraq."

Cam said, "I think it is pretty clear what John's position is."

I pushed back. "Actually, I'm standing here outside the bubble and I am pretty engaged in these issues and I read about Iraq all the time and it doesn't seem that clear to me. I don't know where your brother stands. In fact, I hate to tell you this, but if his position is not clear to me, someone who reads everything and cares, it is probably not clear to the rest of America."

Cam really couldn't clarify his brother's position. So I said

"I am not going to endorse your brother unless he *clearly* states and emphatically believes that he is against the war in Iraq and any foreign policy based on a preemptive war doctrine. And if you're telling me he's already said that, I'm telling you that he has not said it quite clearly enough."

Shortly after that, I got a call from Mary Beth Cahill, the former staffer to Senator Ted Kennedy, who was John Kerry's campaign manager. What started as a congenial phone call turned into a fairly heated confrontation. Mary Beth didn't like hearing what I said about Kerry's message not resonating with the American public. The tack she took with me was that they knew what they were doing and I didn't know what I was talking about. Kerry had made it clear about where he stood on Iraq.

I was not intimidated by what she had to say. People spoke about Mary Beth as though she should be both revered and feared. I had no reason to think she should be either. I'm sure she saw me as this thirty-three-year-old who deserved a pat on the head and a summary dismissal, but I didn't care. "Let me set you straight here, Mary Beth. No matter what you and your campaign people think you are doing, the message is not getting out. You may say John Kerry is against the war in Iraq, but that's not what I'm hearing out here in the real world."

I was as honest with her as I could be. I felt I was making a big decision. I needed some reassurances from her that I wasn't making a mistake. Plans were made for Mindy, Patty, Lorie, and me to meet with Kerry in Allentown, Pennsylvania, at the airport. The meeting was off the record because we still had doubts about endorsing him based on our frustrating contact with his campaign and their inability to articulate his foreign policy position.

The polls around that time had Kerry twenty points below

Bush with voters concerned about terrorism. "Security moms" in this race were what "soccer moms" had been in the 2000 election, and Kerry was losing ground to Bush with this demographic as well. Women who might vote for Kerry because of his stand on other issues were supporting Bush because they thought he was stronger on terrorism.

Kerry came into the room at the Allentown airport flanked by his handlers and advisers and sat down at the head of the table. Let's just politely say that Senator John Kerry didn't have us at hello. The atmosphere was somewhere between meeting your boyfriend's parents and being called into the principal's office. It wasn't totally uncomfortable, but it was awkward. He was trying too hard. We wanted to connect with Kerry the human being, but unfortunately, what we got was Kerry the candidate.

We asked Kerry a few questions he couldn't answer. Despite the rocky start with his staff in the preceding weeks, we had come to Allentown with high expectations. We had been fighting an uphill battle for three and a half years and we were eager to work with someone who would work with us, not against us. We wanted a strong leader who believed what he said—and believed in it because he was smart enough to know *why* he believed in it. I don't always agree with John McCain, but I know his strength and beliefs are genuine and deep.

We told Kerry that we needed to know his position on Iraq, specifically, disavowing its linkage to 9/11. We told him that we were against preemptive wars such as the one in Iraq because they made us less safe. We cited specifics from the 9/11 Commission hearings where a CIA agent testified that the war in Iraq actually gave bin Laden what he could not achieve by murdering our husbands: namely, an increased recruitment of al Qaeda operatives. Such recruitment of terrorists worldwide meant that we were much less safe post-9/11 due to President Bush's own bad decision to start a baseless war in Iraq.

We then asked Kerry some specifics on the 9/11 report and its recommendations. He assured us that when he was president he would enact all the recommendations as soon as he could—the first week. We asked him what he thought about the report itself. In other words, did he think it was comprehensive and well written? Kerry said that he thought it was a solid accounting. We told him that we weren't so sure. We asked him whether he would consider impaneling another 9/11 Commission to continue this commission's unfinished work if he became president. He said he would.

While we came away from the meeting with little personal enthusiasm for John Kerry, he was still the only alternative to four more years of George Bush. Lorie joked that she would have supported Big Bird or Elmo against Bush. The thought of prolonging the war in Iraq sickened me. Ron had died a senseless death. Knowing thousands of American families were going to suffer the senseless deaths of their sons or daughters in Iraq infuriated me. As far as I was concerned, the Iraq war was linked to 9/11 only by revenge, lies, oil, and the arrogance of individuals.

But we had come by our political pragmatism the hard way. Four days later, on September 14, Patty, Lorie, Mindy, and I went down to Washington to endorse Kerry. We were joined by Monica Gabrielle, a 9/11 widow who had worked with us on the Family Steering Committee and grown very close to us. We were also joined by April Gallop. April had been badly wounded in the Pentagon attack along with her two-month-old son, Elijah, whom she'd taken with her to work that day.

We walked into campaign headquarters early in the day. The news conference was scheduled for that afternoon. We were told to write out our remarks. Mindy was annoyed. The campaign had led us to believe that we'd have support from their staff. One of the jokes from the girls about teaming up with the Kerry campaign was that we would no longer have to do everything on our own. But once again, we found ourselves alone. They didn't even have pen and paper ready for us. The widows were growing restless and worried.

Mindy had four versions of what she wanted to say, Patty had a notebook full of stuff, and I had an outline and note cards. We met with Mary Beth. The campaign didn't want us to focus on terrorism. But that made no sense. What else could we talk about? We were good at speaking from our hearts, and that's what we were determined to do. However, we felt like we were flying solo when we walked into the news conference.

I began by explaining that I had voted for George Bush four years earlier but could no longer support him. "The truth is, after watching the Republican Convention in New York, I am scared. I am scared of the mentality of accepting a war for a lifetime. I am a mother of a five-year-old who has already lost her father to terrorism. I don't want her to be working in a building someday and get blown up as payback for our current policy in Iraq. As her mother, I owe it to her to do everything I can do to provide her with a safe and happy future. A future full of war is not the future I have envisioned for my daughter. And that is why I am here today endorsing John Kerry."

Patty, who had also voted for Bush, spoke of how hard it was for her to shift her allegiance. "It has been a painful process to accept that President Bush failed us," she said. Then it was Lorie's turn. Ironically, Lorie ended up making policy in her remarks when she said, "The reason I'm supporting John Kerry for president is because I have a sixteen-year-old son and I don't want him drafted." A reporter asked if she meant that

John Kerry would never institute a draft and she said, "That's why I'm supporting him."

The widows and I joked after the press conference that the campaign had gotten their first taste of dealing with us. They learned the danger of leaving us to our own devices. We laughed and joked that if they were not going to help us, they might be sorry, because we could end up writing a whole new set of Kerry policy objectives—starting with there being no draft under a Kerry administration.

By four o'clock that afternoon there had been some Republican response to our endorsement. Some of the other 9/11 family members were having a counter news conference to talk about their support for President Bush. I went back to Kerry headquarters. Joe Lockhart, head of Kerry campaign communications, was there with a baseball bat, walking around like the king of the castle. By then, it was around 7:00 P.M. and it seemed way too quiet. I had envisioned a real working war room. What I saw was Lockhart walking around like the lone sentry guarding the abandoned castle. Where the hell was everyone?

I told Joe that about two hundred families for Bush were going to rally or do something. Where was the war room? Who was going to draft the response? Lockhart didn't know what I was talking about. I told him that when we were fighting in Washington, we always responded immediately to whatever broke. In a 24/7 news cycle, it was essential. We knew we'd get clobbered in the press for supporting Kerry, and we wanted some backup from the campaign. For three years we'd been attacked whenever we spoke out. We were told by the Kerry campaign that if we were ever attacked on the campaign, we'd be supported. The first attack was headed our way. Where was the retaliation? There wasn't any. Lesson learned.

That first day was repeated over and over in different permutations, as in the movie *Groundhog Day*. The campaign just didn't know how to benefit from our experiences in Washington, to use the past three years of our fighting for a 9/11 commission as a way to wake people up and make them realize that the current administration was doing nothing in the way of making us less vulnerable to terrorists.

A candidate who was mocked for being out of touch and too aloof should have recognized that we, the 9/11 widows, were able to connect with everyday voters effectively mostly because we were normal real people just like them. But the campaign relied so much on polls and testing and focus groups that they lost any ability to connect with life outside their own rarefied political bubble. We offered them pure oxygen, but they insisted on breathing the same dank, recycled air.

We were moms with teenagers and toddlers. We had spent several years focused on the issue of national security—the issue that was paramount in the minds of voters. For three years we'd battled against every obstacle the Bush administration had thrown at us. We succeeded in getting the commission established in the first place followed by subpoena power; better funding; Condoleezza Rice's testimony; access to the PDB; testimonies from the president and vice president—however limited they were; and finally, we received a two-month extension for the commission (not quite the full six-month extension we'd asked for and needed). We achieved those results because we believed passionately in our pure motive and objective: to make the nation safer.

Maybe we hadn't worked on the last thirty-five congressional races, maybe we hadn't been policy wonks for Senate leaders, but we knew something about being in guerrilla warfare. If the upper echelons of the campaign had book learning, we had radical and effective street smarts. We didn't need to do a focus group to figure out where we stood on an issue. We simply spoke and acted from our hearts and souls. And it worked for us over and over again.

I could stand up in front of an audience and say, "Before 9/11, I was just like you. After 9/11, I turned into this woman who went to Washington at four A.M. for three years straight to lobby to make sure people like you are safe. I'm standing here and telling you to support John Kerry because I know in my heart of hearts that after three and a half years of fighting this administration and fighting the Republican Congress that the only way we are actually ever going to be any safer is if we have a new president." To me it was about saving and protecting lives, not wasting them as collateral damage in baseless preemptive wars.

There were exceptional moments when we all saw the potential for how great a candidate Kerry could be. One of those glimmering examples was Kerry's speech at New York University on September 20, 2004. He introduced us by saying that not only had we suffered unbearable loss, but we had fought to create the independent commission to help us learn the lessons from that terrible time.

Kerry's speech was good—tough, passionate, and unequivocal. He made points we had been pushing him to make since our first meeting with him when we argued that people did not understand where he stood on the Iraq war. It was gratifying to hear him say things like this:

We know Iraq played no part in September 11 and had no operational ties to al Qaeda.

The President's policy in Iraq precipitated the very problem he said he was trying to prevent. Secretary of

State Powell admits that Iraq was not a magnet for international terrorists before the war. Now it is, and they are operating against our troops. Iraq is becoming a sanctuary for a new generation of terrorists who someday could hit the United States.

We know that while Iraq was a source of friction, it was not previously a source of serious disagreement with our allies in Europe and countries in the Muslim world.

The President's policy in Iraq divided our oldest alliance and sent our standing in the Muslim world into free fall. Three years after 9/11, even in many moderate Muslim countries like Jordan, Morocco and Turkey, Osama bin Laden is more popular than the United States of America.

Let me put it plainly: The President's policy in Iraq has not strengthened our national security. It has weakened it.

After the NYU speech, the campaign seemed alive in a way it hadn't before. We were all fired up. I was raring to go and had come to my moment of truth. I had to get on an airplane. I had not flown since 9/11. Once I canceled the Christmas trip to Amelia Island with Caroline, I felt like I'd never fly unless I absolutely had to. Now, to campaign for John Kerry, I did.

I'd decided that passing the commission's recommendations was a matter of life and death. I thought, and still think, that there will be another major attack in this country and that too many people will die unnecessarily, simply because we aren't better prepared. Looking at the realities of campaign travel and knowing that it involved a lot of flying on planes, I knew I had to deal with the fact that I hadn't flown since 9/11. To me, even to this day, flying on a plane is a life-or-death decision. I know how completely unsafe and compromised the airlines are when it comes to terrorism. And that makes flying very difficult. Getting on a plane has to be worth it. I asked myself: If I got killed in a plane crash while supporting Kerry on the campaign trail, would it be worth it? I felt strongly that it would. At that point in time, I knew the only way we would be safer as a country and less vulnerable to terrorists was with a new president who brought along with him the full endorsement of the 9/11 Commission recommendations and a new foreign policy. That decision took care of the philosophical part of me, but there was still the rest of me, which needed to be able to physically board an airliner.

I developed a ritual that I used throughout the campaign. I had a Walkman—still no iPod—that I put on as soon as I got on the plane, and there was a Dave Matthews CD that stayed in. I would always hit song 7, lean back, and close my eyes. I knew from my research that the most dangerous point in a flight is during takeoff; the jet is carrying 10,000 gallons of fuel and can easily be hit by surface-to-air missiles until it reaches a certain altitude. With my eyes closed, I visualized a stream of images of my daughter, Caroline, saying, "I wuv you, Mommy," and Sam, with those soulful eyes that hid his bad-boy spunk, staring at me while I kissed his nose. I kept those images in my head until I knew we were safely at the cruising altitude and beyond the reach of surface-to-air missiles. If I died before then, it would be with the faces of those I loved most beaming at me. It's a stupid and superstitious ritual I still use to this day because I've convinced myself that once I stop, something bad will happen to me.

It was hard to be away from Caroline so much for the two and a half months I would be campaigning. Ron and I had never used babysitters during her first two and a half years of life. Now I was going to be away from her for days at a time. I promised to fly home whenever I could and to take her along with me whenever possible. I would sacrifice my time with Caroline for two and a half months to try to help ensure that she and every other American child had a safe world in which to thrive. What was two and a half months in return for a lifetime of us being together—and being safe?

The campaign assigned a handler to me because of my concerns about flying. Monica and I were traveling together for a few days when we first met Liz Ryan, who had taken a leave of absence from her job as a children's advocate in Washington, D.C. Liz looked twenty-five but was actually closer in age to forty. Monica and I were initially put off by her serious, nononsense demeanor. But oh, were we wrong. By the end of the first day we knew Liz was fabulous and we told the campaign we wanted to work with her all the time. Not only was she smart and organized, she had a wickedly irreverent sense of humor.

Campaigning captivated me. As pathologically shy as I am, I still fell in love with it all. Even when I was just rolling out words at the end of a seventeen-hour day with not enough sleep or food in me, I still understood the opportunity given to me to do something that really mattered and to connect with people. I had never been to places like Iowa, Minnesota, or Nevada. As a sheltered suburban housewife, I hadn't ventured far outside my world. After 9/11, I'd logged thousands of miles driving back and forth to Washington, D.C. But otherwise, I traveled in a small orbit.

The campaign was a mind-boggling, exhaustive vortex; it felt like we were held together by nothing more than centrifugal force as we flew from one city to another, jumping on and off planes. As tiring as it was, I never wanted to stop shaking hands with dozens and dozens of people and hearing snippets about their lives. It was also healing for me to see that people outside New York cared about those who had died on 9/11. Of course I knew that 9/11 had "happened to America," but when it happens to you, it's hard to really believe that others share your burden with their own equal sincere compassion and concern.

When we finally had gotten around to making business cards for our treks to Washington, we used a quote from Edmund Burke on the cards: "The only thing necessary for the triumph of evil is for good men to do nothing." On the campaign trail I felt that thousands of people cared about doing something, and that was gratifying.

But the downside of campaigning is that it is a physically grueling ordeal. You're on so many planes with so many people that your resistance is low and you catch colds and your skin breaks out and your hair looks like hell and with only a few hours of sleep a night you feel like shit a lot of the time. Monica and I were convinced for a time that the reason we lost the swing states was because we scared the voters with the way we looked: like a duo of haggard widows. We weren't pretty.

I loved campaigning with John Edwards. No matter how tired and depleted I felt, he always made me and everyone around him believe in the power of what we were doing. His energy was unfailing, his enthusiasm was heartfelt. And he was fun.

We campaigned together often. I loved the Edwards campaign team. They were the best. Young, intelligent, smart, and lively. Unlike Kerry, Edwards and his campaign did have me at hello. His smile was spontaneous, and his ability to connect with people was genuine. Edwards had a foothold in the real world. He had two young children, a daughter in college, and a wife, Elizabeth, whom he clearly adored. The spirit of their marriage was contagious; because they were outwardly still nuts about each other, it was easy to relax and laugh with Elizabeth and John Edwards.

People would often ask me what Teresa Heinz and Elizabeth Edwards were like as people. I told them the truth. Teresa is a woman of serious achievement. But when she walks into a room, everything has a tendency to tighten up. With Elizabeth Edwards, everything lightens up. Elizabeth is the one you'd want to sit and drink wine with in the kitchen. With Teresa, you'd be careful not to spill. Both women were extremely confident and comfortable in their own skin. It was enjoyable and always interesting to share their company.

For the widows, spending time with Elizabeth Edwards was always a blast. At times during the campaign when we'd feel our energy flagging while we sat waiting on tarmacs or driving endless distances between campaign appearances, Monica would say to me, "Let's call Lizzie!" Or we might be in some remote locale and discover a Starbucks and say that we needed to call Lizzie and report that, indeed, there was a Starbucks in Des Moines. (In fact in all of Iowa, the *only* Starbucks was in Des Moines.)

John Edwards and I made a great team. When we appeared together, Edwards always spoke first. He'd then introduce me and I would talk for about ten minutes and then take questions from the audience. We would get feedback from campaign headquarters. My favorite person to talk to on the campaign was Joel Johnson. Joel was one of the campaign's senior advisers. He was young, smart, and fun. Mostly, he would always boost my confidence by calling up and shouting, "You did great! Just keep it up."

I was continually moved by how deeply engaged people had become with the commission's work. People were asking serious questions about policy, which told me that they had actually taken the time to read the commission's report. I would very often call the widows who were home in New Jersey to tell them how much I wished they were with me so they could bear witness to how many people were grateful for our hard work. It truly made me realize that the endless nights and long miles of traveling while we fought for the commission had all been worth it. And I always shared that sentiment with every audience I met by thanking them for being such engaged, educated, and caring American citizens.

I usually began my speeches by saying that on September 10, my life had been much like theirs. But 9/11 changed everything, and I didn't want any other family to endure a loss like the one my daughter and I suffered if it could be prevented. I didn't want anyone ever to walk in our shoes. Then I went on and talked about the report and how much more needed to be done to keep us safer.

While we always received great feedback on our appearances from the Washington staff—"You're great; you hit the cover off the ball!"—terrorism was still an issue the campaign did not want to take on directly. National security was ceded to Bush. To me, that seemed like a fatal mistake.

The Mary Beth Cahills and Bob Shrums wanted to win on traditional Democratic issues like jobs and the economy. But the Bush camp made it a race that played on people's fears about terrorism and national security. Cheney kept dealing the fear card from the top of the deck, practically equating a vote for Kerry with a vote for bin Laden and another 9/11.

There was a real split in the campaign about how to get our message on national security out to the American people. A large percentage of the undecided voters were women, and terrorism was the pivotal issue for many. One faction in the campaign felt strongly that the widows needed to be in television ads. But apparently others were adamant about *not* shooting a commercial. One week late in October, a rebellious faction led by Cam Kerry decided to meet in New York City to film a commercial.

It was simple and straightforward. I appeared on camera and said,

> My husband, Ron, was killed on September eleventh. I've spent the last three years trying to find out what happened to make sure it never happens again. I fought for the 9/11 Commission, something George W. Bush, the man my husband Ron and I voted for, didn't think was necessary. And during the commission hearings we learned the truth: We are no safer today. I want to look in my daughter's eyes and know that she is safe, and that is why I am voting for John Kerry.

We had the commercial ready on a Monday. The Friday before, the Bush campaign released an ad known as "The Hug," in which the president wraps his arms around a fifteen-year-old Ohio girl whose mother was on a business trip and was killed on the 104th floor of Tower One on 9/11. Her father snapped a picture of the president at the moment he gave Ashley Faulkner a hug. That then became the basis of an emotional sixty-second commercial. In the ad, Ashley says about President Bush, "He's the most powerful man in the world and all he wants to do is make sure I'm safe, that I'm okay." Her father continues, "What I saw was what I want to see in the heart and in the soul of the man who sits in the highest elected office in our country."

Mindy responded to "The Hug." She said it was nice that

Ashley Faulkner had gotten a hug from the president, but that Mindy's three children needed more than a hug and a promise to feel safe; they needed real reasons and proof. My commercial was already in the can and ready to air. But the problem was, all the commercial time in the big swing states had already been purchased by the Bush campaign. So while our ad had the potential to be an effective response to "The Hug," it did not appear in enough key battleground states to make a meaningful difference.

The impact of "The Hug" was huge. The conservative group that produced it, Progress for America, spent $20 million running it in eleven of the battleground states. In Ohio, the ad ran 7,000 times in the final weeks of the campaign. Tad Devine, a leading Kerry strategist, said, "We lost the election because of 9/11 and terrorism. I think that ad might be why we lost Ohio, and because we lost Ohio, we lost the election."

I always believed that Kerry could win. I felt the depth of the energy in the crowds and knew how much people wanted to feel that America belonged to them again. People wanted to know the truth about their lives, about their nation's security, about what we could do to make it better. I'm not just saying that—it was something I felt deep in my bones and it made me hope in a way I hadn't since 9/11.

When I lived inside my bubble, I was naïve. I didn't think I had to worry about my government. Foolishly, I assumed my government was doing its job in keeping us safe and protected. Part of the reason Ron loved and respected Dick Cheney so much was because he felt he was a strong and courageous leader who would never be dissuaded from doing the right thing. I knew how wrong that was by the time we were in the thick of the battle for the independent commission—it was Cheney who was our greatest opposition from the very outset.

I really meant it when I told campaign audiences that the battles we fought for the commission were battles launched by the White House and its administration. To be among thousands of people who felt the same way and cared as passionately as I did was energizing in a way I could not have imagined.

People came up to me with tears in their eyes to thank me for the work we had done on their behalf. I never expected that. I really felt the momentum was there to build a better world, to recapture some of the spirit many of us felt after 9/11.

I relayed this feeling during one of my campaign speeches given at the vice presidential debate, which was held at Ohio's Case Western Reserve University. The gymnasium was packed with several thousand people. After I was introduced, I talked about Ron's last phone call and about how in the weeks following his murder "it was clear that there were failures in our nation's security if this nation could be brought to its knees by nineteen hijackers with box cutters."

There was a roar of applause as people rose out of their seats, wiped tears from their eyes, and began cheering.

I then said that after Pearl Harbor a commission began investigating the attack within eleven days. "This administration stonewalled for over one year. It was a battle. We gave President Bush every opportunity to do the right thing. The Senate voted ninety to eight to allocate funds for such an investigation, but then we had to have negotiations on how to investigate.

"We were given only three million dollars to investigate the worst terrorist incident in this nation's history. By comparison, fifty million dollars was allotted for the space shuttle. We had to negotiate with the White House all summer before they finally gave us thirteen or fourteen million dollars for the investigation to go forward."

I talked about how the war in Iraq, in my view, had made

the country less safe; in fact, it had accomplished what the terrorists on 9/11 had failed to achieve: It increased recruitment
for al Qaeda. The 9/11 attacks were designed in part to be
"spectacular," as a way of luring new recruits into the terrorist
network. The day before we spoke at Carnegie Mellon, the
Iraqi president had talked about the terrorists flooding into his
country and had said Iraq was now a "magnet" for terrorists.

What happened at Carnegie Mellon happened in varying
degrees as Monica and I hopscotched across the country. We
felt euphoric at the promise the crowds contained. The number
of volunteers who supported us along the way was awe-
inspiring. Watching these volunteers was like witnessing
democracy at work. I was bowled over that people would be
so committed that they took leaves of absence from their families and work to volunteer for months on the campaign. They
ran phone banks and met us at the airport, often briefing us on
local issues. Sandwiches were passed out that volunteers had
made, people pitched in as drivers—it was all such a gift from
the heart, as corny as that might sound. I still get e-mails from
people I met along the way, updating me on their lives and
children.

But sadly, I feel that John Kerry squandered the efforts of
thousands of people who gave their all to try to get him in the
White House. He squandered that collective hope by not listening to his own heart and worrying more about what other
people would think than about what he really believed.

Four days before the election, Osama bin Laden released a
videotape that put 9/11 right at the forefront of the campaign.
Going into the final sprint, the two candidates were neck and
neck in the polls. Osama had not been seen publicly for fourteen months. Seeing him alive and well made terrorism the

number-one issue again, which turned out to be a plus for the president.

Kerry needed to hit back with everything he had. I was campaigning in Reno with Monica and Peggy Kerry. We were sitting in a restaurant scarfing down some food, waiting to catch the next flight to Las Vegas for another campaign stop when the Osama tape came over the airwaves of CNN. Frankly, it was chilling. Chilling not only because seeing bin Laden always scares us and makes us yearn to have our children safely within reach, but also because this time his words sparked. Bin Laden looked tanned and rested. He didn't look like a trapped rat on the run from the almighty wrath and reach of the U.S. military. He looked calm and relaxed as he delivered his comments censuring President Bush for his shady Halliburton deals in Iraq and his failure to rise out of a school chair on the morning of 9/11:

> No one except a dumb thief plays with the security of others and then makes himself believe he will be secure. Whereas thinking people, when disaster strikes, make it their priority to look for its causes, in order to prevent it happening again. . . .
>
> But I am amazed at you. Even though we are in the fourth year after the events of September 11th, Bush is still engaged in distortion, deception and hiding from you the real causes. And thus, the reasons are still there for a repeat of what occurred. . . .
>
> So he [Bush Sr.] took dictatorship and suppression of freedoms to his son and they named it the Patriot Act, under the pretense of fighting terrorism. In addition, Bush sanctioned the installing of sons as state governors, and didn't forget to import expertise in election fraud from

the region's presidents to Florida to be made use of in moments of difficulty. . . .

That being said, those who say that al Qaeda has won against the administration in the White House or that the administration has lost in this war have not been precise, because when one scrutinizes the results, one cannot say that al Qaeda is the sole factor in achieving those spectacular gains. . . .

Rather, the policy of the White House that demands the opening of war fronts to keep busy their various corporations—whether they be working in the field of arms or oil or reconstruction—has helped al Qaeda to achieve these enormous results. . . .

And so it has appeared to some analysts and diplomats that the White House and us are playing as one team towards the economic goals of the United States, even if the intentions differ. . . .

It is true that this shows that al Qaeda has gained, but on the other hand, it shows that the Bush administration has also gained, something of which anyone who looks at the size of the contracts acquired by the shady Bush administration-linked mega-corporations, like Halliburton and its kind, will be convinced. And it all shows that the real loser is . . . you. . . .

It never occurred to us that the commander-in-chief of the American armed forces would abandon 50,000 of his citizens in the twin towers to face those great horrors alone, the time when they most needed him. . . .

But because it seemed to him that occupying himself by talking to the little girl about the goat and its butting was more important than occupying himself with the planes and their butting of the skyscrapers, we were given three times the period required to execute the operations—all praise is due to Allah. . . .

And it's no secret to you that the thinkers and perceptive ones from among the Americans warned Bush before the war and told him: "All that you want for securing America and removing the weapons of mass destruction—assuming they exist—is available to you, and the nations of the world are with you in the inspections, and it is in the interest of America that it not be thrust into an unjustified war with an unknown outcome."

But the darkness of the black gold blurred his vision and insight, and he gave priority to private interests over the public interests of America. . . .

So the war went ahead, the death toll rose, the American economy bled, and Bush became embroiled in the swamps of Iraq that threaten his future. He fits the saying "like the naughty she-goat who used her hoof to dig up a knife from under the earth."

So I say to you, over 15,000 of our people have been killed and tens of thousands injured, while more than a thousand of you have been killed and more than 10,000 injured. And Bush's hands are stained with the blood of all those killed from both sides, all for the sake of oil and keeping their private companies in business. . . .

Be aware that it is the nation who punishes the weak man when he causes the killing of one of its citizens for money, while letting the powerful one get off, when he causes the killing of more than 1,000 of its sons, also for money. . . .

In conclusion, I tell you in truth, that your security is not in the hands of Kerry, nor Bush, nor al Qaeda. No.

Your security is in your own hands. And every state

that doesn't play with our security has automatically
guaranteed its own security.

Monica and I were visibly upset—trembling, in fact. I
wanted to get home to Caroline immediately. I needed a bug-
hug. Jumping on the red-eye from Vegas to New York, I re-
treated to Long Island and was happy to be home safe with
Caroline the very next morning.

The last campaign rally was in Cleveland on the eve of the
election. It was a Bruce Springsteen concert. Earlier in the day I
was in Cleveland and some of its smaller suburbs giving
speeches and making some phone calls at various phone banks.
I had hooked up with Cam Kerry and James Boyce, Cam's assistant, who were traveling with Larry and Laurie David. Larry
David was the producer of *Seinfeld*. He also has an award-
winning show on HBO, *Curb Your Enthusiasm*. Laurie David is
an impassioned and articulate environmental activist who works
for the organization called NRDC—Natural Resources Defense
Council. Laurie is one of those people who doesn't talk the talk
and not walk the walk. She is committed to alternative energy
resources and saving our environment by stopping global
warming. After spending only an afternoon with her, I was convinced that she should run for office. She is intelligent, fearless,
and driven. Larry, of course, is exactly the way he is on his television show on HBO. He is hysterically funny, smart, and witty.

We met at the hotel and then headed over to the huge outdoor concert being thrown by Bruce Springsteen. While waiting
to enter, we were ushered into the back-lot area and I had the
opportunity to spend some time with Springsteen. As a girl who
grew up in New Jersey and was also dubbed one of the "Jersey Girls," I felt this encounter was a memorable one. He gave
me a huge hug. Told me that he read about the Jersey Girls in

the *New York Times* and local papers and was always cheering for us. He was our biggest fan. Hearing that come from Bruce Springsteen required an immediate "patching" with the widows. I called Lorie first. Bruce got on the phone with her and spoke to her for about ten minutes. In fact, I had to tell him to get off the phone with her. But he wasn't lying when he said that he was our biggest fan; he sat and discussed minute details of the commission and the hearings and rehashed all of our battles, with Lorie listening and adding anecdotes throughout the entire conversation.

Springsteen and I both lived in the same neighborhood in New Jersey. My daughter was scheduled to start school in the same school his kids attended. So we made some small talk. I then said that I had considered moving out of New Jersey and didn't know whether I would be returning. He looked sad and immediately asked why. I told him the truth. I didn't feel comfortable living in my mostly Republican county and town any longer. While I'd been away on the campaign trail someone had placed Bush/Cheney signs along my property, and I felt that I was no longer welcome.

Later that evening while the concert was under way, I was busily talking to some volunteers when Larry David slapped me on the shoulder. He said that Springsteen had just mentioned my name. Bruce announced that I was in the audience and that he wanted to sing a song for the Jersey Girls, who were great Americans, but more important, true Jersey Girls. He then went on to play "Thunder Road." It was awesome to be serenaded by Bruce Springsteen before a crowd of at least 50,000. I had tears in my eyes as I quickly called the widows on my cell phone.

Afterwards, I thanked Springsteen profusely and gave him a huge bear hug. He pulled me aside, saying, "I can't play 'Jersey Girl' because I didn't write the song, but anytime you want a private rendition, call me and you got it. I will sing it to you over the phone. You girls keep fighting, now, and take good care of yourselves." Laurie David snapped a picture of us standing together with our arms around each other's shoulders. The photo hangs on my refrigerator to this very day.

The next morning, Cam, James, Laurie, Larry, and I flew to Boston to meet up with the rest of the campaign. As I disembarked, I was told that I was scheduled to talk that night at an outdoor rally in Copley Square. Panicking a bit about what I would say in the speech and being a bit overtired from the late night before, I immediately headed to the hotel to start jotting down some words for my speech.

By late afternoon, the mood in the hotel at campaign headquarters was electric. The exit polls showed Kerry not just ahead, but winning. People were slapping each other on the back and watching a huge television monitor.

Larry David was off to one side and did not seem to be as enthusiastic. I walked over to him and asked him what was going on. "Everyone is celebrating, but I'm not there yet, I'm just not there yet." I wasn't sure I was either and told him so. "Larry, I'll get there when you get there. When you allow yourself to get happy, I'll allow myself to get happy." We had a deal.

I had written a very short speech. By that point in the campaign, I was certainly comfortable with what I had to say, but the thought of getting up and saying it still made me quiver. My shyness had survived the campaign trail. Knowing I was going to be on live national television on election night, speaking about the man who could be president of the United States the next day, didn't help my nerves, either. I decided that Patty, Mindy, Lorie, and Monica should be there with me. We had started this long journey together, and I wanted them there to end it together, too. Carole King sang "You've Got a Friend" as we all stood backstage waiting to go out. The song brought forth a well of emotions for us. And then we all walked out arm in arm and I took the podium.

I got back to the hotel around nine o'clock. I was riding the up escalator and someone said to me, "We lost it." "Wait a minute," I said. "I just went out to give a speech and we had won it. What do you mean? We *lost* it?" I felt overwhelmed and all I heard in the explanation was something about exit polls.

I walked into the room in the Hyatt that was headquarters. Laurie David was sitting on the floor transfixed by the television that was tuned to CNN's *Super Desk*. The rest of the famous people were all commiserating on the other floors, half partying and half playing politics.

"What happened?" I said.

"It's awful. We lost it." Laurie was crying.

I went over to find Larry. He was speechless. Liz Ryan was dragging celebrities over to us to have our pictures taken. "These are the Jersey Girls," she said. "They are fabulous." But I felt anything but. I walked away and returned alone to my hotel room.

Mourning Ron was a sorrow about losing something I knew I had and suffering the acute knowledge of knowing that I could never have that life again. The election was the defeat of hope, optimism, and the promise of the future. I knew how high the stakes were. I wanted to believe that all of our efforts had meant something that could be translated into pouring a new foundation for the future. This loss of hope felt cruel.

At 4:00 A.M. I woke up and turned on the television. I was hoping against hope. The election hadn't been called when I went to sleep, but the news was not good. At eight-thirty I went upstairs to the floor where all the senior Kerry campaign people were meeting. They had just made the decision to concede.

I was upset. I wanted Kerry to contest the results. I had seen for myself how fervent his supporters were. Why give up without a fight?

We sat in the fourth row and listened to John Kerry and John Edwards concede victory to President Bush. Patty was in tears. My eyes didn't even water. I was far too upset. We walked back to the hotel, stopping at Starbucks. It was cold, dreary, and sad. The defeat was awful, the news about Elizabeth Edwards having breast cancer unbearably cruel. All the color seemed drained from the world.

Monica, Patty, and I made the long drive home together. We got lost a number of times but just didn't care. What were we rushing home for, anyway—it was going to be a long four years, and we were in no rush for them to start. We felt totally crushed and depressed.

Getting home and seeing Caroline, my little doodlebug, made me smile. She seemed so full of joy and laughter. She was always busy. Sam had no concept of defeat. He was one big hooray, too. Being surrounded by their love and constant motion carried me.

But still I felt as though I'd fallen into a dark and cold abyss.

Two days after I got home there was a message on my cell phone. "Kristen, it's John Edwards. I just want to tell you I had a great time traveling with you and think you're the best. Elizabeth loves you, I love you, and if you need anything, I am still in the Senate office, closing up shop here, but still available and around. Take good care of yourself and your little girl and stay in touch."

Classy. I never heard from John Kerry.

The widows and I don't regret supporting John Kerry for

president. We believed that we needed a new president who would run our country differently from George Bush. We wanted a president who would understand what needed to be done to fight the war on terror, a man who didn't defend his bad foreign policy choices and national security decisions with "booga-booga" scare tactics and speeches. We had spent three long years trying to get President Bush to understand and learn the valuable lessons of 9/11. And he never did.

The widows and I live our lives so as to not have any regrets at the end of each day. If John Kerry had run for president and lost without our involvement in his campaign, we would always have wondered if we could have made a difference in the outcome. We tried our best and followed our hearts when we joined the Kerry campaign. For us, it was the right thing to do. In doing so, we took part in democracy; we tried to change the course of our country, tried to move it toward becoming a better and safer place. We feel proud and good about that. We certainly have no regrets.

CHAPTER EIGHT

─────

Your Right Arm Returns

THE END OF THE Kerry campaign was demoralizing and depressing. It brought me almost to a complete halt and forced me back into reality. The fast-paced life of the 24/7 campaign trail was exhausting, but it had also been an enormous distraction for me.

Ever since the first few months after Ron's death, I'd been fighting for something: fighting to make the Victims' Compensation Fund more equitable, fighting for the independent commission, fighting for access, fighting for public hearings. Then there were the times I testified and the enormous preparation that went into those presentations. Then there was gearing up for the release of *The 9/11 Commission Report*, fighting to get its recommendations implemented into law, and then the campaign.

I had moved out of the house on 268 Monmouth Avenue back in the summer of 2004. It was the end of the school year, and I knew I didn't want to live in New Jersey any longer. The house seemed too sad. The woods no longer gave me solace. I felt like the house was cursed. I decided that Caroline and I would spend the summer elsewhere, and if we didn't feel like returning home once Labor Day rolled around, we would just never return to New Jersey. It was a good time for a fresh start. When we left in June, I grabbed photos and scrapbooks and left all else behind. Food remained in the freezer, cereal and grains in the pantry, clothes in the laundry basket, DVDs in the DVD player.

Obviously, deciding to go on the Kerry campaign delayed my decision about where Caroline and I should reside. Now I really had to figure out how and where we would live.

As it turned out, Caroline needed to get more specialized and professional care for her speech and learning delays. Her current school couldn't provide a good enough support structure for the kind of reading specialists, occupational therapists, and speech therapists she needed. After talking it over with the widows, I decided it would be best to move into New York City. It was a logical choice, but one that filled me with dread. I didn't like moving back into the heart of the terrorists' strike zone. I was wary of the noise and congestion and the throngs of people. The thought of being part of the daily chaos of Manhattan seemed overwhelming to me. But I knew we had to try.

We moved into Manhattan in January 2005. It was a new start and a new year. I found a small apartment a few blocks away from one of the city's best public schools. Caroline was enrolled for kindergarten, and the movers made plans to deliver our furniture.

By definition, moving is stressful. But I decided to plow through the day with as much focus and concentration as I could and just get the job done. Sam was not exactly a city dog. Trying to corral him, keep him from barking, and avoid any damage to the building in the process was not an easy task. He was like a rat in a cage. Caroline was a lot more adaptable. She is extremely easygoing. She loved the idea of living in New

York and being so close to Central Park. She adored the elevator men and doormen (in fact, she knew everyone's name
within a week). She was eager to get her new city life under
way. She bounded around the apartment, hanging up her art-
work, unpacking bags and boxes, giggling with delight.

And then the phone rang.

Paul (the same Paul who had taken me to Ground Zero and
handled the whole body-part-recovery process) was on the
phone. Paul called me regularly, but I could tell something was
wrong immediately when I heard his voice. "Kris, I have some
bad news. More of Ron's body parts were recovered." My heart
sank. "You need to call my uncle Frank at the funeral home." I
got dizzy, tried to right myself, stumbled, dropped the phone,
and puked. It was too much. How was it possible that I could
get a call about my husband's remains on the one day of the
year when I was completely drained, emotionally and physically? I really couldn't take it. Sam was still pacing the empty
floors. Caroline was still bounding around. I was becoming
undone.

At that moment the buzzer went off. The furniture was there.
When I opened the front door of the apartment, the moving
guy looked startled. He asked me if I was okay. With tears
streaming down my face, vomit still on my shirt, I wiped my
face with my shirtsleeve, saying that I was okay, and motioned
for him to start bringing in the boxes.

I took the phone off the floor. Paul was still there. I told
him that the moving men had just showed up and that I had to
get off the phone. I promised him that after I had unpacked the
125 boxes, taken Sam for a walk, found something for Caroline
to eat, made a makeshift bed for her, and gotten her to sleep,
I would give his uncle Frank a call. I told myself, "There. Lock
it out of your brain, Kristen. Shut it out. Don't think about it.

Suck it up. Unpack the boxes. Take a deep breath. Lock it out. You don't have the liberty to think about this now. Later. Later you can break down."

When the boxes were partially unpacked, I finally called the widows. My black humor had returned and I was now ready to deal with reality. I dialed Mindy first and asked her to patch the other pods, saying, "We are going to need complete patching for this one." Mindy got nervous. She knew I was already depressed after the Christmas holidays. She knew I was totally stressed from the idea of having to move into New York City with Caroline and Sam. She knew I was at the end of my rope.

Once patched, I told the widows what had happened. They were speechless. They could not understand how I could have received more body parts, since two weeks before, we had all been told by the City of New York that all body parts had been identified and that the 9/11 families would no longer be notified about finding any more. How was it possible?

"Well, what did you get?" was the next question. I didn't know the answer to that one. I still didn't have the stamina to call the funeral director. The girls understood. They knew that receiving Paul's phone call had been a sucker punch directly to my gut. They were really worried about me. Apparently I wasn't sounding so clearheaded on the phone. They suggested that we all patch into the funeral director the next morning. But in the meantime, "Well, what do you think it could be?"

"Torso," Patty said confidently. In unison we all said, "Torso? How could it be his torso? How is that possible?" One of the more macabre things that many 9/11 families deal with is not knowing specifically how our loved ones died. We look at the images of that day. They are horrific. Unbearable. We desperately want to believe that our loved ones did not suffer in their final moments. But the devastating images of that day are always there to remind us. And the phone calls that very rarely discuss full bodies but rather only scattered body parts make it very difficult to expect anything but the very worst. Oddly, I'd thought immediately of torso when Paul had first called me. I always think worst-case scenario, and to me receiving my husband's torso would be the most unbearable body part to accept. Then, we all began to get angry that we'd been told two weeks ago not to expect any more phone calls about body parts. It seemed cruel for me to receive one now.

The next morning I called Paul's uncle Frank. He told me that he'd first been notified a week before Christmas but decided to wait until after the holidays to tell me. He wanted to save me from the devastation of receiving his phone call a week before Christmas. Frank nearly died when I told him that the day I'd been notified had been my moving day. He felt terrible. I asked him what I needed to do. He told me that it was all very perfunctory: He could fax me a form, and they could cremate Ron's remains in New York City and FedEx the ashes to his funeral home in New Jersey. I agreed that it was the easiest thing to do.

I then asked Frank what body parts were found. Frank told me it was Ron's right arm from the shoulder on down, with his hand and fingers intact. He told me that it was a large body part. Frank suggested that I speak to the medical examiner, since he couldn't understand how it took so long to identify such a large body part that had Ron's hand, and therefore his fingerprints, attached. He gave me the name and number I needed to call.

I called the widows and we decided that we should all call the medical examiner together. When we did, what we learned infuriated all of us. We were told that Ron's right arm had been tagged and identified at nearly the same time as his other arm. For some unexplained reason, the medical examiner had lost his right arm in the freezer for three years. The gentleman we spoke to was very cordial. He laid out the facts as best he could. He told me that each of the arms had been found in the same quadrant of Ground Zero. There were only one hundred body parts that were tagged in between. They were found a day apart. He could give me no explanation as to why the delay in identification had occurred.

Mindy then asked if I would be getting notified again. She raised the possibility of more of Ron's body parts lying around in the freezer. Was that likely? If so, when could I expect a call? Six months? A year? The medical examiner said that I could possibly receive another call. He suggested that I not bury Ron's remains for at least six months.

After getting off the phone with the ME's office, the widows and I discussed the situation in our inimitable way. Patty started by saying that she thought it was Ron's way of sending me a helping hand on moving day. Mindy said that she thought it was his way of sending a hug. Lorie said she was pissed that I now had a complete set of matching arms and she still had nothing from Kenny.

Things started to settle down after that. I mean, how much worse could they get? By February, Caroline, Sam, and I had finally settled into a routine. Caroline was happy at school and Sam enjoyed his three long, daily walks in Central Park. Both of them really took to city life.

And then one day while Sam was out walking in the park, he was bitten in the eye by another dog. I rushed him to the vet. The vet noticed that Sam had a cyst on his throat. He suggested we take a needle biopsy. When he extracted the fluid he said he thought it looked fine. I told him I wanted it sent out to a lab, explaining that Sam was like a child to me and I was worried it could be cancer; I knew that cancer was rampant in golden retrievers. I had already lost my mother to cancer; I wasn't prepared to lose Sam to the disease.

The lab results came back and it turned out that Sam had lymphoma. The positive news was that it was not even a stage 1. The doctor suggested we remove the tumor and place Sam on a course of chemotherapy. While stunned and horribly upset, I felt reassured that we had caught the cancer so early on. From everything the doctor was telling me, Sam had an excellent prognosis.

I ended up taking Sam to a veterinarian-oncologist every three weeks for a physical examination and chemo treatments. I wanted to make sure Sam survived. The last thing Caroline and I needed was for Sam to die young. Neither one of us was ready for the one male left in our life to disappear. By June, Sam was thriving. His blood work looked excellent. He was gaining weight and had a great appetite. He even began swimming again. In fact, his oncologist remarked that he thought it was incredible that a dog on chemotherapy actually gained weight. I was ecstatic. We had beaten it.

In August we decided to drive back to New Jersey to see my family. Sam was in the back of the car. He was quieter than usual. I was talking to Patty on the phone as I drove through Brooklyn and joked that I thought Sam might be dead in the back. I called his name and he perked up his head. He was fine.

When we pulled up to my dad's house, I walked around to the back of the SUV to get Sam out. He was limp and unable to raise his head. I looked into his eyes. They looked strange. He was straining for breath. I pried open his mouth and heard air sucking in. His tongue didn't move. I slammed the door shut, started the car, and raced to the oncologist's office, which was twenty minutes away. While driving about a hundred miles an hour, with my heart racing and Caroline asking me what was wrong, I dialed the vet. "I've got a golden retriever, eight years old, currently on chemo for lymphoma. He's a patient of Dr. Clifford's. He is very sick. I can't lift him out of the car. I am on my way and will be there in five minutes. Please have someone outside waiting."

When I pulled in the parking lot, the gurney was waiting. I jumped out. Caroline was upset by this point. She knew something was seriously wrong with Sam. I had been preparing her in the early stages of Sam's chemo treatment for the possibility that Sam might die. But when I was told Sam had beaten the cancer, I reassured Caroline that he was going to live a long life and be with us for more years to come. This was not looking good. When I opened the back, Sam lifted his head. Caroline jumped out of the car and ran to the back. He did his thump wag. I told her to pet him and give him a kiss on his nose. She did. She told him that she loved him.

After they took Sam inside, a doctor showed up within three minutes and said that Sam had had a massive hemorrhage and needed to be put down. There I was with my six-year-old daughter who'd had her father murdered by terrorists and now she was at the vet with me when her dog—who was like a brother to her—had to be put to sleep. It was awful. The color washed from my face. I asked if there was anything they could do. I told them I didn't care how much it would cost. Anything. Anything to save his life. The vet told me he was in extreme pain. His spleen had exploded. He needed to be put down.

The vet arranged for an assistant to take Caroline to another room to look at baby squirrels. As she walked down the hall, I entered the triage room. Sam was lying limp on the table. Still alive, but clearly in tremendous pain. I bent down. I kissed him on the head and placed his face in my hands. I went nose to nose with him, looking him in the eyes. I told him I loved him. And that he had to go to find Ron in heaven. I just kept saying over and over again, "Go on, go find Daddy. Go find him now." Within thirty seconds his eyes turned gray and he was gone. I was devastated.

I gathered up Caroline, signed the release forms for Sam's remains to be cremated and sent to me in a cherry urn, left the building, drove to my father's house, dropped Caroline off, got back in the car, and drove to the beach. I broke down and cried like I hadn't cried in years. I sobbed. I wept. I hyperventilated. I screamed. I just kept crying and crying and crying. It all felt so unfair. So goddamn unfair.

Want to know the damage of 9/11 on children? This should sum it up: Caroline initially handled Sam's death like a seasoned war veteran. At the age of six, she looked me in the eye, took my face in her hands, and told me, "Mommy, don't be sad. Sam is in heaven with Daddy now. He's with Daddy up in the moon. They're playing. Don't be sad." I asked her if she felt sad. She looked at me and said, "Mom, Sammy is in the moon. He died liked Daddy died. It's just the way life goes." Her comments rattled me. They scared me. Was she the most put-together and resilient kid in the world or was she incapable of feeling normal emotion? I said to the widows, "Oh, yes, we are going to be racking up some huge therapy bills in the near future." I wasn't joking.

As it turned out, Caroline just delayed her grief. She wanted to be strong for me, I guess. I feel bad about that. But Sam's early death was a severe blow to me. I had known Sam for more years than I had known Ron. Sam had been like a child to me. I referred to him as my son. Sam had known my mother and Ron. He was by my side with his sloppy kisses and dirty paws through both of their horrible deaths. And now I was alone.

Within a week of Sam's dying, my colitis came back with a vengeance. A month after the fourth anniversary of 9/11, my gastroenterologists recognized that my usual medication was not working. The colitis was getting worse. We needed to either significantly increase my current dosages of corticosteroid medication or try something else. The doctors were already upset that I had been on corticosteroids; years of treatment had already depleted my bones. They wanted me off them as soon as possible. It was time for drastic action.

The doctors suggested a low-grade chemotherapy treatment. I didn't have a choice. It was that or hospitalization and the possibility of removing my colon. I opted for the chemo. After seeing how well the chemo had worked for Sam, I wasn't holding out much hope. But I was tired and in a lot of pain. I wanted and needed to feel better.

In the midst of my chemo treatments, I received an offer on my home in New Jersey. The buyers were motivated. They wanted to close in a month. I needed to empty the house in time for that closing. How was that going to happen? I was sick. I was depressed. I missed Sam. I hated living in New York City. And now I had to clean out the home that Ron and I had shared. Once again, life felt unfair.

My chemo treatments were spaced three weeks apart. For the first couple of days after each infusion I felt tired, nauseated, and pretty crappy. I knew I had to schedule the move and cleaning-out of the house in New Jersey in a non-chemo week. Cleaning out my life in New Jersey was the last thing I felt emotionally or physically ready to do at that point. But it wasn't like I had a choice.

Mindy captured the way I needed to view my post-9/11 life this way: "You know, I think before 9/11 we had happy lives with sad moments. Since 9/11 we have sad lives with happy moments. That's the difference. Just expect to have more sadness than happiness. And then you can't get angry and disappointed." Mindy nailed it on the head. But, chemo and dead dog aside, I wasn't going down without a fight.

CHAPTER NINE

⊶⊶⊶

The Dumpster

T HEY WERE LARGE. They were ugly. But they were mine: two rented thirty-yard-long Dumpsters that would become his-and-her coffins for the life Ron and I were supposed to share. I'm not so dramatic that I called the Dumpsters that at the time, but in retrospect I see that's what they were. Unbeknownst to me, I was about to unleash a purge and catharsis with a fury that would astonish me.

I called my closest non-widow friend, Sara Travers, who loves me enough not to judge what others might have easily called an extremely irrational act. A more "normal" widow, whoever she might be, would have called the Goodwill and the Salvation Army and donated her items and possessions. I did that for Caroline's toys. But not for everything else. I laid waste to it instead.

When I returned to the house in New Jersey in autumn 2005, I realized that whatever I'd left behind from the year before I didn't really need. I hadn't missed any of it. It was all just ornamentation for a life I no longer had. What was the sense in keeping it? As I walked from room to stale room, I looked over everything. I touched everything. I sat down on the sofa

and the beds. I smelled the pillows. I allowed myself to remember what my life had been. The memories were just too
painful to bear. I wanted them gone.

Slowly and carefully at first, and then more and more
wildly, I hurled almost everything I owned into the two ugly,
rusty steel containers that were the size of boxcars. Smoothly
polished teak chairs were splintered to pieces with a huge
sledgehammer and tossed into the Dumpsters. Bookcases were
hacked apart along with end tables, coffee tables, couches, and
beds. Lamps with shades in muted earth tones made shattering
sounds as they crashed into the wreckage. The microwave,
coffeemaker, Acme Juicer, and food processor were heaved
onto the mess along with fine bottles of wine, sherry, scotch,
and cognac. In went the aperitifs, the wineglasses and champagne flutes. Cheers! Adios to the bottles of first cold-pressed
extra virgin olive oil and aged balsamic vinegar picked up on
a friend's trip to Tuscany.

And in went the peanuts from Costco. Those goddamn
peanuts. I chuckled and had tears running down my face as I
tossed those in. I remembered when Ron and I had been shopping in Costco and he spied the restaurant-size container of
peanuts. I had said they were bad for his heart. He had bought
them anyway. A week later he was dead—eating those peanuts
hadn't mattered much. In fact, a lot of things didn't matter
much. And that's why I took great pleasure in choosing to
throw all of those things out. It was wrong, wasteful, and
illogical—just like the murder of my husband. But this time it
was my choice.

Perfectly good and perfectly gone: Fleecy blankets, European pillow shams, and soft cotton sheets went into the Dumpster along with the Christmas hand towels, those damned

decorative pillows, the reindeer, snowmen, and Santa Claus. Ho ho ho. I had been a very good girl. But the laugh was on me.

Those pretty pottery casseroles that seemed so indestructible were now Dumpster debris along with the cookware and the carving set. The cookbooks and cocktail napkins; the crystal decanter; the dozens of place mats; and tablecloths, fine linens, and bold cottons from Provence: all now part of the dregs of my life. Au revoir to the fucking muffin tins and cookie cutters, the KitchenAid mixer and the handmade mixing bowls. Out went the gardening books. You know, I guess I'll never figure out how to get roses to grow in the shade. China crashes in such a predictable way. It's not nearly as satisfying as taking a sledgehammer to your television set. And that, of course, pales in comparison to smashing one dozen pink cups made out of very pretty glass. Sara and I enjoyed those the most. And bye-bye to the bicycles we'll never ride again. In went the skis, the golf clubs, the hiking boots, the tennis rackets, and of course, the softball mitts.

I'd already extracted whatever pleasure could be had from my possessions. I didn't need them around to taunt me with what might have been. Grief will have its way with you. My way won't be your way, and if you think you can predict or judge what another should do, then quickly say a prayer of gratitude for not having been struck down by a loss of unimaginable proportions. Be glad there is still gravity in your world, because when it's gone there isn't one damn thing you can buy that's going to make you feel any better.

If I couldn't enjoy my things, I didn't want anyone else to either. Childish, perhaps, but honest. Out went the table and supplies I had set up in a basement for scrapbooking, a cozy corner I had made where Caroline and I were going to put our memories into books and organize our pictures on acid-free paper. The wrinkled piece of paper with the blue fingerprints and handprints of Caroline and Ron still hung on the wall. They had messily painted it during our last vacation together, one week before Ron died. I have photos of them. Sam was licking the paint, his tail wagging and knocking over the little jars of bright paint. Ron's shirt was covered in blue. Caroline's face was beaming. One of the pictures shows the two of them looking directly at me with their blue hands in the air, proudly showing me what beautiful art they had made. I snapped myself back from the memory and carefully rolled up the paper, tucking it safely away in the backseat of my car. It is odd what things become worldly possessions. That fingerprint art is one of mine. It represents a time of innocence and happiness. A time I doubt I will ever find again.

Next it was Ron's clothes. I had taken them out of our closet about one year after 9/11. I'd carefully packed them away in clear plastic bins, not wanting to part with any of them. Even his well-worn shoes got packed away along with his undershirts, his boxers, his socks. All of it. I wanted to keep it all. And now I had to decide what to do with everything. I couldn't bear the thought of another woman telling the man she loved how handsome he looked while wearing Ron's sports jackets or business suits. The tuxedo still had its tags. In a flash, I decided: never worn; never should be; never would be. Away it went.

Lose what is priceless and everything else is cheap. When I hurled something into the Dumpster, like Ron's Burberry coat, I thought, Fuck it. Not the poetry of Job, perhaps, but my perverse prayer. Job's rage got God to speak. Mine got everything I'd ever owned into a landfill. My black humor came through when Sara asked me if I was really sure about throwing everything out. I looked at her and said, "You know, it is sort of fitting. Why shouldn't all of it get thrown out and taken to some landfill in Staten Island? After all, that is where Ron is. Maybe he could use his golf clubs or his tux?" Sara looked at me nervously. She was wondering whether I had gone completely around the bend. I hadn't. For the first time in four years, I was starting to feel relieved.

My prior life was now officially garbage, all of it worthless except for Caroline and a few family heirlooms. I saved our kayak, my surfboard, and a pair of Ron's shoes so Caroline could put her hands where his feet had been. I kept his hound's-tooth jacket for her so she could touch something he wore and loved. Immediately after 9/11 I had put a few of the T-shirts and shorts he wore to the beach in a Ziploc bag so I could hold on to the smell of him. That got carefully squirreled away in the car, too. Saved. Everything else wound up at the dump.

The kind of resurrection I needed wasn't happening in three days and didn't come in pastel colors. Where was I now in the grieving process? Was I bargaining? Don't think so. Denial? Not a chance. Acceptance? No way. Ron's death is completely unacceptable. I live with the reality of it in my life, but I won't accept it like a package from UPS. I didn't sign up for this. And I will certainly never accept it. It's more like learning to tolerate its ever-looming presence in my life.

Caroline alone was reason enough to live and believe in love. In my heart I knew that with laughter and love we'd make a new life for ourselves—just the two of us. As I pulled out of the driveway, I breathed a huge sigh of relief. Sara and I had worked hard. We had emptied out almost the entire home. We did it alone. When the Dumpster guy came to pick up the Dumpsters, he was awestruck by the fact that two young women filled those huge Dumpsters to their very tops with so much stuff and in such a short time.

As I checked in with the widows on the drive home, they asked me if I was sure I hadn't mistakenly thrown out something I should have kept. I told them I was sure that I hadn't mistakenly tossed anything of value. And I was fine with that notion until I got into bed that night and realized that I'd made an awful mistake. Where were Caroline's baby sweatshirts? I had placed them in a black garbage bag; did they get mistakenly thrown out? I called Sara. She didn't know where they were. As I talked to Sara on the phone, I paced back and forth in my apartment. I kept looking at all of my photos of Ron and Caroline. In almost every single one she was wearing a Gap sweatshirt. I felt sick. I wanted those sweatshirts back.

Yellow, pink, purple, green . . . we had them in every possible color. One day I wanted to show Caroline a picture of herself with her dad at the beach and say, "Here's the sweatshirt. This is what you were wearing when Daddy was alive." I was obsessed by the thought of finding the sweatshirts. There was nothing else I regretted throwing out.

While I was trying to go to sleep, a mental image came into focus. I could see the sweatshirts and see where they had lodged in the back corner on the right-hand side of the Dumpster. It was neither a dream nor a vision, but it was a strong intuitive sense about where those sweatshirts were. I had to try to get them. I called Sara back. She had never tried to dissuade me from anything before, but she tried to talk me out of this. "You'll get hurt. There's all that broken glass and all the broken pieces of wood and metal. It's too dangerous."

I didn't care. The next morning I drove back to my house and climbed into the Dumpster, into the muck and wreckage of my life. As I began to tear my way through garbage bags and over mountains of debris that scaled eight feet high, I realized I didn't have my cell phone with me. If I got hurt or trapped I was on my own and perfect tabloid fodder: 9/11 WIDOW FOUND DEAD IN DUMPSTER: MURDER OR SUICIDE? I kept slicing open garbage bags and finding nothing but my clothes and Ron's. The Dumpster was wet and gross. I felt like an idiot, but not as stupid as I would feel if I gave up. Finally, in the bottom of the pile, exactly where I sensed they should be, I found my little girl's pastel sweatshirts. My heart literally soared with relief.

It was finished. I was done. I climbed out and went home to New York. A few days later the Dumpsters were hauled away. It felt strange and good. I felt cleansed. I felt relief. Unburdened. Now that I had given up on happily ever after, I just wanted to concentrate on the hereinafter.

CHAPTER TEN

⊶⊷

Where to Go? What to Do?

REALIZING THAT CAROLINE had never really experienced a true Christmas, I set my sights high for making Christmas 2005 the best ever. It started during the first week of November, when I began unpacking the holiday decorations. Almost immediately I found myself overwhelmed and utterly swept up by the Christmas spirit. By Thanksgiving, every corner, bookshelf, window, nook, and cranny in our home was literally dripping with Christmas. Then I turned my attention to the outdoors. Lights, bows, wreaths, garlands, and wooden figures were strewn about decorating the columns, windows, fences, and of course Caroline's playhouse. I joked that our home and gardens were vomiting Christmas. It was out of control.

I also decided to get a puppy. Caroline and I felt unbalanced and lonely without Sam in our lives. So after waiting a respectable amount of time to let both of us grieve for Sam, I contacted a golden retriever breeder on Long Island. The delivery date for the puppy was December 23. Once I heard the date, I knew that Santa had to make the delivery—on his sled with his reindeer. And so he did

We left New York City for Christmas vacation on the

morning of December 23. I had been hinting to Caroline for weeks that Santa might bring her a new puppy. As we pulled into the driveway to our home, I threw the house keys to Caroline and told her to open the front door. As she did, she immediately noticed that the Christmas tree lights were on. The entire house was illuminated in twinkling lights. As she walked toward the tree, she heard the cry of a puppy. She screamed at the top of her lungs, "Mommy! Mommy! There's a puppy under our tree! A puppy! Santa brought us a puppy!"

She was ecstatic. And of course I was exhausted. Getting the puppy under that tree took two weeks' worth of running around, planning, ordering, and driving all over Long Island. It wasn't easy. But it was worth it to see the joy and surprise on Caroline's face. As she picked up her new puppy, she found a letter written from Santa:

Dear Caroline,

This puppy is for you. I had to deliver him early because I didn't have enough room on my sled with all the presents I have to deliver. Please take good care of him and love him with all of your heart. Love, Santa.

P.S. Make sure you feed him. He was so hungry that he was eating poor Rudolph's food!! Silly puppy!

I desperately wanted Caroline to have a special Christmas—to be dazzled by the magic of Santa Claus. Since Ron died in 2001, we had never really celebrated Christmas. In fact, this was our first Christmas tree in four years. Knowing that I had only a few more years left before Caroline would learn that Santa is only make-believe, I wanted to maximize them. Will I be able to top the puppy that Santa brought in 2005? We will have to wait and see.

Caroline was given a choice of three names for the puppy. She chose Cooper. We affectionately refer to him as Super-Duper-Cooper-Dog. Truth be told, he should be called Super-Duper-Pooper-Dog because that seems to be all he does. But puppies are puppies, and Cooper has already wheedled his way into our hearts. We haven't invited him to sleep through the night on the bed yet, but I can't wait for that day to come. It will be nice to feel his warmth and hear his soft little snoring puppy sounds.

So far Cooper is a very good dog. Much calmer than Sam. And maybe a bit smarter, too. He has become my new reason to bring out the camera and camcorder—something I've rarely done in the past five years. Sure, I have some pictures and video from the past five years, but for the most part I just never felt like I wanted to document our new life without Ron. It makes me sad, though, that I missed documenting so many years of Caroline's life. My little girl has gone from a toddler in diapers to a beaming seven-year-old who likes to make her own peanut butter and jelly sandwiches. Documenting our lives in the hereinafter is a commitment I have newly made to myself. And the little "duper dog" is the perfect inspiration for doing just that.

My best friend Sara's boyfriend, Cam, recently asked Sara a question: "What would Kristen do if bin Laden were captured, the United States pulled out of Iraq, and Bush was impeached? Do you think she would just go on a permanent vacation?" Cam asked this question while he and Sara were watching me on the *Today* show. I was being interviewed about the bin Laden audiotape that was released in early January 2006. Cam, once a rabid Republican, has started to open his eyes in the way I did immediately after 9/11. Of course he was joking with Sara when he raised the question. But when Sara told me about it, I started to wonder: What would I do? Truth? I would go to sleep—for about a month. Now, that would be fabulous.

Would I wake up? Of course, because too many issues still remain that need to be addressed and fixed by our elected officials in the White House and Congress. And sadly, I know from firsthand experience that unless the American people rise up and open their mouths, those issues will be ignored.

Unfortunately, my to-do list is fairly long: better border security, better chemical plant security, better nuclear power plant security, better port security, better mass transportation security, better securing of loose nukes and biological components, the overhauling and updating of our justice system so that we can effectively and successfully prosecute terrorists, ending human rights abuses and torture, prioritizing alternative energy resources and thereby becoming less dependent on foreign oil, putting an end to global warming, better equipping our local responders, drying up terrorist funding from foreign nations, and finally, protecting civil liberties while at the same time adequately maintaining homeland security. While lengthy, this list is in no way lofty. It represents a realistic appraisal of what needs to be done in the wake of the 9/11 attacks and the aftermath of the Bush administration's bad judgments and actions.

Regarding air travel, clearly we have issues in securing our airlines from a terrorist attack. Putting aside vulnerabilities from shoulder-launched missiles, too small a percentage of the cargo that gets transported in the belly of commercial airliners gets tested for bomb materials. Why? Does it make any sense that we make airline passengers go through airport security and baggage screening when the commercial airliner they are flying on most likely has unchecked cargo from Company XYZ that was never screened for explosives? Nearly every commercial flight that takes off has a cargo hold that is not fully tested or screened for bombs. It presents an enormous vulnerability to airline security and a huge opportunity for the terrorists.

But airline cargo holds are not the only area of vulnerability. One of the plots that al Qaeda was interested in prior to 9/11 was setting electronic timers on explosives planted on aircraft. If al Qaeda wanted to stage a simultaneous attack, its operatives could simply board selected aircraft, assemble bombs in the bathroom, set the timers of those bombs to explode a year in advance, hide the bombs under the seats or in the ceiling panels of the lavatory, and disembark. Think about how many flights this technique could have been used on in the past year. What is the date selected for twenty planes to simultaneously blow up in midflight?

Clearly, we would never catch the bombers, since they could have assembled and planted the timed bombs in the lavatories months before and would now be safely ensconced in the mountains of a far-off country such as Afghanistan or Pakistan. But is there anything that we could do today to better protect our airlines against such an attack? And more to the point, how much would it cost?

It is my understanding from anecdotal information that the entire airlines industry is compromised. From reservations to food service to baggage to flight attendants to mechanical crews—al Qaeda has spent years infiltrating our aviation system. Of course, we are not told this information outright because no American would accept a transportation system so compromised. After all, who would want to fly on a commercial airliner knowing that the reservations agent, the flight attendants, the pilots, the ground crew, the food services crew, the baggage crew, or the mechanical crew had al Qaeda terrorists among them? This information cannot make you feel comfortable as you board your next flight. But what can we do?

Why don't we start demanding that every airport have a team of bomb-sniffing dogs and that prior to every takeoff, those dogs walk down the aisle of the plane and through the cargo hold? At a bare minimum, before that plane takes off, you know that there are no bombs on board.

Do you live in a state with an airport? Do you use that airport? Do any planes that fly into and out of that airport fly over your home? Would you be willing to donate money—say, twenty dollars a year—to support a team of two dozen bomb-sniffing dogs at your local airport? I sure would if it meant that something—hell, anything—would be done to better protect our commercial airliners. Wouldn't you feel better knowing that your plane was bomb-free?

This I know: Dogs can't be infiltrated by al Qaeda. When they are trained to sniff out bombs or explosives, they are also our best defense—because we can *trust* them. That's something that can't be said for either our airline industry executives or our government, all of whom have left us terribly vulnerable when it comes to airline security.

Recently, the widows and I met with an intelligence agent to discuss some issues revolving around the Pentagon's special operation, Able Danger. The meeting was mind-boggling. What we learned was that if Able Danger existed prior to 9/11 (which I believe it did), there is simply no excuse for the attacks not being prevented by our government. At the time of this writing, Congress is scheduled to hold hearings on Able Danger, and I am hopeful that the truth will come out during those hearings.

Able Danger was a data-mining operation that allegedly identified several of the nineteen hijackers before 9/11: Mohamed Atta, Khalid al Mihdhar, Nawaf al Hazmi, and Marwan al Shehi. The Able Danger operation was supposedly shut down in May 2001 because it had conducted illegal surveillance on U.S. citizens. This argument is illogical since, according to the media accounts I have read, Able Danger used all "open source" data—in other words, it used public information to create its targets. Moreover, the hijackers identified by Able Danger were not U.S. citizens and therefore not entitled to the same rights and privileges as Americans. Rather, they were in this country illegally since their visas had inherent flaws and/or certain indicators that should have barred their entry into this country or been grounds to deport them. Nevertheless, according to media reports, when the Able Danger team raised these very same points with the Defense Department attorneys, the attorneys apparently ignored their arguments and shut down the program.

The Able Danger surveillance techniques were apparently transferred to the NSA, however, and quite possibly the CIA; how these two agencies might have used the data-mining technique remains classified. Regardless, what remains disturbing to me is that the Able Danger files containing all the gathered evidence about al Qaeda sleeper cells inside the United States in May 2001—a mere four months before the 9/11 attacks—were reportedly destroyed and not shared with other intelligence agencies like the FBI. Why?

Perhaps even more alarming, the identified sleeper cells (the four identified 9/11 hijackers) were left alone (and alive) to carry out their final plans and preparations. To reiterate, in May of 2001, four known al Qaeda killers who were identified and targeted by our intelligence community (specifically Special Operations Command at DOD, where Able Danger was created) to be "taken out" were ignored and thus allowed to finish their final preparations for the 9/11 attacks. All the files and information about these four al Qaeda killers were permanently destroyed and not capitalized upon, and even the presence of these killers within this country was a fact not shared with the FBI.

Recall that at this very time, late spring of 2001, people like George Tenet, Richard Clarke, and Condoleezza Rice were anticipating an imminent terrorist attack from Osama bin Laden. Also recall the August 4, 2001, Presidential Daily Briefing titled "Bin Laden Determined to Strike the United States." How is it possible that these four men were just left alone to continue their plans and preparations for the 9/11 attacks that would occur a mere three months later? Particularly when at least two of these identified sleeper cells had direct involvement in the USS *Cole* bombing that killed seventeen sailors in October 2000.

As previously stated, the four hijackers identified by Able Danger were inside this country with U.S. visas that were inherently and/or patently flawed. So, even if Able Danger was shut down at DOD, the question must be asked: Why were four known and dangerous al Qaeda operatives not immediately detained and deported for their visa violations? Unfortunately, at this point we have no answers as to why that did not happen. Moreover, questions remain as to whether the program was shifted to another agency like the NSA or CIA; and if so, whether this other agency continued to carry out surveillance on these four men for the remaining four months preceding the 9/11 attacks.

As more information is uncovered regarding Able Danger, my worst nightmare is not that the 9/11 attacks should have been prevented, but that we might learn another country other than Afghanistan was complicit in the 9/11 attacks. This information would be explosive because we went to war with Afghanistan and then Iraq and no other country after 9/11. Obviously, one big question would be why we might have ignored factual evidence linking a country to the 9/11 attacks and decided to invade another country (Iraq) that had no connection. A bigger question is whether at this point in time the American people would be willing to go to war with another country that really *did* participate in the 9/11 attacks while we're still bogged down in a war, which we chose to enter with no justification, against a nation that had no connection to 9/11.

Raising the stakes, of course, is the fact that the country I speak about, unlike Iraq, is arguably a real, credible threat when it comes to weapons of mass destruction. Would I want to start a war with such a nation? Probably not—not after seeing how poorly the administration has handled the debacle and quagmire unfolding in Iraq. And I say that because I simply do not think our military, under its current leadership with its guiding policies and principles, would be able to win such a war. That is not being unpatriotic. That is not failing to support our troops. It is being rational and realistic. It is *valuing* the human lives of our fighting men and women.

Of course the image of nuclear bombs exploding in Chicago, New York City, Houston, Los Angeles, or Des Moines as a result of going to war with such a country terrifies me. But would a terrorist country bomb those cities, whether we started a war with them or not? In other words, is there a real risk that terrorists would use their WMDs on U.S. soil? Who knows? To answer that question, I guess we would need to rely on our intelligence community to prepare a threat assessment. And we all know how reliable such a threat assessment can be. Witness the war in Iraq, which was based on flat-out, dead-wrong lies.

That is not to say that I am soft or indecisive about the need to deal with terrorists—any terrorists, including those who facilitated the murder of my husband. My feeling is that because of the mess created in Iraq; because of my lack of faith in the judgment and decisions of our Congress and president; and because of the absolute ineptitude exhibited in every area when it comes to securing our homeland during the past five years, it scares me to think how poorly we would handle a war with a nation like Iran. After all, look how poorly we handled a goddamn hurricane that was forecast five days prior to hitting landfall in the Gulf Coast. With the Bush administration's track record—9/11, Iraq, Katrina—I simply don't have much faith in our nation's ability to do *anything* right. Forget about protecting lives during a terrorist attack from a nation that might have real WMDs.

I will pose some hypothetical questions. Should President Bush or President Clinton be held accountable if we were to find out: That Able Danger was a program started during the Clinton administration? That the Clinton administration had plenty of warnings about the USS *Cole* bombing and yet did nothing to prevent it? That the Clinton administration did not name al Qaeda as being responsible for the *Cole* bombing when it clearly had evidence to prove such a connection in November 2000? That the Bush administration was handed all of this information in January 2001? That the Bush administration did not identify al Qaeda as the group responsible for the *Cole* bombing during the nine months preceding 9/11? That the Bush administration was responsible for shutting down or transferring Able Danger, the program that identified some of the key operatives for the *Cole* bombing and the 9/11 attacks? That the Bush administration failed to detain and deport four known al Qaeda killers in the months preceding 9/11 (even knowing that al Qaeda had already cost the lives of seventeen sailors in the *Cole* bombing)? And finally, that the Bush administration failed to use the vital information that had been gathered about these four future hijackers to prevent the 9/11 attacks? Would this rise to the level of dereliction of duty for either President Clinton or President Bush—or both? I think so. Yet neither has been held accountable.

During the meeting the widows and I had with some of the people involved with the Able Danger operation, Patty asked one of the men what he feared most regarding a possible future terrorist attack in the homeland. Here is what he said: "You know what a PT Cruiser is? It is a car. You know where they are assembled? Mexico. Do you know that Chrysler has a cargo ship carrying those PT Cruisers that goes from Mexico to Tampa every week? If I were a terrorist, I would put a nuke in a PT Cruiser. Money goes a *loooong* way in Mexico. You would be surprised what a little money can get you in Mexico. Once that ship pulled into Tampa, I would detonate the bomb. Putting aside the civilian damage, do you know where our nation's overseas military command is located? Tampa. If al Qaeda or any other terrorist group detonated a nuclear bomb in the port of Tampa they would dismantle our nation's ability to coordinate, communicate, and support our military troops overseas. It would utterly paralyze every military operation. If I was a terrorist and I was smart, that's what I would hit. That's my worst nightmare."

Yikes. We asked him if he thought it was truly possible. He said he thought it was a distinct possibility. And truthfully, when you examine whether our president or Congress has done anything in the way of securing our ports, cargo ships, or the many loose nukes that are floating around the world since the dismantling of the Soviet Union, we learn that far too little has been done to decrease our vulnerabilities in these areas.

Speaking of port security, Americans recently learned that the Bush administration favored giving management of at least six of our nation's largest ports to the United Arab Emirates.

The UAE was named at least twelve times in the Moussaoui indictment. Large amounts of money were transferred from UAE banks to the 9/11 hijackers while they were living as sleeper cells inside the United States. (Why such wire transfers were not tracked by our Treasury Department or the Able Danger data-mining program remains unknown.)

Frankly, I don't think it sounds rational to give control of our ports to any foreign government. But I think it is *totally* irrational to give control of our ports to a nation that was named at least twelve times in our own Justice Department's 9/11 indictment of Zacarias Moussaoui. These facts are known to President Bush and Attorney General Alberto Gonzales; yet according to both, the UAE is now our ally in the war against terrorism. Does President Bush define the word "ally"? No, he does not. Just like he does not give a definition of who qualifies as our "enemy."

Why would President Bush be cutting business deals with the UAE? Perhaps because we need nations like the UAE for their oil? Essentially, we will have to continue to conduct business and remain friendly with many nations like the UAE because of our dependency on their oil supplies.

Americans consume vast amounts of oil. We use it to heat our homes, run our electric plants, fuel our cars. Since America has such a small percentage of the world's oil supply, we must import our oil to support our needs. These oil imports come from oil-rich countries in the Middle East like Saudi Arabia and the UAE. Those same oil-rich countries maintain ongoing relationships with, and in some cases outright support of, terrorist organizations. Because Americans are dependent on these nations for their oil, we are unable to sever economic relations with them. As a result, we pay money to these foreign nations for their oil; they take our money and fund the terrorists, who then use that same money—*our* money—to plan, prepare, and carry out terrorist attacks against us. It makes no sense, particularly when our Congress and president have committed themselves to drying up terrorist funding. But until Americans are willing to make sacrifices in their daily lives by reducing their use of oil, we will continue to fund the terrorists with our own money.

Here is how I like to boil it down: If you approve of our nation doing business with nations that fund terrorists and organizations that want to kill Americans; if you like driving your monster SUV (as I admit I do) and living in your six-bedroom home; if you don't care about investing in environmentally sound alternative energy resources; if you do not want to demand that our government truly make a concrete, concerted, and real effort to bankrupt the terrorists; and if you are unwilling to make sacrifices in your own life so that we as a nation can cut our dependence on foreign oil, then which one of your loved ones are you willing to lose to the terrorists?

It is reprehensible that five years after 9/11, President Bush still has not decreased our dependence on foreign oil. True, during his State of the Union address in January 2006, President Bush laid out a plan for America to become less dependent on foreign oil—by 2025! Do you realize how many thousands of lives will be lost to terrorism between today and 2025? Do you recognize that it is virtually impossible for us to dry up terrorist money lines while at the same time we continue to buy oil from Middle Eastern countries?

It's fairly simple: Americans must become less dependent on foreign oil. We must invest in alternative energy resources like wind power, solar power, even soy power. We must invest in our automobile industry so it can compete with the Japanese automakers and match their enormous strides in the development of hybrid vehicles. We must provide subsidies and tax breaks to companies and individuals who choose to fuel their homes and businesses with alternative/clean energies like solar or wind power. Since 9/11, it is inexcusable that none of these things have been seriously promoted or undertaken by Congress or the Bush administration.

Regarding the UAE port deal, President Bush stated that he was concerned about sending a bad message to our Middle Eastern allies. He wanted those Middle Eastern allies of the United States (read: oil-rich nations) to know that the United States wants to conduct business with them. Frankly, I don't think the refusal to turn management of our ports (or any part of our nation's infrastructure, for that matter) over to a foreign nation sends a bad message. I think it sends a strong message that we do not conduct business with any nation that directly or indirectly funds, aids, or supports the terrorists who want to kill us. But when President Bush speaks of sending bad messages, he should be more concerned about the bad messages his administration's torture policies have spread throughout the Arab world.

Why do I care about torture? Because it is inherently wrong. Because it runs counter to our democratic principles. Because it does not work. And because it actually harms our ability to effectively fight and win the "war on terror."

We have three individuals in our custody—Ramzi bin al Shibh, Khalid Sheikh Mohammed, and Khallad bin Attash— who are all implicated in the *Cole* bombing and the 9/11 attacks. In fact, bin al Shibh made a self-admission on al Jazeera that he participated in the planning of the 9/11 attacks. Yet none of these terrorists have been prosecuted in a United States court of law. Why? Because we have tortured them. Have we received any valuable information from their torture? In other words, have we prevented any attacks? No. So then what is the point of torture? There is none, which is probably why it was outlawed by the Geneva Convention.

To sum up, we are holding terrorists in our custody, treating them as badly as Saddam Hussein treated his own people, having gleaned no valuable information or actionable intelligence from them to prevent another attack—yet we know they were directly connected to carrying out the 9/11 attacks—and we cannot hold them accountable in a court of law because our intelligence officials (with the consent of the president) have tortured them. Does that make any sense? Is that President Bush's definition of "bringing terrorists to justice"? Is that President Bush's way to send a positive message to our allies in the Arab world?

Torture harms our reputation in the world. Torture puts our intelligence agents who are behind enemy lines and gathering HUMINT (human intelligence) in grave danger, since they no longer have the protections of the Geneva Convention in their back pocket. If they get captured, the United States cannot say to their captors: "The United States doesn't torture prisoners, please don't torture our agent." Unfortunately, now it's quid pro quo. And don't think that every intelligence agent infiltrating enemy groups or nations overseas is not patently aware of the fact that there is not one thing that our nation can do or say if they get captured behind enemy lines. Essentially, they are on their own.

When it comes to the Bush administration's torture policies, we have lowered ourselves to the level of the thugs. And that is a very bad message to send to the Arab world.

These policies have barred us from bringing terrorists to justice. At the same time, it is highly questionable whether these policies have prevented any terrorist attacks. What they have done is harm our reputation in the world and place our soldiers and intelligence agents in grave peril, making it harder for them to gather the kind of important information we need to keep America safe against future terrorist attacks. Are we told the truth about any of this? Is this openly and honestly debated? No, because the man who wrote the memorandum to the president that sanctioned the use of torture on "enemy combatants" (the man who called the Geneva Convention "quaint") is now sitting as our attorney general. And what does he tell us? Trust him. Torture works. When asked by the media to prove that his form of torture works, we are offered no evidence. We are told once again to trust him.

With a laundry list of items that clearly indicate the poor judgment of the Bush administration, is it a wise decision to continue to blindly trust these current leaders?

Isn't it true that instead of fixing airline security, border security, port security, mass transportation security, and local response, and securing loose nukes and biological components, President Bush and Congress have spent billions on starting a war with Iraq—a nation that posed no real threat and had nothing to do with 9/11? Instead of capturing Osama bin Laden in Afghanistan, thereby decapitating al Qaeda's symbolic leader, President Bush captured Saddam Hussein in Iraq—a despot, yes, but a man who posed no real threat. And because of President Bush's preemptive war with Iraq, al Qaeda's recruitment and training have increased enormously, making the entire world less safe and more destabilized. Alarmingly, isn't it also true that our focus in Iraq has enabled other more lethal regimes, like those in Iran, Syria, and North Korea, to grow even stronger and more capable of attacking America with real WMDs?

If we cannot stabilize Iraq, if Iraq continues to grow worse even with (and perhaps because of) the U.S. military's presence there, then how can President Bush expect to handle a real threat posed by another nation, like Iran? If Iraq is in any way an indication of our ability to fight and defend ourselves against terrorist groups, regimes, and governments, then I think we are in serious trouble. When we can't defend ourselves and save lives when it comes to a forecasted hurricane like Katrina, how are we to defend ourselves and save lives when it comes to a surprise terrorist nuclear attack from a nation like Iran?

We—the American public—find ourselves stunned and overwhelmed. Every day brings a new scandal swirling around the Bush administration and Congress that trumps the prior day's scandal. And it seems that every time a scandal erupts, a well-timed audiotape or videotape from one of the many al Qaeda operatives (or "Number 2s") suddenly surfaces to scare us into submission.

Preoccupied with that constant fear, the American public fails to confront the truth about anything (terrorist threat or otherwise). We never come to understand why the Bush administration and our Republican Congress have made the bad choices or taken the dangerous actions they have. Alarmingly, most of the public blindly accepts the many lies being perpetrated in the name of "national security" and our "ongoing fight against the enemy." Most of us fail to realize that with a timeless, faceless, nameless, and stateless enemy, President Bush's "ongoing fight against the enemy" will never end. We will never return to our sensibilities, the truth, and a peaceful future.

How are we to *really* know if our government's choices since 9/11—all in the name of "national security"—have truly made us any safer when the only proof the Bush administration offers is hollow rhetoric? What if our current leaders really *don't* know what they are doing? What if our leaders really *don't* have our best interests at heart?

Sadly for me, I no longer trust President Bush or Congress to look out for my best interests. I can no longer assume that everything will be okay. I can no longer close my eyes, stick my head in the sand, and hope for the best. The death of Ron woke me up to that fact—that something is terribly wrong with our country's leadership. Spending the past five years in Washington lobbying for change has seared this frightening truth into my DNA.

Before 9/11, I, like most of America, lived my life as if this country was a safe place, in which the chances of a personal catastrophe befalling me or my husband were on a par with a lunar rock hurtling out of the heavens and bonking me on the head. I blindly assumed that my government could take care of itself—and take care of me and my family. I felt that my responsibility began and ended at the voting booth and in writing occasional checks to charities.

Ron and I truly appreciated our life together. We noticed nature and beauty. We enjoyed sharing our lives with each other. We exercised together, ran errands and did chores together, ate dinners together, and raised our daughter together. We were an all-American family. And in many ways, I thought that our all-American family would be protected against bad things happening to us because we knew that we were blessed; we knew that we lived our lives as good, responsible people. So how could anything bad ever happen to us?

And then came the horror and devastation of 9/11. The day that my eyes were peeled open. The day that my beloved husband was brutally murdered by terrorists. My blind ignorance and blithe innocence were shattered and lost. Forever.

Five years later, I am still scared. Probably more scared than I was immediately after 9/11 because I know a lot more now. I know all the problems that still exist, and I know enough to predict future problems. More important, I know how very little has been done to fix the problems that leave us so recklessly, senselessly, and perilously vulnerable to terorrist attack. It is our current leaders' bad judgment, dangerous policies, and failure to fix homeland security that pose the most significant risk to our country's *real* safety. If you doubt what I say, just look at the facts and study the track record of this Republican Congress and the Bush administration.

I remain totally frustrated that our homeland security apparatus has been so ignored in the past five years. Too many failures have been neither addressed nor remedied by President Bush and Congress. I wish more than anything that I could end this final chapter on a positive note—that I could honestly tell you that everything is being done to keep you and every American as safe as you can be from terrorist attack. But there is no happy ending here. At least not yet.

Some days I feel like packing it all in and running away to again stick my head in the sand; living in that pre-9/11 bubble wasn't such a bad way to live. I miss the bubble and that life. I miss it very much. And let's be honest, it can be overwhelming to realize how many years it will take to fix the damage that has been done to our country in the past five years. But we can't give up.

Truth is, most days the widows and I feel like we are just hitting our heads against the wall as we continue to fight the good fight—the right fight that needs to be fought to keep this country and all of our loved ones safe. But in the end (business cards or not), the widows and I will continue our fight because we've got children (and new puppies) to raise, teach, and protect. And for us, they are the lives, hearts, and minds worth fighting for.

Sweets,

I miss you. It's been five years since you left. I've gone from being a thirty-year-old wife to thirty-five-year-old widow. Sometimes I feel more like I am sixty-five because I am so tired, sweetheart. Often I wish that I could close my eyes and go back to living in our dream.

The world has changed since you were killed. We are a nation at war. Soldiers are dying in the dusty streets of Afghanistan and Iraq. We are told to fear everything, from more deadly terrorist attacks to a deadly strain of the flu virus called the bird flu. It is crazy to live like this.

Caroline continues to live with sunshine and happiness on her face. Her eyes sparkle with love and delight. Her giggle is still present but carried by a nearly toothless grin. The tooth fairy has visited us on at least six occasions. When Caroline looks at me now through her bright eyes, I see a glimmer that suggests an all-knowingness. It's that same look that older children give to their parents about Santa Claus—they know that he doesn't exist, but they can't bring themselves to let go of believing in the hope and happiness that the magic of Santa Claus brings to them.

Sam died this past summer. It was awful. Because you weren't here, I had to be there when he was put to sleep. When he took his last breath, I kissed him on his nose and told him to go find you in heaven. Did he? Are you two together? I think you are. So does Caroline. And it gives us comfort to believe that there is indeed a heaven and that you are no longer alone; that your little boy, Sam, is now bounding beside you, licking your face and keeping you warm at night.

We have a new puppy now. His name is Cooper. I went to pick him out at the breeder and he was the troublemaker from the minute I saw him. There were about eight puppies running around. I had three to choose from. I looked at the three tiny little bundles of love and studied their personalities. One was quite docile and a bit overweight. One had a shorter tail yet a beautiful face. And the last one was squirreling around, knocking things over and trying mightily to escape through the puppy fence. With a sparkle of trouble in his eyes, he was clearly the rabble-rouser: intelligent, bursting with love and abundant, exuberant energy. He bounded over to me, plunked down, and looked intently into my eyes. I took him in my arms and went nose to nose with him. He tried to squirm free and then suddenly relaxed and licked my nose. I knew immediately that we just fit. He was the one for Caroline and me to share our lives with. I wanted to name him Jack, but Caroline decided to name him Cooper. And we are now a happy family of three.

Caroline's seventh birthday is coming next month. Unbelievable, isn't it? I think we are going to Disney World to celebrate. Last year we went to Disney World for the first time. You know how I always dreaded going to places like that? Well, it was the best time in my life since you died. We had an amazing time together. Sara went with us and she was the perfect person to take because she was so totally into the entire Disney experience! She and Caroline went on all the rides together, wore Minnie ears, and took pictures with all the Disney characters. We saw the fireworks, the parades, played in the pool, went on safari, and even had breakfast with Cinderella in her Magic Castle. I wish you could have been there to watch Caroline run around like a maniac and giggle with such delight.

We live in New York City now. I know, I know. But we like it here. In fact, Caroline absolutely loves it. She rides her scooter through Central Park, swings from the ropes in the playground, hails cabs, swipes her MetroCard to ride the bus, and loves her school that is right around the corner. She thrives on the noise and people and vitality that surround us. On the weekends we go to the beach, where we take Cooper swimming and Caroline enjoys riding her favorite horse, Ben. We make cupcakes and cookies. We play dress-up. In summer, Caroline loves to go fishing. She tells me that when she grows up she wants to be either a "fisher-girl" or a veterinarian.

Sweetheart, our life is carrying on. The years are moving forward. But our memories of you and the life we shared together will never be forgotten. It is sad without you here and it's hard to raise Caroline alone. But we are still doing okay. And I have learned to know that being okay is good enough. I now look forward with hope to having a future where the good things outnumber the bad. I have been listening to a song lately that has a lyric, "because it's the happy little moments along the way, that make everything in the end seem okay." And that is how I want to live out the rest of my life. Simply being happy for those little tiny moments along the way.

We will still look for you amongst the moon and stars. And Caroline and I will continue to blow our kisses to

*you and Sam each night. But our tears will no longer
taste so bittersweet. Because I've learned that even our life
without you is too short and precious for that.*

*Sweetheart, keep a close and watchful eye on us,
because knowing that you are watching and smiling
down on us will make it all worth living for.*

—January 2006

The Hereinafter

Someone I loved very dearly once shared a secret with me about an enchanting place located on the eastern end of Long Island. After 9/11, I ended up buying a home there, and it is the most precious piece of advice I have ever followed in my life. It was a place he held dear in his heart. A place he knew I would love. A place he knew Caroline and Sam would cherish. The kind of place where memories can now be made anew:

Its long, empty beaches filled with small rocks and shells to collect, its crystal-clear waters that allow you to see your toes as they dance with the gray sands that shift with the changing tides. Sweeping, breathtaking sunsets and silly blankets of stars laughing on the horizon just beyond reach. A moon that is always brilliantly and majestically laid out overhead, smiling down through the darkness of night and perfectly poised for capturing shooting stars and whispering dreams and wishes.

I now know that the truest island of shelter is love. One day I might fall in love again, but I know that it will never be the same. How can you replicate the moon and the stars and everything a girl could ever love? The smiles, the laughter, the simple happiness that exuded from us and abounded between us with such incredible ease. The blueness of his eyes, the sparkle of his grin, the touch of his hand in mine. And his handsome face smiling back at me with absolute love—all of them now memories that I will forever hold sacred in my heart, be thankful for in my mind, and yearn for in my soul.

AFTERWORD

A Letter to Ann Coulter

Dear Ann,

But for the murder of our husbands on 9/11, we would not have gone to Washington to fight for an independent 9/11 investigation. Our involvement in national security would have begun and ended at the voting booth, like most citizens.

But for the initial failure of our leaders and elected officials to create an independent 9/11 Commission to investigate the terrorist attacks, we would not have not been forced to publicly fight for it.

An important part of that fight required us to demand the attention of our elected officials by speaking out in the media. Sadly, in many cases, such public pressure (and its possible effect on Election Day) is needed to inspire elected officials to do the right thing. That is not my opinion. That's reality. Had President Bush and Congress impaneled an independent commission on their own, we would not have needed to lobby Washington. Likewise, had Congress thoroughly investigated the attacks and not limited its investigation into intelligence-only areas, we would not have needed to fight for the 9/11 Commission.

We wanted the 9/11 attacks investigated thoroughly and competently so that fewer terrorist attacks would succeed in the future and more lives would be saved on the day of the next attack. When you study the events of 9/11, you learn that many more lives should have been saved, and many damages and injuries could have been mitigated. We wanted to hold the government accountable so that, going forward, our nation would be better prepared for future attacks and disasters.

Fighting for national security—securing the homeland or wanting to make the nation safe—ought to be an unassailable objective, similar to the Amber Alert, Megan's Law, and providing body armor for the troops. Regardless of who the messenger raising these issues might be, the goals are inarguable because they are pure, true, and right. Will these issues receive more focused attention if the message is delivered by people who speak passionately because they have been personally affected? Yes, absolutely. But it's the issue that is unassailable— not the people espousing that issue. If your conservative Republican friends are on the wrong side of the issues, that's their problem.

Ann, the Jersey Girls are moms. We have children. Perhaps one day if you have a child, you may understand the sense of duty and obligation that parents feel toward their children to provide them with a safe and secure environment, both in the present and the future. There were many, many times when we wanted to give up. We were tired and frustrated. But we didn't. The reason? Our children. We were left as their sole protectors; we wanted them to know that even though their fathers were brutally killed, they could be and would be safer living in America.

You complained to many interviewers that they hadn't taken the time to read your book. But did you take the time to look at the Family Steering Committee Web site (www.911 independentcommission.org)? You might discover that we shared some of the same disappointments, concerns, and grievances that you have expressed with regard to the 9/11 Commission. *The difference is that we made those concerns known while the*

Commission was doing its work—that is, when it could have made a difference. Why didn't you?

We could have used some more support back then, when we were fighting against individual commissioners' apparent and very possible conflicts of interest and the need for more hard-hitting hearings. We needed more help in fighting for an extended deadline, so as to remove the Commission's final report from the politics of the 2004 election, and a budgetary increase so the Commission could complete its unfinished work on questions about Able Danger. (You see, I did read your book.)

But frankly, I wonder how much you really know about the 9/11 Commission. You don't seem to understand that President Bush picked Tom Kean to be the chairman—not the "co-chairman." You don't seem to be aware that Philip Zelikow was the Commission's staff director or of why that position was so important. You also seem ignorant of the fact that Zelikow had served previously on the Bush National Security Council transition team and on the President's Foreign Intelligence Advisory Board. (Do you even know who the current members of PFIAB are or what PFIAB does? Probably not.) I wonder whether you even know that Zelikow is currently serving as Secretary of State Condoleezza Rice's Special Counsel. Finally, and most important, are you aware that the White House exercised the "final edits" on the Commission's report? Tell me, Ann, how does that add up to a Democratic whitewash?

Because I was one of twelve family members who lobbied fiercely for an independent commission, I was invited to meetings in the White House and on Capitol Hill. I testified before Congress, as well. I wish you knew about the battle that occurred behind the scenes because then you might not make silly statements such as "nobody could ever debate the Jersey

Girls." Ironically, it is because we kept most of those meetings confidential that you probably don't know how nastily certain elected officials behaved behind closed doors. Trust me, we were countered, rebutted, and challenged in almost every meeting we attended. Did we go on the record about those incidents? No. We could have, and I can assure you that some of your conservative Republican friends would not have come off well.

When I kept my mouth shut about the way a certain Republican official spoke to me merely because it would have made people in your party look bad, was I being "political"? I'm sure there are some Democrats who would say yes. Did that mean I was being manipulated by your right-wing friends? No. It meant that I had a job to do and I found no reason to distract attention from our cause by dragging people through the mud. There was plenty that I could have spouted off about then, and there still is to this very day. But I don't—mostly because my mother and father taught me to rise above bullies rather than stoop to their level.

You branded the Jersey Girls media whores, a bunch of celebrity-seeking widows who enjoyed their husbands' deaths. Had your friends—including many elected officials in the Republican Party and conservatives in Washington—not put up a fight, and a very nasty fight, we wouldn't have needed to raise public awareness through the media. So if you want to blame anyone for our appearances on television, you should blame your own coterie, not us. We simply wanted to inform the nation about what needed to be done. And we still intend to do that.

Earlier this year, some of us were invited to appear on television to discuss the verdict in the Zacarias Moussaoui case. We agreed to do that because the U.S. has in custody three individuals with a more direct connection to the 9/11 attacks than Moussaoui. To us, it is important to show the world that we are a nation of laws and that the U.S. can successfully bring terrorists to justice. Does that matter to you, Ann? If so, then you ought to support us in our goal of bringing Khalid Sheikh Mohammed, Ramzi Bin al-Shibh, and Khallad bin Attash to trial. Our judicial process should hold these madmen accountable for the deaths of nearly 3,000 innocent people on 9/11.

I am truly puzzled by your accusation that we were operatives of or used by the Democrats. We were never paid for television appearances, we did not drive around in limos, we did not have publicists or PR people, and we wrote all of our own press releases, talking points, letters to the editor, statements, and testimony. (I don't know if the 9/11 family members who chose to support the Republican Party can say the same.) At any rate, your statements are false and defamatory, although that is nothing new for you.

As a public figure I'm in a poor position to hold you legally accountable for your lies. But I will take the time to set the record straight here. The Democrats were nearly the only people in Washington willing to help us. That is not my opinion; it is a fact, notwithstanding a few honorable exceptions, such as Chris Smith and John McCain. We worked with anyone of either party who supported an independent investigation.

For some unknown reason—and as a seasoned right-wing operative maybe you can enlighten us—most Republicans we encountered were completely opposed to learning any lessons from 9/11. It's a shame, too. After all, the Republican Party has been in total control of Washington for the past three years. Had they made true national security a higher priority, perhaps our cities would be better protected against terrorist attacks and disasters. Again, the sorry conditions in our cities and across our nation are a matter of fact, not opinion. Please don't blame me for that failure. Assign the responsibility where it belongs.

Similarly, one of the reasons we are still fighting for national security reforms (and encountered so much resistance in fighting for an independent commission) is that very few people actually read commission reports. They often sit on bookshelves gathering dust. Have you read the *9/11 Commission Report*, along with its accompanying footnotes? Have you read the Robb-Silverman report on the Iraq intelligence failures? What about the Joint Inquiry of Congress report on 9/11? How about the Hart-Rudman report? Or even the Bremer report? Probably not. If you haven't, you should, because I think you would find those volumes illuminating.

You have expressed outrage that few of your critics actually read *your* books. You complain that they merely cherry-pick your most inflammatory comments while missing your overall message. Frustrating, isn't it?

You also wrongly accused us of being in the pocket of former president Clinton. The obvious reason for why we always directed our questions and requests to President Bush was simply because Clinton was no longer in office. The former president had no power to commence an investigation into the 9/11 attacks, nor did he have any power to effect change to make the nation safer after 9/11. That power lay in the hands of President Bush—you know, the guy who in your opinion has supreme authority.

Ann, I don't want to get into a debate with you. It's not because I am afraid of you or your nasty bullying tactics. I'm not going to debate you because we have many, many more important issues to deal with in our country right now.

But I will leave you with this: We live in America, the world's oldest democracy. Democracy can prevail (is that what you and your friends really fear?), but that requires hard work, as President Bush might say. Every citizen in this country is entitled to his or her beliefs, and every citizen is entitled to participate. We still have the right to speak our minds to effect change (within the parameters of the law, of course). So don't try to silence the voices of victims or anyone else, merely because you disagree with them or feel threatened by their political choices. In my opinion, your method of using intimidation and insults to "win" a debate is truly unpatriotic.

Actually, I expect that you will continue to scream and shout and smear as nastily as you want, so long as you think that that kind of behavior sells books. But we have tackled bigger bullies than you and lived through far worse circumstances than your book tour. We're not intimidated by you. We're not running away.

And under no circumstances will we be silenced by your "godless" rantings and ravings.

> Kristen Breitweiser
> New York City
> June 2006